MODERATE OR MILITANT

In 2001, of the 138 million Muslims in India, 31 million, or 22%, lived in Uttar Pradesh. West Bengal, Bihar and Maharashtra also had over ten million Muslims each. Most Muslims live in these four states. Besides, Kerala, Andhra Pradesh, Assam, Jammu and Kashmir, and Karnataka had five to ten million Muslims each, Rajasthan, Gujarat, Madhya Pradesh, Jharkhand, and Tamil Nadu 3 to 5 million each, and Delhi, Haryana, and Uttaranchal one to two million each. Punjab and Orissa, with populations of over twenty million each, had fewer than one million Muslims. Even though the Muslims uniformly share the tenets of their faith, they are rooted in various ecological niches and cultural systems. They are also thus heterogeneous and differ from one another in biological, linguistic and cultural traits. The Muslims are mainly situated in rural-urban situations followed by those living exclusively in rural and urban settings. Five Muslim communities such as Withal, Lalbegi, Madari/ Kalander claim the status of the Scheduled Castes and 19 communities have been returned as the Scheduled Tribes. Of the total number of Muslim communities, a very large number, 60.8 per cent, migrated to their present habitat in recent years. While Urdu has been returned as the mother tongue by a majority of the Muslims, 46.27 per cent of the Muslims have also returned the scheduled/regional languages as their mother tongues. Social divisions among Muslims exist on a relatively smaller scale in the form of clans (22.4 per cent), sects (9.4 per cent), sub-castes (10.6 per cent), bands and sub-tribes. Hierarchy with social divisions also exists. Differentiation is reported at social, economic, religious (sects), occupational and territorial levels. [K.S. Singh, *People of India: An Introduction* (New Delhi, 2002, revised edition), pp. 44–5]

MODERATE OR MILITANT
IMAGES OF
INDIA'S MUSLIMS

MUSHIRUL HASAN

OXFORD

UNIVERSITY PRESS

OXFORD

UNIVERSITY PRESS

YMCA Library Building, Jai Singh Road, New Delhi 110 001

Oxford University Press is a department of the University of Oxford.
It furthers the University's objective of excellence in research, scholarship,
and education by publishing worldwide in

Oxford   New York

Auckland   Cape Town   Dar es Salaam   Hong Kong   Karachi
Kuala Lumpur   Madrid   Melbourne   Mexico City   Nairobi
New Delhi   Shanghai   Taipei   Toronto

With offices in
Argentina   Austria   Brazil   Chile   Czech Republic   France   Greece
Guatemala   Hungary   Italy   Japan   Poland   Portugal   Singapore
South Korea   Switzerland   Thailand   Turkey   Ukraine   Vietnam

Oxford is a registered trademark of Oxford University Press
in the UK and in certain other countries

Published in India by Oxford University Press, New Delhi

© Oxford University Press 2008

The moral rights of the author have been asserted
Database right Oxford University Press (maker)

First published 2008

ISBN-13: 978-0-19-569531-1
ISBN-10: 0-19-569531-3

Typeset in GoudyOlSt BT 11/13.6
by Jojy Philip, New Delhi 110 015
Printed in India by Rajshri Photolithographers, Delhi 110 032
Published by Oxford University Press
YMCA Library Building, Jai Singh Road, New Delhi 110 001

Contents

Preface

'O you who believe, steer well clear of supposition,' states the Quran. The aim of this book is to take stock of the readings and interpretations of 'lived' Islam. It is to appreciate how social scientists and creative writers have been guided by certain assumptions or suppositions about the Indian Muslims in a world now and ever in flux and transition. Even though some offer a slightly different point of view, the glue that binds my narrative together is the war of words around secularism. The battle lines are drawn, for at stake is the very survival of a society that prides itself on nurturing a substantial tradition, Hindu and Muslim, of argument and pluralism. As for style and presentation, I can only draw comfort from the following verse of Mohammad Iqbal:

> Symbol and allusion are not suitable of this time,
> And I have not got the art of word-making

Nitasha Devasar put the idea of writing this book into my head and graciously waited for me to complete it. Over the years, Zoya has been a source of strength, support, and encouragement. She has created the very favourable conditions in which I have been able to write. Rakhshanda Jalil, with whom I have co-authored *Partners in Freedom: Jamia Millia Islamia* (2007), took time off from her own commitments to comment on the book at various stages of completion.

Dedicated to the present
And
the sorrow of present times
which is alienated from the
Rose-garden of life,
The forest of yellow autumnal leaves
That is my country
The assembly of griefs.
Dedicated to the benumbed souls of officemen
the moth-eaten hearts and tongues,
To the postmen,
the tonga drivers,
the railway engine drivers,
the hungry brave men of factories,
The master of the World, the King
of the beyond, deputy of God on earth—
The peasant;
Whose cattle have been driven away by the rogues
Whose daughters have been abducted by the dacoits,
Whose field, not even of arm's length—
a part of which has been taken away by the Patwari,
Another part by the revenue officer,
whose turban, under the feet of the oppressor,
is in shreds

To the grief stricken mothers—
whose children cry in nights
sleepless, refuse to be consoled, do not tell their grief.

To those dames—
whose flowers of eyes

blossom in vain behind screens and corridors
only to be withered away.

To those married women
whose limbs
got exhausted at loveless
decorative nuptial beds.

To the widows—
lanes, by lanes and pockets
where in the profane places
the moon is often seen performing ablution.

Where under the shadows—
one may hear sighs
the henna of hem
the sound of bangles
the fragrance of locks of hair
the burning smell of the aspirations—
suppressed in the hearts.

To the seekers of knowledge
those who reached the
gates of powers that be
with offers of the pen and the book
and did not return to their homes;

To those innocent souls
who, in their naïveté,
with lamps lit in their hand,
aspiring for high ideals,
landed up where there
was darkness, endless,
To the prisoners
whose hearts lit with
night-burnt fire of tomorrow's
dreams, turned into stars.

To the brightness of future days
which like fragrance of roses
has been lost in its own world.

—Faiz Ahmed Faiz (1914–84)*

* Translated from the Urdu by Humayun Zafar Zaidi, in Javed Akhtar, 'Progressive Writers' Movement in Urdu Literature', *Indian Literature* (New Delhi), no. 234, 2007, p. 142.

MODERATE OR MILITANT

1

Introduction

Christopher Hill (1912–2003), the English Marxist historian, reminded us that history has to be rewritten in every generation, because although the past does not change the present does; each generation asks new questions of the past, and finds new areas of sympathy as it relives different aspects of the experiences of its predecessors. This book, written at the dawn of the twenty-first century, is about India's Muslims. It offers a look at certain aspects of their past and their reflection in current discourses. This timely and significant subject remains an ever-open field of enquiry for understanding the dynamics of their politics and social change, and a book like this can hope to do little more than present some vital issues to readers and whet their appetites for further discussion.

Rabindranath Tagore (1861–1941), whose work and life were closely interwoven with India's own, noted that 'what is radically wrong with our rulers is this: they are fully aware that they do not know us, and yet they do not *care* to know us'.[1] These words could as well apply to the appalling ignorance about Islam and the culture associated with it today. Even though Islam is widely perceived and experienced as a dynamic way of life consisting of praxis and ideology, the literature on its followers in the subcontinent, who are regarded as a part of the repository of many events that make up its complex history, is woefully inadequate.

[1] Edward Thompson, *Rabindranath Tagore: Poet and Dramatist* (Oxford, 1926), p. 291.

Mohammad Iqbal (1877–1938), the poet-philosopher, observed at a Muslim League session in December 1930: 'It is no exaggeration to say that India is perhaps the only country in the world where Islam, as a people-building force, has worked at its best.'[2] Yet a book published a few years ago and carrying a chapter entitled 'Islam matters to the West' excluded the histories and contemporary predicaments of India's Muslims.[3] This is an example of how the twenty-first-century historian sees the 'Muslim world'.

My aim, then, is to put an end to the neglect that Barbara Metcalf, renowned American historian on South Asia, calls 'too little', a phrase that runs as a motif throughout this narrative causing me to ponder, time and time again, both its reasons and its woeful consequences. If the place of Islam in the twenty-first century is permanent and living with it as a political phenomenon is a certainty for the foreseeable future,[4] we need to work on a history that does not make 'Islam' prior—the stereotypical thinking Barbara Metcalf calls 'too much'.[5] Make no mistake, those who are unwilling to confront the past will be unable to understand the present and unfit to face the future.[6]

Today, vital issues impinge on Muslim lives, not least their interaction with other communities. Globalization is another issue; it causes the old traditional points of reference to disappear here and elsewhere and re-awakens passionate affirmations of identity often emerging from withdrawal and self-exclusion.[7] There is also the challenge of Western ascendancy being met on a daily basis not uniformly but variously.[8] There is, finally, the struggle between modernists and traditionalists for the Islamic heritage and the search for a place in post-colonial societies. Issues touching deep-seated chords of feelings are raised over and over

---

[2] Sharifuddin Pirzada (ed.), *Foundations of Pakistan: All-India Muslim League Documents 1906–1947* (Karachi, 1970), vol. 2, p. 154.

[3] Bassam Tibi, *Islam between Culture and Politics* (Harvard, 2001), Chapter 4.

[4] Beverly Milton-Edwards, *Islam and Politics in the Contemporary World* (London, 2004), p. 217.

[5] Barbara Daly Metcalf, Presidential Address: 'Too Little Too Much. Reflection on Muslims in the History of India', *Journal of Asian Studies*, 54, 1995, pp. 51–67; and her *Islamic Contestations: Essays on Muslims in India and Pakistan* (New Delhi, 2004), p. 210.

[6] Bernard Lewis, *Islam and the West* (New York, 1993), p. 130.

[7] Tariq Ramadan, *Western Muslims and the Future of Islam* (New York, 2004), pp. 4–5.

[8] Khalid Bin Sayeed, *Western Dominance and Political Islam: Challenges and Response* (Karachi, 1995).

again as every single Muslim—from North America to South East Asia—
is under scrutiny to either reinforce or revise the only two images that
are in vogue, 'Good Muslim' and 'Bad Muslim'.[9]

However, at the heart and soul of this book is an endeavour to
articulate a vision of Islam, rather the many different kinds of Islam
instead of the frightening monolith of popular perception, living in
harmony with other faiths and of the Muslims, inheritors of the great
Indian civilization, living in a pluralist milieu. I expand on a single
thread that runs through my earlier studies, including an anthology of
stories, in which the multicultural realities are presented in regional
languages and in local cultures. In this specific case, the variegated
perceptions got further accentuated with the time-span covered in the
book, in its linearity, for over the whole of the twentieth century.[10] If this
effort sounds unduly optimistic, it is in part because of the vast resource
of religious and intellectual tolerance embedded in 'Hinduism' and partly
owing to the diversity in Islam. When all is said and done it ought to be
possible to locate the diminishing value of divisive ideologies and the
ultimate dissolution of primordial loyalties.

To Jean Paul Sartre (1905–80), French existentialist philosopher,
dramatist, novelist, and critic, writing in 1946, freedom of choice was
axiomatic. But freedom to choose what sort of goal? To the argument
that there seems to be no objective grounds for choosing anything in
particular, Sartre replied that 'man finds himself in an organized situation
in which he himself is involved: his choice involves mankind in its
entirety, and he cannot avoid choosing.'[11] Taking my cue from these lines,
I offer a series of generalizations bearing upon India's essentially inclusive
and tolerant nature. For example, in a society where religion plays a
dominant role in virtually every walk of life, it is my business and the
business of every historian to bring secularism into our discussions and
to affirm its validity as a principle guiding the nation. To renounce this
claim is to surrender the nationalist project to right-wing ideologies, be
it Hindutva or Islamism.

[9] Mahmood Mamdani, *Good Muslim, Bad Muslim: Islam, the USA, and the Global War against Terror* (Delhi, 2005).

[10] Mushirul Hasan and M. Asaduddin (eds), *Image and Representation: Stories of Muslim Lives in India* (New Delhi, 2000).

[11] Quoted in George Lichtheim, *Europe in the Twentieth Century* (London, 1974), p. 435.

In Chapter 2, I lay bare the strains and stresses resulting from, in their past and currently fashionable forms, the images of Muslim communities,[12] partition, and a series of shattering events such as the demolition of the Babri Masjid on 6 December 1992 and the Gujarat catastrophe in February–March 2002. In recent years, the media has discovered and interpreted Islam as posing a counter alternative to the West. It is, consequently, obsessed with theories on the clash of civilizations, the imperative of *jihad* for contemporary Muslims, and the theoretical roots of 'Islamist political terror'. This is lamentable enough; but the more worrisome development is that some sober historians are also influenced by the global image of Islam based on observation rather than systematic empirical evidence.[13] Given that India is neither a centre of *jihadi* terrorism nor the battlefield for the future of Islam, they are reluctant to lay stress on India's civilizational identity that is against any totalitarianism—Hindutva or Islamism. This exercise would make sense, especially in the light of the 'too little' emerging during the last few decades.

In Chapter 3, I have introduced the debates triggered by the writings on nationalism and communalism, on identity politics, on social reforms, and on the administrative definition of the Muslims as separate and homogenized. This image of Muslims as separate and homogenized had important implications; as David Gilmartin points out, 'It represented a sharp break from the networked mode that had shaped medieval thinking, and it is little wonder that it generated considerable ferment in Muslim thinking in India.'[14]

Anyone who embarks upon my kind of enterprise is bound to rely heavily on sociologists and political scientists and the literature they generate. Their tools or concepts can sometimes secure insights into the past. This chapter indicates where I have done my own research, and where I have relied upon others. Occasionally, I use excerpts from my own writings for reiterations; they are recast or expanded, enlarged and strengthened (I seek the reader's indulgence for a few long citations).

[12] I have discussed the communal images at length in 'The Myth of Unity: Colonial and National Narratives', in David Ludden (ed.), *Contesting the Nation: Religion, Community, and the Politics of Democracy in India* (Philadelphia, 1996), pp. 185–208.

[13] On this theme, see Shahid Amin, 'Representing the Musalman: Then and Now, Now and Then', in Shail Mayaram, M.S.S. Pandian, Ajay Skaria (eds), *Muslims, Dalits, and the Fabrications of History: Subaltern Studies XII* (New Delhi, 2005).

[14] David Gilmartin, 'A Networked Civilization', in Miriam Cooke and Bruce B. Lawrence (eds), *Muslim Networks: From Medieval Scholars to Modern Feminists* (New Delhi, 2005), p. 57.

That such an exercise is badly needed can be ascertained by examining any of the standard reference works on South Asian history, politics, sociology, and comparative religion.

In Chapter 4, I contest theories on civilizational fault lines by introducing the voices of diversity in the writings of Aziz Ahmad (1913–78) and Mohammad Mujeeb (1902–85) on the one hand, and Nirad C. Chaudhuri (1897–1999) and the Trinidad-born V.S. Naipaul (b. 1932), on the other. Having seen something of the world in which they lived and wrote and of their plan to face the 'green peril', one is confronted with the infinitely more difficult task of assessing their impact. To do this is not to indulge in idle speculation. Of the four, Mujeeb alone showed awareness of the all-inclusive nature of the historical process of which he was part. The other three are naturally conservative, extol as knowledge what is already prejudice, and defend ways of thought and action that undermine democratic values. Nirad Chaudhuri seems to me to have a crucial position in the history I am tracing: he was heir to a great intellectual tradition in Bengal, with a mind moulded by the dominant ideas of his age.

Chapter 5 discusses the synthesis being worked out between the high Islamic custom-centred traditions which exist as complementary and integral parts of a common religious system and bestow upon Indian Islam a distinctive character.[15] The same story is taken up, with a shift in emphasis, in the next chapter on education and faith, education and the West, education and politics. Thererin I discuss some of the seminal writings on nineteenth- and early-twentieth-century Indian Islam.

In the chapter on partition I seek to situate—to borrow the jargon of the times—the discussion within the context of currently competing arguments and connect the many-layered partition history with the story previously told—the story of pluralism and composite living and its sudden collapse. Some recent works by Ravinder Kaur and Yasmin Khan force us to look again, and from a most uncomfortable angle, at the partition debates.

Fresh facts on post-colonial India have enforced fresh thinking, though historians stop at a point in time dictated by the transfer of power on

[15] Imtiaz Ahmad, 'For a Sociology of India', in T.N. Madan (ed.), *Muslim Communities of South Asia: Culture, Society and Power* (Delhi, 2001, 3rd enlarged edition), p. 18. For a contrary view, see Dipankar Gupta, *The Context of Ethnicity: Sikh Identity in a Comparative Perspective* (New Delhi, 1996), Chapter 7.

15 August 1947. The late Professor Sarvepalli Gopal (1923–2002) gave up the time-honoured practice in his three-volume study of Jawaharlal Nehru (1889–1964). Ramachandra Guha and Sarah Ansari have followed in his footsteps. My book, *Legacy of a Divided Nation: India's Muslims since Independence*, carries the story until the demolition of the Babri Masjid; another, *The Nehrus: Personal Histories*, closes with the assassination of Rajiv Gandhi (1944–91).[16] This book, too, moves back and forth into contemporary times. In Chapter 8, I use the recommendations of the government-appointed Sachar Committee to debate aspects of minority rights.

Socrates (470?–399 BC) suggested that the first task of philosophy was to clear away confusion and misrepresentation by defining the meaning of words. Let us therefore start with nationalism. Even though the idea which lies at its core is the 'nation',[17] most prevailing judgements tend to describe nationalism as 'a dark, elemental, unpredictable force of primordial nature threatening the orderly calm of civilized life'.[18] Nehru would not have agreed with this postmodern critique. To him, nationalism was inevitable in the 1930s and 1940s, and national freedom was the first and dominant urge, more so for India with her intense sense of individuality and past heritage.[19]

Like nationalism, 'secularism' is one of the most evocative themes of our time. This is not the place to attempt to say what secularism means. There have been enough attempts already. Dissected relentlessly in all quarters by generalists as well as social scientists of all hues, secularism is sometimes derided as a Western import unsuited to Indian soil where indigenous traditions of tolerance have a long-standing presence.[20] The secular project is itself questioned for its denial of collective, cultural identities in the past.[21] Without going into the nitty-gritty of these

[16] Ramachandra Guha, *India after Gandhi: The History of the World's Largest Democracy* (New Delhi, 2007); Sarah Ansari, *Life after Partition: Migration, Community and Strife in Sind 1947–1962* (Karachi, 2002); Mushirul Hasan, *The Nehrus: Personal Histories* (New Delhi, 2006).

[17] Liah Greenfeld, *Nationalism: Five Roads to Modernity* (London, 1992), pp. 3, 4.

[18] Partha Chatterjee, *The Nation and Its Fragments: Colonial and Postcolonial Histories* (New Delhi, 1994), p. 4.

[19] Jawaharlal Nehru, *The Discovery of India* (Calcutta, 1946 reprint), p. 33.

[20] Rajeev Bhargava, 'India's Secular Constitution', in Zoya Hasan, E. Sridharan, and R. Sudarshan (eds), *India's Living Constitution: Ideas, Practices, Controversies* (New Delhi, 2002).

[21] Sudhir Kakar, *The Colour of Nothingness* (New Delhi, 1996), p. 22.

controversies, I use the term 'secular state' to describe the relationship which exists, or which ought to exist, between the state and religion.[22] As Jawaharlal Nehru put it succinctly:

The word 'secular' perhaps is not a very happy one. And yet, for want of a better, we have used it. What exactly does it mean? It does not obviously mean a state where religion as such is discouraged. It means freedom of religion and conscience, including freedom for those who may have no religion. It means free play for all religions, subject only to their not interfering with each other or with the basic conceptions of our state. It means that the minority communities, from the religious point of view, should accept this position. It means, even more, that the majority community, from this point of view, should fully realize it. For, by virtue of numbers as well as in other ways, it is the dominant community and it is its responsibility not to use its position in any way which might prejudice our secular ideal.[23]

From secularism we move on, inevitably, to its antithesis, communalism, 'a narrow and disruptive creed', based on hatred and violence and the narrowest bigotry. Used as a pejorative term to denote narrow and parochial ideologies, it bears a striking resemblance to the various forms of fascism in other countries. It is in fact the Indian version of fascism.[24] And yet communalism was primarily the Hindu–Muslim problem, the Nehru Committee Report (August 1928) stated in its preamble to one of the chapters.[25] It referred to religious communities organizing themselves separately for promoting their specific interests. While discussing Sind's separation from the Bombay Presidency, the Report observed:

To say from the viewpoint of nationalism that no communal provinces should be created is, in a way, equivalent to saying from the still wider international viewpoint that there should be no separate nations. Both these statements have a measure of truth in them. But the staunchest internationalist recognizes that without the fullest national autonomy, it is extraordinarily difficult to create the international State. So also, without the fullest cultural autonomy—and communalism in its better aspect is culture—it will be difficult to create a harmonious nation.[26]

[22] D.E. Smith, *India as a Secular State* (Princeton, NJ, 1963), pp. 3, 454.

[23] Uma Iyengar (ed.), *The Oxford India Nehru* (New Delhi, 2007), pp. 65–6.

[24] Ibid., p. 385.

[25] *All Parties Conference 1928. Report of the Committee Appointed by the Conference to determine the principles of the Constitution for India* (Allahabad, 1928), p. 27.

[26] Ibid., p. 68.

While Nehru regarded communalism as an essentialy political, economic, and middle class phenomenon that did not affect the masses,[27] Iqbal considered it indispensable for the formation of a harmonious whole in India.[28] Still others see communalism as one aspect of the pre-modern, which is central to the reality and ideology of fundamentalist movements.[29] It is pioneered from below, especially in north and central India and much less in the southern region, by the creation of a strong communitarian consciousness pitted against the 'other' and from above by the political demands of mass-based mobilization. This makes possible the entry of the communal groups, Hindus, Muslims, and Sikhs, onto the political stage.

Today of course the motives imputed to 'communalism' are different from those that were imputed in the 1940s. Yet the best definition of communalism is still that given by Wilfred Cantwell Smith in 1946:

Communalism in India may be defined as that ideology which has emphasized as the social, political, and economic unit the group of adherents of each religion, and has emphasized the distinction, even the antagonism, between such groups; the words 'adherent' and 'religion' being taken in the most nominal sense. Muslim communalists, for instance, have been highly conscious of the Muslims within India as a supposedly single, cohesive community, to which they devote their loyalty—paying little attention to whether the individuals included are religiously ardent, tepid, or cold; orthodox, liberal, or atheist; righteous or vicious; or to whether they are landlord or peasant, prince or proletarian; also paying little attention to Muslims outside of India.[30]

India's unity,' stated Iqbal at the Muslim League session in December 1930, had to be sought not in the negation, but in the mutual harmony and cooperation of the many.[31] This is pluralism, pure and simple. It implies adjustment of the masses through a slow but gradual process and their knitting together in a common country and living in perpetual proximity. Concerned to protect and perpetuate particular existing cultures, pluralism respects diversity but promotes affiliation on the narrower grounds of

[27] Jawaharlal Nehru to Lord Lothian, 17 January 1936, in Iyengar, *The Oxford India Nehru*, pp. 123–4.

[28] Pirzada, *Foundations of Pakistan*, vol. 2, p. 158.

[29] Leonard Weinberg and Ami Pedahazur (eds), *Religious Fundamentalism and Political Extremism* (London, 2004), p. 29.

[30] W.C. Smith, *Modern Islam in India* (Lahore, 1946), p. 1.

[31] Pirzada, *Foundations of Pakistan*, vol. 2, p. 159.

shared history. It respects inherited boundaries and locates individuals
within one or another of a series of ethno-racial groups to be protected
and preserved.[32]

Without going into the roots and deeper meanings of terms like
'syncretism', 'public arena', 'public culture', or 'public sphere', I adopt the
commonly accepted textbook definitions. To me, for example, syncretism
is no more than a simple, innocent sentiment expressed by Jahanara
Begum in 'If' by Sunil Gangopadhyay (1918–70). Read in the context of
the tenacious mental divide wrought by partition, this story portrays the
crossing of that invisible barrier of religious prejudice within a middle-
class family where a Muslim son is married to a Hindu girl. However,
the mother wants the grandchild to imbibe the values of Islam. Still,
her memories of syncretic practices are so strong that they are brought
back during a visit to her daughter-in-law's house on a festive occasion.

Jahanara Begum raised herself slowly. Wonder whose bed this was! She kept looking
at Deepa with a fixed gaze. Soon a faint smile appeared on her face. Lowering her
voice to a whisper, she said, 'I hope you've been able to complete your Puja properly?
Deepa, don't you all prepare a ceremonial *prasad* with some *atap* rice, bananas and
batashas? I remember having that when I was a child, I used to love it so much, can
you please bring me a little of that now?'[33]

In *Man and Superman*, Bernard Shaw (1856–1950) wrote that a book's
artistic quality is determined not by the opinions it propagates but by
the fact that the writer has opinions.[34] Without displaying any artistic
quality, I hold on to certain values and, at the same time, propagate them.
For example, whether or not Islamism is the ideology of Islamic
internationalism which has evolved as a variety of religious fundamentalism,[35] I consider its impact to be detrimental to the Muslims
themselves. I say this as a Muslim seeking a place for Islam and for its
adherents in a set-up of democratic peace based on a global civil society
and its civic values.[36] Even though it is misleading to suggest that Islamists

[32] David A. Hollinger, *Post Ethnic America: Beyond Multiculturalism* (New York, 1995),
pp. 3, 79–82.

[33] Bashabi Fraser (ed.), *Bengal Partition Stories: An Unclosed Chapter* (London, 2006),
p. 442.

[34] Bernard Shaw, *Prefaces by Bernard Shaw* (London, 1934), p. 165.

[35] Tibi, *Islam between Culture and Politics*, p. 270.

[36] Ibid. I have amended some words of Bassam Tibi.

are 'nourished by an Islamic tradition that is intrinsically inhuman and violent in its rhetoric, thought and practice',[37] there is no denying that the totalitarian forces seeking redemption through violence cause greater damage to the Muslims themselves and not the West alone.

The same applies to jihad (refers to effort or exertion) which bears no resonance in the minds of the poor and the weak. It can therefore be used as an inclusive concept, incorporating the values in Asoka's *dhamma*, in Sufism, and in the Din-e Ilahi of Jalaluddin Akbar (r. 1556–1605). Why jihad only against the unbeliever? In Islam's true ecumenical spirit, one can think of 'gender jihad' as a weapon for establishing gender justice in Muslim thought and praxis.[38] In fact, it is possible to wage *jihad-e akbar* ('the greater jihad') and restore the egalitarian spirit of Islam with patience, forbearance, and high ethics. After all, the Prophet had proclaimed: 'O believers, be you securers of justice, witnesses for God, even though it be against yourselves, or your parents and kinsmen, whether it concerns rich or poor, for God is nearer to you than both. And do not follow caprice, so as to swerve [from the truth].'

The Urdu poet, Ali Sardar Jafri (1913–2000), wrote:

> Neither Chengiz lives any longer, nor Timur,
> What have survived are the People,
> The youthful waves of the ocean of time,
> Gush and flow from eternity to eternity,
> Ours is a story of the millennia;
> For we are invincible, eternal
> We are the designs and patterns of civilizations,
> We are the aspirations of the hearts,
> We have been over engaged in struggles,
> We are the sharp swords of history.[39]

The general optimism in poets like Jafri is much more likely to lead to positive results than the lazy cynicism which is becoming all too common nowadays. Graduate students and teachers would benefit from

---

[37] Ziauddin Sardar, cited in Hasan Suroor, 'Debate or Denial: The Muslim Dilemma', *Hindu*, 17 July 2007.

[38] Amira Wadud, *Inside the Gender Jihad* (Oxford, 2006), p. 10.'

[39] Squadron Leader Anil Sehgal (ed.), *Ali Sardar Jafri: The Youth Boatman of Joy* (New Delhi, 2001), pp. 77–87.

the following observation of Pieter Geyl (1887–1966), the Dutch historian, if they are committed to tolerance, freedom, and dissent.

History, then, will carry us to the sources of what still is our civilization, the civilization of our time. And it is a work of restoration, it is a work of reconstruction, to devote attention to our past, to study history. It is an escape from the present, it is strengthening ourselves for the struggle that is calling us. I tell you so, and I hope that you will feel it yourselves, or will learn to feel it. But this does not mean that I want to impress upon you that in your study you should be continually animated by present-day occupations. Not a bit of it. On the contrary. Plunge into the subject, work hard, stick to the laws and the rules of the subject, exercise your powers of criticism and of discrimination…. The other thing will come, if it can come, of its own accord.[40]

---

[40] Pieter Geyl, *Debate with Historians* (London, 1985), pp. 277–86; see also his *Encounters in History* (London, 1967), pp. 242–3.

2

Of Bitter Passions

Prejudices, racism, and Islamophobia are tangible expressions of the hard reality of Western societies, and Muslims must not naively think that these will simply disappear, as they become citizens settled in their societies. Increasingly, and for a considerable period, they will have to become accustomed to facing political security measures, discrimination, accusations of 'double-talk', menacing, malevolent looks, and acts of surveillance and control. Distrust is so great and suspicion so widespread that times of mutual trust seem still to be far away. But rather than complaining sadly, it seems to me that there is only one response to this state of affairs: to hold to one's convictions; express one's principles and hopes; make clear comments and criticisms; keep to one, open way of speaking (with Muslims and with one's fellow-citizens); participate in society for good in partnership with all human beings who, in conscience, reject a world without conscience; and, armed with one's faith and a critical mind, reject dualism and keep one's head by cultivating patience and long-suffering.
—Tariq Ramadan, *Western Muslims and the Future of Islam*, p. 230

The University of Edinburgh launched the 'Islamic Surveys' series in 1969 to counteract the relative neglect of the achievements of Islam in the Indo-Pakistan subcontinent. W. Montgomery Watt, General Editor, described South Asia as not a mere frontier of Islam but an integral part of the Islamic world. Moreover, Indian Islam preceded the heartlands in receiving and responding to the European impact. For these and many other reasons, its histories received scholarly attention.[1]

'The story of the Muslims in India has been a long one, with many vicissitudes,' wrote Wilfred Cantwell Smith (1916–2000) in 1957. 'In it has been much of importance, much of grandeur, much of turmoil (both inflicted and suffered). The point is that that story is not yet over.'[2] Well, we have allowed decades to pass without asking ourselves many vital questions, not because we did not have the time but because we were either unconcerned or took for granted that we had all the answers. As a result, wide areas of the Muslim/Islamic movements, institutions, liberal thought, and reformers are represented by only a handful of articles or the occasional book. Peter Hardy, the historian, explained the reason:

Largely for political reasons—the British urge to establish the superior quality of their rule over Muslim, the Muslims' own search for their identity in modern South Asia and the Hindu debate whether to regard Muslims as brother freedom fighters or as deposed conquerors—the study of Islam and of Muslims in South Asia is as yet neither as disciplined, dispassionate nor as sophisticated as the study of Islam and of Muslims in the classical lands of Islam.[3]

The vibrancy of Indian Islam is not in doubt. Richard Eaton refers to the 'double-movement' between the local cultures of South Asia and the 'universal norms of Islam, and points to the enormous variation of Islamic traditions not only across social class and over time, but also across space'.[4] Asim Roy, the author of a classic study on Islamic syncretism,[5] emphasizes 'historical' and 'lived' Islam with its 'breadth, elasticity, tolerance and creativity' that has made the religion 'a rich, vital, living, and great civilization'.[6] Finally, Francis Robinson has

---

[1] Aziz Ahmad, *An Intellectual History of Islam in India* (Edinburgh, 1969), p. v.

[2] W.C. Smith, *Islam in Modern History* (Princeton, NJ, 1957). According to the British historian Percival Spear, Indian Islam is 'a necklace of racial, cultural, and political pearls strung on the thread of religion. One cannot appreciate the necklace merely by studying the thread'. 'The Position of the Muslims before and after Partition', in Philip Mason (ed.), *India and Ceylon: Unity and Diversity* (London, 1967), p. 31.

[3] Peter Hardy, *The Muslims of British India* (Cambridge, 1972), p. 261.

[4] Richard Eaton (ed.), *India's Islamic Traditions, 711–1750* (New Delhi, 2003), p. 6.

[5] Asim Roy, *The Islamic Syncretistic Tradition in Bengal* (Princeton, NJ, 1983).

[6] Asim Roy, *Islam in History and Politics: Perspectives from South Asia* (New Delhi, 2006), p. 17.

suggested that India's Muslims were unique in the intensity of their self-conscious identity, notable in their development of a separate political identity, and famed, at least in the early 1920s, for voicing pan-Islamic concerns.[7]

Despite the greater numbers and more varied intellectual activities of Indian Muslims, it is the Arabs who still constitute the real core of Islam.[8] A book on 'Muslim Politics' refers to 154 million Indian Muslims as many as fourteen times.[9] *Intellectuals in the Modern Islamic World* carries chapters on Egypt, Morocco, Bosnia-Herzegovina, Saudi Arabia, China, Pakistan, and Japan but none on India.[10] Their peoples are among the 'makers of Contemporary Islam';[11] they alone represent 'The New Voices of Islam'.[12] Indian Muslims, on the other hand, survive on the margins of the academic consciousness; nobody even notices their varied social life and organizations.[13]

This is not an uncommon trend, for it is often argued that the classical heritage of Islam remains external to Indian history.[14] Nirad Chaudhuri, an intellectual of standing, believed that upper caste Bengali Hindus ignored the Muslim intellectual ferment until its political consequences became threateningly clear to them.[15] Some other writers find fault with the Orientalists and their absorption in the Arab heartland rather than India such that Indian Islam is not considered part of the great Islamic civilization centring on the Middle East. To the extent the Muslims figure in scholarly works on India, it is to narrate the story of the Mughal decline

[7] Francis Robinson, *Islam, South Asia, and the West* (New Delhi, 2007), p. 142.

[8] H.A.R. Gibb, *Modern Trends in Islam* (Illinois, 1945), p. x.

[9] Dale F. Eikelman and James Piscatori, *Muslim Politics* (Delhi, 1997).

[10] Stephane A. Dudoignon, Komatsu Hisao, and Kosugi Yasushi (eds), *Intellectuals in the Modern Islamic World* (London, 2007).

[11] John L. Esposito and John O. Voll (eds), *Makers of Contemporary Islam* (New York, 2001); Mark Sedgwick, *Islam and Muslims: A Guide to Diverse Experiences in a Modern World* (Boston, MA, 2006). Olivier Roy, *Globalised Islam: The Search for a New Ummah* (London, 2004).

[12] Mehran Kamrava (ed.), *The New Voices of Islam: Reforming Politics and Modernity—A Reader* (London, 2006).

[13] Imtiaz Ahmad, 'For a Sociology of India', *Contributions to Indian Sociology*, vol. 6, 1972, pp. 172–8; Nasreen Fazalbhoy, 'Sociology of Muslims in India', *Economic and Political Weekly*, 28 June 1997, pp. 1547–51; Akbar S. Ahmed, *Discovering Islam: Making Sense of Muslim History and Society* (London, 1988), especially Chapter 10.

[14] Partha Chatterjee, *The Nation and Its Fragments: Colonial and Postcolonial Histories* (New Delhi, 1994).

[15] Nirad C. Chaudhuri, *The Intellectual in India* (New Delhi, 1967), p. 7.

and not to showcase a highly cultured, and in many respects tolerant, society.[16]

In contrast to Europe where Islamic scholarship had developed, by the second half of the nineteenth century, an organization—methods of teaching, publication, and communication—and acquired a self-perpetuating authority which has continued to exist until today,[17] M.N. Roy (1887–1954), a leading Indian intellectual-activist of the first half of the twentieth century, drew a picture of the two communities—Hindu and Muslim—living together for centuries without being aware of each other's culture and religion. The Hindus were by and large ignorant of the 'immense revolutionary significance' of Islam and the varieties of the 'Islamic spirit'. This being the case, Roy wanted to awaken interest in Islam's contribution to human culture.[18]

In an earlier work (*The Historical Role of Islam*, 1918) Roy had emphasized that the Muslims had adopted India as their own, forming an integral part of the society, and the combined Hindu–Muslim support sustained the Sultans of Delhi (1206–1526) and the Mughals (1526–1857). Overseas travellers represented their reign as prosperous and socially tranquil,[19] where in the absence of a 'drain of wealth' the people and not foreign exploiters benefited from whatever limited progress took place. 'All conquerors are conquered in turn,' observed Halide Edib (1884–1964), the Turkish author visiting India in 1935. 'But,' she added,

there is a difference between the conquerors who are attached to some outside Power and thereby retain their individuality, and the conquerors who have no outside attachment and must settle down on the land of their conquest and make it their permanent home. The Muslim conquerors of India were of the second kind, therefore destined to a greater degree of assimilation.[20]

Roy insisted that the medieval era of Muslim dynasties was as much a part of India's history as any other previous era,[21] and that Islam and

[16] Peter van der Veer, *Religious Nationalism: Hindus and Muslims in India* (California, 1994), p. 20.

[17] Albert Hourani, *Islam in European Thought* (Cambridge, 1991), p. 2.

[18] M.N. Roy, *The Historical Role of Islam* (New Delhi, 1981 reprint), p. 57; Sibnarayan Ray (ed.), *Selected Works of M.N. Roy* (New Delhi, 1997), vol. 4, p. 401.

[19] Ray, *Selected Works of M.N. Roy*, vol. 1, p. 99.

[20] Halide Edib, *Inside India*. With an introduction and notes by Mushirul Hasan (New Delhi, 2002), pp. 210–11.

[21] Ray, *Selected Works of M.N. Roy*, vol. 1, p. 98.

Hinduism had to find a mutual settlement whether the conquerors and the conquered so desired or not. This fact alone had to be agreed upon by all and interpreted objectively in order to bridge the psychological Hindu–Muslim divide.[22]

Jawaharlal Nehru, who met Roy during his brief visit to Moscow in 1927 on the tenth anniversary of the Bolshevik Revolution, explained the neglect of Islam in terms of the upper castes regarding Islam as a rather crude approach to the problems of philosophy and metaphysics.[23] His own tone, both in *An Autobiography* as well as *The Discovery of India*, is generous and reflective. Indeed, he agreed with Abdullah Yusuf Ali (1872–1955), also educated in Cambridge, that the Hindus and Muslims had failed to work out a synthesis in their everyday life, and that it was essential to create a solid and enduring understanding 'based on the inner dictates of our own hearts'.[24]

Some early-nineteenth-century British writings villified Islam to establish the rightness of their rule by contrasting it with the evil deeds of their Muslim predecessors, so as to discourage Indians from developing distorted ideas about their own past and consequently about their present and future. With notable exceptions and with significant regional variations, the Indian literati, too, bought the theories woven around this agenda. In the process they positioned Islam outside their frame of reference and subordinated the entire historical process to an abstract theory rooted in the tyranny of Muslim rulers, their disruption of Hindu culture, and the destruction of the sacred unity of the motherland. In many fictional histories, medieval rule is only about the rape and abduction of Hindu women, the slaughter of sacred cows, and the defilement of temples. Writers like Bharatendu Harishchandra (1850–85), the Hindi poet, went to the extreme of belittling Urdu as 'the language of dancing girls and prostitutes'.[25]

---

[22] Ibid., vol. 4, p. 400.

[23] Jawaharlal Nehru, *The Discovery of India* (Calcutta, 1946 reprint), p. 225.

[24] Stephen N. Hay, *Asian Ideas of East and West: Tagore and His Critics in Japan, China, and India* (Bombay, 1970), p. 302.

[25] Vasudha Dalmia, *The Nationalization of the Hindu Traditions: Bharatendu Harischandra and Nineteenth-century Banaras* (New Delhi, 1997), pp. 208, 212. The mosque built by Aurangzeb (1658–1707) beside the sacred Vishvanath temple in Varanasi, kept fresh the 'wounds in his heart'. See also Sudhir Chandra, 'Communal Consciousness in Late 19th Century', in Mushirul Hasan (ed.), *Communal and Pan-Islamic Trends in Colonial India* (New Delhi, 1985 revised and enlarged edition), pp. 180–95, and his *The Oppressive*

The printing of books and pamphlets contributed to the negative representation of Islam and to the perpetuation of the view that the Hindus and Muslims belonged to the most diverse and mutually incomparable spheres. The virtuous were represented as those who had tried to obstruct Muslim rule. Historians, writers, poets, publicists, and reformers used religious symbols to implant and nurture a 'national' sentiment. Such initiatives in late-nineteenth-century Maharashtra or Punjab militated against the Congress ideology, but their true implications for the emergence of communitarian identities have not been examined even by later-day intellectuals, trained in argument and analysis.

Every attempt at historical interpretation, wrote Alfred Cobban (1901–68), the historian of the French Revolution, must stand or fall by its consistency with evidence.[26] Let us see how this might hold true for Nirad Chaudhuri, who, one presumes, converted a good many English and Bengali readers to his credo.

Intellectually, the Hindus outraged the 'European mind' precisely in those three principles which were fundamental to its approach to life, and which it had been applying with ever greater strictness since the Renaissance: that of reason, that of order, and that of measure. Discussing A Passage to India by E.M. Forster (1879–1970), Chaudhuri is uncomfortable with Aziz and the other supporting Muslim characters. In his view, Forster created sympathetic Muslim characters because he shared the liking the British had for the Muslims, and the corresponding dislike for the Hindus. So Dr Godbole appears a clown rather than an exponent of Hinduism.

Gifted enough to distinguish between good and evil, Chaudhuri disregards the commonly accepted social and cultural norms. He therefore finds himself in moral conflict with existing institutions and defends himself by his own convoluted logic. The noteworthy points are: Why does Aziz fluster him? Is it not rather that he began with a conviction and then set out to prove it? More generally, it is worth asking why Muslim characters did not figure, with some notable exceptions, in Bengali

---

Present: Literature and Social Consciousness in Colonial India (New Delhi, 1992). On the stereotypical recollection of Muslim conquest and its impact on 'Hindu India', see Shahid Amin, 'On Retelling the Muslim Conquest of North India', in Partha Chatterjee and Anjan Ghose (eds), History and the Present (New Delhi, 2002), pp. 25–43.

[26] Alfred Cobban, The Social Interpretation of the French Revolution (Cambridge, 1964), p. 162.

literary writings (outside the circle of Muslim writers) for well over a century. I seek answers to these questions in this chapter.

History can be made to supply the plot and the setting for a mind already made up. One of Chaudhuri's central arguments is that the Muslim intellectual tradition ran wholly independent of and without being influenced by the Hindus.[27] It is glaringly obvious that this proposition does not rest securely on the kind of historical foundations he had built up so laboriously in his biographies of Robert Clive (1725–74) and the Oxford-based German Orientalist Max Mueller (1823–1900). Census reports and Gazetteers alone testify to the scale and depth of cultural and religious intermingling in rural as well as urban Bengal. The Baul singers of Bengal indicate a strong undercurrent of non-conformist popular materialism in the remote villages of Bengal.[28]

Reviewing Chaudhuri's *The Autobiography of an Unknown Indian*, Susobhan Sarkar (1900–82) commented that the true determinants of medieval Indian civilization were not pure Islamic religion, language, or social practice, and that Chaudhuri erred in disregarding the medieval coexistence of the Hindu and Muslim religions and their mutual influence, especially in rural Bengal. According to him, the way of life of the masses, the village organization, the social structure remained largely the same throughout the ages.[29]

Mahesh by Sarat Chandra Chatterjee (1876–1938), Bengal's most popular novelist and short story writer, is a narrative of the deprivation in peasant life as seen through the life of the landless peasant, Gafoor. Within the story, the author deftly weaves the web of inter-community life. The choice of the title *Mahesh*, another name for Lord Shiva, brings out in stark terms his indictment of the Hindu priest–zamindar combine as against Gafoor's simple and unalloyed love and devotion for Mahesh. In the end, the zamindar's oppression compels Gafoor to leave the village and seek employment in the jute mills of Fulbere where he had refused to work earlier, because 'there was no religion, no honour and privacy for women there'. The story concludes on the following note:

[27] Chaudhuri, *Intellectual in India*, p. 5.

[28] Rajat Kanta Ray (ed.), *Mind, Body and Society: Life and Mentality in Colonial Bengal* (Calcutta, 1995), p. 14; Sumit Sarkar, *The Swadeshi Movement in Bengal, 1903–1908* (New Delhi, 1973), pp. 408–9.

[29] Susobhan Sarkar, *Bengal Renaissance and Other Essays* (New Delhi, 1970), p. 192.

Gafoor set out holding the hand of his daughter in the darkness of the night. He had no one to call his own in the village; he had nothing to say to anyone. As he crossed the courtyard and reached the acacia tree, he stopped dead in his tracks and burst out crying loudly. Lifting up his head to the star studded black sky he said—'Allah, punish me as much as you like ... But Mahesh died with his thirst unquenched. They did not leave the tiniest patch of land for him to graze. Don't forgive the person who robbed him of the grass and the water that are your gifts to all creatures.'[30]

In *Gora*, Rabindranath Tagore's celebrated novel, the barber feels solidarity with the Muslims rather than with their Hindu oppressors.[31] Chaudhuri knew this, but it suited him to disregard the energy behind any form of cultural synthesis and the fact that such energy is derived not from any external, unintelligible force, but from the sheer experience of living together in a village. Cultural synthesis is, in the words of Mujeeb, 'an invitation to live and feel in a larger world, to see in love and suffering, beauty and indifference, grace and elusiveness a universalism that resents and rejects the bondage of time and space'.[32] Chaudhuri, by contrast, resented such a synthesis with unruffled serenity. Evidence of fraternal living inspired him with distrust, composite culture invoked immediate rejection. Notice the following passage:

In certain parts of India, notably the Punjab and Hindustan, the Hindus were so crushed by the Muslim conquest that they could just save their religion and social organization, but could not save their culture and its external features. Clothing, language, script were some of the things over which they had to accept compromises. So many Hindus took to wearing the Muslim costume, speaking Urdu, and writing in the Arabic script, and by doing all these things they gradually lost the sense, not only of the uncleanliness of these things from the Hindu point of view, but even of the unnaturalness. This was particularly true of the Punjab. I have seen Hindus belonging to such a strict sect as the Arya Samaj reading the Gita in an Urdu translation. It should also be recalled that the Rajputs, Marathas, and Jats, all of whom rose in revolt against Muslim rule, did not mind wearing the Muslim costume, even though they called the Muslim a Yavan in contempt.[33]

---

[30] Introduction, in Mushirul Hasan and M. Asaduddin (eds), *Image and Representation: Stories of Muslim Lives in India* (New Delhi, 2000), p. 9.

[31] Ashis Nandy, *The Illegitimacy of Nationalism* (New Delhi, 1994), p. 38.

[32] Mohammad Mujeeb, *Islamic Influence on Indian Society* (Meerut, 1972), p. 137.

[33] Nirad C. Chaudhuri, *Culture in the Vanity Bag* (Bombay, 1976), p. 92.

The author of these views did not ever admit the falseness of his kind of argument. The smouldering fire of bigotry blazed in the romances of Indian chivalry, of which several were published in the early twentieth century. The facts of history mattered little, if at all, to Nirad Chaudhuri.

As much as any of the other works, *The Autobiography of an Unknown India* (1951) owed its conception as well its tone and spirit to the impressions created by the partition of Bengal in 1906 and of India in 1947. Chaudhuri projected his interpretation, a mixture of fear and enmity, backwards and onwards. His literature of denunciation began with an appraisal of the Sultans and the Mughals and extended to a generalized hostility towards the Muslims. Even though Chaudhuri would have known of Muslim participation in virtually every aspect of the swadeshi movement,[34] he still nursed 'a new kind of hatred' for Muslims at that time.[35] 'We as children,' he recalled, 'held the tiny mustard in our hands and sowed it very diligently. In fact, this conflict was implicit in the very unfolding of our history, and could hardly be avoided.'[36]

Chaudhuri lambasted Muslim clerics without reflecting on the role of those, notably Abul Kalam Azad (1888–1956), who had revolutionary links in their early days.[37] He should have known that a number of them also worked towards the overthrow of the British in the 'Silk Letter Conspiracy' of 1915 (letters urging revolt against the British were wrapped in a piece of cloth), in which the students, teachers, and the head of Deoband's Dar al-ulum, proudly called 'the Azhar of the East',[38] took active part.

One day I saw a procession of Muslim divines trooping into Sarat Babu's house. I was quite familiar with the modern Muslim dress, but had no idea that these learned

[34] Sarkar, *Swadeshi Movement*, p. 426.

[35] Nirad C. Chaudhuri, *Hinduism: A Religion to Live by* (New Delhi, 1979), p. 232.

[36] Nirad. C. Chaudhuri, *The Autobiography of an Unknown Indian* (New York, 1951), p. 225.

[37] Rajat Kanta Ray, 'Revolutionaries, Pan-Islamists and Bolsheviks: Maulana Abul Kalam Azad and the Political Underworld in Calcutta, 1905–1925', in Hasan, *Communal and Pan-Islamic Trends*, pp. 103–18.

[38] A group of *ulama* established, after 1857, the most important *maktab*, which later developed into Dar al-ulum (an institution of high learning). As a seminary, this institution aimed at resisting social and religious changes introduced by the British and maintaining the cultural and religious identity of the Muslims. Rashid Ahmad Gangohi (d. 1905), one of its founders, strongly opposed the introduction of Western education and supported the Indian National Congress in order to counter the activities of Syed Ahmad Khan.

Muslims wore different clothes. They did, for they had green gowns on and big turbans on their heads. ... We, the educated and urban Bengalis, with not a fraction of Westernization in our manner of living, did not even imagine that such persons existed in Bengal. I with my knowledge of Islamic painting could only assume when I saw them that they were crude incarnations of the Muslim divines I had seen portrayed in Persian or Mughal miniatures. Their faces were grave, and even stern. One face struck me very forcibly. It was pinched and peevish, but of an incredible ferocity. The eyes were large, black, and burning, and in that emaciated face they looked even blacker and larger. ... He looked like an ill-dressed Robespierre, the sea-green Incorruptible. Sarat Babu's house was not only crowded for the occasion with these survivals of Islam, but even reeked of them.[39]

This was the man who claimed to have eagerly drunk in the message of 1789, the year of the French Revolution. In one of his celebrated books, Chaudhuri wrote:

Muslims are now expiating for their short-sighted arrogance, which makes me observe that whatever clever people might say in defence of unscrupulousness in politics, and about its success, there is some power in the universe which sees to it that such cynicism does not pay, and that nothing but what is inherently right ever succeeds. Define it as you like, as theodicy or the justice of history, it is there, irrespective of any name. We see the operation of that power in the sad fate of the Muslims of India, both in the Hindu and in the Muslim state. What gave them victory in 1947 was not the opportunistic policy of their leaders, but their fanatical devotion to a cause which was a lost one in history. So, there is no escape for them today from that lost cause, and still less from the intolerable burden of fighting to the last for a lost cause.[40]

Here, again, Chaudhuri is guilty of disregarding common sense to feed his own petty prejudices. Otherwise, why speak of 'victory' in 1947? Victory for whom? India's 'tryst with destiny' apart, that year brought tragedy rather than triumph.

Why demonize the Muslims? What is the cause of such pettiness and intellectual poverty? Bhudeb Mukhopadhyay (1827–94), a thinker of stature, blamed British historiography and bureaucratic machinations for the deterioration of inter-community relations.[41] Chaudhuri would

[39] Nirad C. Chaudhuri, *Thy Hand Great Anarch! India, 1921–1952* (London, 1987), p. 469.
[40] Nirad C. Chaudhuri, *The Continent of Circe* (London, 1965), p. 252.
[41] Amiya P. Sen, *Hindu Revivalism in Bengal 1872: Some Essays in Interpretation* (New

not admit that this was so. 'Nothing was more natural for us,' he states, 'than to feel about the Muslims in the way we did.' His teachers in school impressed upon their students that Islam spread by force, Muslims abducted women, and their rulers desecrated temples and forcibly converted Hindus to their faith. They also talked about the wars of the Rajputs, the Marathas, the Sikhs, and the oppression of Aurangzeb.[42] Later in life, Chaudhuri (and perhaps his classmates as well) says he became aware of the enormity of destruction of places of worship. It was impossible to judge, he wrote, what Hindu temple architecture was like in its homeland in the greatest age of Hindu civilization.[43] During all those centuries all over northern India, he asserted absurdly, only the ruins of the temples survived.[44]

Looking closely, Chaudhuri's 'liberalism' was heavily laden with Bengali revivalist consciousness. Writing in *Thy Hand Great Anarch!*, he recalled—without showing the slightest awareness of the resistance movements against the West in many parts of the world—celebrating Italy's attack on Tripoli in 1911, although his own father called it downright robbery, which indeed it was, and exulting at the victories of Serbia, Bulgaria, and the other Balkan states. After Turkey joined Germany at the end of 1914, he felt that the Muslims would be taught a lesson.[45] The British defeats in the Dardanelles and Mesopotamia upset him, 'as strongly as any Englishman', whereas the Treaty of Sevres, despite being 'unfair', did not.[46]

Delhi, 1993), p. 172; Tapan Raychaudhuri, *Europe Reconsidered: Perceptions of the West in Nineteenth Century Bengal* (New Delhi, 1988), pp. 41–2.

[42] Chaudhuri, *Thy Hand Great Anarch!*, p. 226.

[43] Chaudhuri, *Hinduism*, p.126.

[44] Ibid.

[45] Chaudhuri, *Thy Hand Great Anarch!*, p. 37.

[46] Ibid., p. 37. The Turkish peace terms (14 May 1920) produced a blaze of resentment among every section of the Muslim community and gave a new dimension to the Khilafat agitation. Under the peace terms, Turkey was to be shorn of its Arab possessions—Syria, Palestine, Mesopotamia, Hijaz, and other Turkish provinces in the Arab peninsula. The portion of the Bosphorus on the Asiatic and European shores was to be internationalized. The other half, extending from St. Stefano to Dalma Bagtche, was declared a port of international interest under a commission on which Turkey was not even represented. In fact, the peace terms proposed to sever from Turkey provinces and districts predominantly inhabited by the Turks, and to impose suzerainty over the Turkish sovereign which, according to the Indian Muslims, would affect his status and prestige as the religious head

At the time of the annulment of Bengal's partition in 1911, Maharaja Manindra Chunder Nundi lamented that in East Bengal 'the Muslim population will preponderate (and) the Bengali Hindu will be in a minority. We shall be strangers in our own land.'[47] Chaudhuri agreed. History for him meant celebrating British rule as an age of liberation from Muslim despotism; its key objective being to prevent this 'despotism' from returning to Bengal when the British withdrew from their Indian Empire and to deny that Muslims could be Bengalis and, by extension, Indians.[48] 'Repelled' by the prospect of living in a Muslim-dominated Bengal,[49] he talked of the Muslim menace growing from minute to minute. The moral was simple enough: confront the devil now; for tomorrow it may be too late.

Bengal's partition unleashed the resentment of the poor, mainly the Muslim peasantry,[50] against the rich and the Hindu landlord–money-lender combine. After the tremors of Swadeshi subsided, the landlords and their allies struck a deal with the government to bolster their influence in society and administration. They took advantage of the benefits accruing from the Montagu-Chelmsford Reforms of 1918, and wrested control of the Bengal Congress, the party of the dominant classes, chiefly the Hindu jotedars. Soon enough, the 'Congress of the poor' treated the

---

of the community. Finally, the terms were designed to retain the protectorate of the sacred cities of Islam in non-Muslim hands.

[47] 'Proceedings of the Town Hall Protest Meeting, 7 August 1905', in All about Partition, India Office Library, London, Track 1037.

[48] Joya Chatterji, Bengal Divided: Hindu Communalism and Partition, 1932–1947 (Cambridge, 1995), p. 268.

[49] Ibid., p. 466.

[50] The vast majority of Bengali Muslims were peasants. Among ordinary cultivators, Muslims were almost twice the number of Hindus, but among landlords there were nearly twice as many Hindus as Muslims. The Permanent Settlement had resulted in many families, mainly Muslim, losing their lands to a new class of Hindu landlords. The Resumption Proceedings between 1828 and 1846 not only further impoverished the few Muslim families that had survived the Permanent Settlement but also destroyed the economic basis of Muslim educational institutions, which were almost entirely maintained by revenue-free grants. By the end of the nineteenth century, Hindus owned most of the land in Bengal. This was most strikingly evident in eastern Bengal, a Muslim-majority area. Muslims formed 80 per cent of the population in Bogra district, but there were only five Muslim zamindars. Muslims were 64.8 per cent of the population in Bakargunj district, but they owned less than ten per cent of the estates and paid less than nine per cent of the total land revenue. Anil Seal, The Emergence of Indian Nationalism: Competition and Collaboration in the Later Nineteenth Century (Cambridge, 1971), pp. 301–2.

other political formations, albeit weak, the parties of the masses, with a mixture of fear, contempt, and indifference. Of particular interest in all this was the defence of privileges and alliance with the landed classes, whose interests and aspirations were markedly different from those of the Hindu or Muslim peasantry.

More spectacular were the open collisions in the Bengal Legislative Council. In 1928 and 1937–9, the lines of division were clear-cut: whereas the Muslim members backed the motions against the landlords who cowed and browbeat the *raiyats*/sharecroppers, the Hindu members, especially Congressmen, tended to be pro-landlord.[51] Fazlul Haq (1873–1962), a product of Calcutta University, resigned from government service to join the Bar in 1912, entered the Bengal Legislative Council in 1912, and took a leading part in the Congress–League negotiations of 1916. Starting public life as a 'nationalist', he served as secretary of the Congress from 1918 to 1919. An upwardly mobile commoner who reached the top of the social ladder, he found the traditional image of the Muslims in which social mobility was an unacceptable anomaly, and substituted a new image for it, that of a *community* as it came to be understood by the colonial government. As the founder of the Krishak Proja Party in 1927, he championed the interests of an oppressed and impoverished peasantry. Precisely because the peasants were becoming more conscious of their rights, the old feudal survivals and privileges appeared all the more vexatious and intolerable.

Paradoxically, though, Fazlul Haq was condemned, especially after becoming Bengal's chief minister from 1 April 1937 to March 1943, as 'communal' and 'separatist' whereas his detractors, who whipped up religious passions for personal gains, were extolled as 'nationalists'/ 'freedom fighters'. People like Nirad Chaudhuri categorized Fazlul Haq as communal and drew certain conclusions, mostly erroneous, from the growing polarization in Bengal's polity. 'No one will grudge Mr. Chaudhuri seeking his own consolation,' observed Sarkar. 'But,' he added, 'the path of history is indeed devious. And in all probability, his firm conclusions will break down in the process of its unfolding.'[52]

---

[51] Partha Chatterjee, 'Agrarian Relations and Communalism in Bengal, 1926–1935', in Ranajit Guha (ed.), *Subaltern Studies I: Writings on South Asian History and Society* (New Delhi, 1982).

[52] Sarkar, *Bengal Renaissance*, p. 193.

Chaudhuri insisted that Muslims constituted a society of their own with a distinctive culture, and that they could therefore not be absorbed into a unified nation which could be called India. This being the case, 'no historical argument was too false or too foolish to be trotted out by the Hindus to contest the demand of the Indian Muslims to have their own way of life'. By 1939, he had lost all hope of Hindu–Muslim reconciliation, and actually wrote that, short of a miracle, the Hindu–Muslim question had passed beyond the possibility of a rational solution. In all this he was profoundly mistaken.[53]

CULTURAL DILEMMAS

The concluding note and message of Bankim Chandra Chattopadhyay (1838–94) in *Anandmath* is that it is the Muslim who vanquished past generations of Hindus who will be the great adversary of the new Hindu.[54] The celebrated writer looked upon medieval India as a period of bondage, saw in Islam a quest for power and glory, and felt its followers to be devoid of spiritual and ethical qualities and characterized by irrationality, bigotry, deviousness, sensuality, and immorality.[55] In *Sitaram* (1887), Bankim's last novel, Shree, the female warrior, acquires the mantle of a violent mother goddess in the climactic scene where she urges the killing of Muslims.[56] This kind of rhetoric was often accompanied by very harsh, even coarse, language and popularized the use of terms of abuse such as *mlecchas*. While we know that this particular language infused the rhetoric and aspirations of violent Hindu communalism of the next century,[57] we can only guess its psychological impact on those for whom the term was frequently used.

Bankim would not qualify for Bernard Shaw's view that the lesson intended by an author is hardly ever the lesson the world chooses to learn

[53] Chaudhuri, *Thy Hand Great Anarch!*, pp. 38, 331.

[54] Tanika Sarkar, 'Imagining Hindurashtra: The Hindu and the Muslim in Bankim Chandra's Writings', in David Ludden (ed.), *Contesting the Nation: Religion, Community, and the Politics of Democracy in India* (Philadelphia, 1996), p. 177.

[55] Vernacular histories often reinforced the stereotypical figure of 'the Muslim' fanatic, who was bigoted, warlike, and cruel. Chatterjee, *Nation and Its Fragments*, p. 102.

[56] Pradip Kumar Datta, 'Bangla Sahitya and the Vicissitudes of Bengali Identity in the Latter Half of the Nineteenth Century', in Sambudha Sen (ed.), *Mastering Western Texts: Essays on Literature and Society* (New Delhi, 2003), p. 237.

[57] Sarkar, 'Imagining Hindurashtra', p. 179.

from his book.[58] Some, if not all, Bengali writers used him to validate their polemics against the Muslims about falling male population among Hindus, abduction of Hindu girls, and clashes over the playing of music before mosques.[59] By the end of the nineteenth century, there was more and more talk of 'Hindu cowardice', a major ideological component of the dominant Hindu communitarian discourses. The myth of Hindu cowardice, always counterpoised against the militancy and aggression of Islam and its followers, acquired salience and a raison d'être for Hindu outfits.

But the tide of hate and calumny did not sweep the whole of Bengal. Rabindranath, the eclectic poet-writer, shared neither Bankim's anti-Islamic virulence nor the anti-Islamic polemics of Swami Dayanand Saraswati (1827–83), the high priest of the Arya Samaj movement.[60] Susobhan Sarkar cites several examples from Tagore's writings after 1907 reflecting his universal humanism, his eclectic message, and his quest for the larger universe.[61] Tagore also contrasted the egalitarian principles of Islam with the injustices inherent in the Hindu caste system. He referred to 'the unconventional code of life for our family has been a confluence of three cultures, the Hindu, Mohammedan and British'.

Rabindranath set the first stanza of 'Vande Mataram' to music and sang it at an early Congress session in Calcutta. The anthem had, after all, acquired a separate individuality and an inspiring significance of its own.[62] Yet he conceded that the poem, along with its context, could

[58] Bernard Shaw, *Prefaces by Bernard Shaw* (London, 1934), p. 151.

[59] Pradip Kumar Datta, *Carving Blocs, Communal Ideology in Early Twentieth-century Bengal* (New Delhi, 1999).

[60] The Arya Samaj reacted powerfully to colonial subservience and to the Muslim majority in Punjab. It, therefore, underlined the moral and spiritual degeneration of the Hindus, and their inability to defend their hearth and home, their temples, or the honour of their women against the Christian–Muslim onslaught. Such an evaluation of 'Hindu character' was neither supported by contemporary events nor by some of the protagonists of Hindu revivalism, such as Madan Mohan Malaviya, who maintained that Hindus were not weak and that in all conflicts with the Muslims, 'when they were equally matched they were never vanquished'. Yet the Arya Samaj set out to provide a vision of and pride in the Hindu nation, and make Hinduism a new living force, both defensive and even militant if necessary. Lala Lajpat Rai, its leading figure, stated that the tiny barge of the Arya Samaj was at that time to him the barge of Hindu nationality.

[61] Sarkar, *Bengal Renaissance*, pp. 73–81.

[62] 'Vande Mataram', 30 October 1937, in Sisir Kumar Das, *The English Writings of Rabindranath Tagore, Vol. 3: A Miscellany* (New Delhi, 1996), pp. 824–5.

offend Muslim sensibilities. On 26 September 1932, he urged Gandhi, who had broken his fast against separate electorates for the dalits, 'to make a desperate effort to win over the Mahommedans to our common cause'.[63]

During a debate in the Lok Sabha over the linguistic reorganization of states, Jawaharlal stood against monolingualism (and the homogeneity of culture it engenders). He informed the House that he sent his daughter, Indira Gandhi (1917–84), to Santiniketan so that she could imbibe the culture of Bengal. But it is in his tribute to Rabindranath on his birth centenary at Visva-Bharati that one gets a real sense of the reasons that may have moved Jawaharlal to send Indira to Santiniketan. The institution built by Gurudev exemplified the values that Jawaharlal himself held so dear: the confluence of nationalism and internationalism, tradition and modernity, the importance of developing the spirit over sheer material gains, the necessity of breaking down the narrow barriers of caste, race, and creed. 'I have a fear,' he says to his daughter,

that in this year of Gurudeva's birth centenary his message and ideals might be swept away in the flood of words and eloquence and that we may imagine that we have done our duty by him. That is a dangerous delusion which comes over us often. I should like you specially here at Santiniketan and the Visva Bharati to remember that the test of your homage is not what you may say about him but the way you live, the way you grow, and the way you act up to his message.[64]

Rabindranath had much in common with his contemporary, the Urdu poet Iqbal, the 'Poet of the East'. The former received knighthood in 1915, the latter in 1922. Urdu and Persian speakers like Motilal Nehru (1861–1946), Tej Bahadur Sapru (1875–1949), and H.N. Kunzru (1840–92) recited Iqbal's verses; Rabindranath's poems were, likewise, read and sung by all Bengali speakers, Hindus and Muslims alike. Qazi Nazrul Islam (1899–1976) called Rabindranath his guru and compared himself to a comet shooting away from the radiance of the sun (*rabi*, Rabindranath).[65] Rabindranath's influence on Humayun Kabir (b. 1906), author-educationist, is deep and pervasive: his poetry bears striking resemblance to the thoughts and sentiments of some of Rabindranath's

[63] 'To Gandhi', 30 September 1932, Krishna Dutta and Andrew Robinson (eds), *Selected Letters of Rabindranath Tagore* (Cambridge, 1997), p. 417.

[64] Mushirul Hasan (ed.), *Nehru's India: Select Speeches* (New Delhi, 2006), p. 16.

[65] Hay, *Asian Ideas of East and West*, pp. 256–7.

early poems.[66] Even outside Bengal, Tagore had a long list of admirers; his books were translated into Urdu. In *Gandhi and Communal Unity*, Abid Husain, professor at Delhi's Jamia Millia Islamia, interpreted the ideas of Gandhi and Tagore, the two figures he admired most, arguing that 'if we loved our country, the human race and the pursuit of Truth, we had to dream with Tagore and realize our dream in action with Gandhiji—to see Truth with Tagore and *live* it with Gandhiji'.

Rabindranath's and Iqbal's images of the West and its civilization are not dissimilar. Both (Rabindranath all through his life; Iqbal in his early years) sought a synthesis of the best qualities of East and West. Both advocated Hindu–Muslim comradeship. They met in 1935 and again in 1938, just before Iqbal's death. Gurudev sent a message of appreciation at his death: 'The death of Sir Mohammad Iqbal creates a void in our literature that, like a mortal wound, will take a very long time to heal. India, whose place today in the world is too narrow, can ill afford to miss a poet whose poetry had such universal value.'[67]

Given such secular sensibilities, why did the sage of Bengal not raise his voice against the slandering of his own people? Why did he not depict Muslim social and cultural life with his usual insight? Why did he not express the grievances of the lower classes and therefore more dissatisfied elements amongst Muslims in town and country? The only major Muslim character in his oeuvre that instantly springs to mind, Kabuliwallah, is more a stock character than a 'real' protagonist; the rest are peripheral. The conclusion to which we find ourselves forced is that, with some exceptions, it is not just the poor or *ajlaf* but the *ashraf* Muslims as well who struggled valiantly to figure in the otherwise expansive worldview of the dominant landed and professional classes.

The composer of 'Jana-Gana-Mana' did, in fact, make some concessions to the prevailing Hindu orthodoxy and social conservatism,[68] advising his followers not to completely cut themselves off from 'the great Hindu community' and the 'highest truths of Hindu Shastras'.[69] Elsewhere

[66] Frank Moraes (ed.), *Science, Philosophy and Culture: Essays Presented in Honour of Humayun Kabir's Sixty-Second Birthday* (Bombay, 1965), p. 49.

[67] This paragraph is based on Hay, *Asian Ideas of East and West*, pp. 298–302.

[68] Lakshmi Subramanian, 'Tagore and the Problem of Self-Esteem', in Ray, *Mind Body and Society*, p. 468.

[69] T.N. Madan, *Modern Myths, Locked Minds: Secularism and Fundamentalism in India* (New Delhi, 1998), p. 207.

he talked of Hindus and Muslims having 'full consciousness of their individuality' expressing itself in 'mutually exclusive and antagonistic' ways,[70] but he also pointed out that Hindus and Muslims in the past were not so obviously conscious of their differences. In some of Rabindranath's early writings, the latter emerge as the first great outsiders. This is true of his obituary of the Arya Samaj leader, Swami Shraddhanand (1856–1926), perceived by the Muslims as their inveterate enemy. Unlike the Hindus who are divided into so many sects, 'whenever the Muslim has attempted to unite Islamic society for any purpose, he has never experienced any hindrances—he has cried out, Allah O Akbar, in the name of one God,' he wrote.[71]

Whenever Tagore dwells upon India's glories, moreover, he tends to elide over nine hundred years of Muslim presence, ignoring the unforgettable lines of Iqbal: *Ai Ab-e rude/Ganga wo din hai yaad tujko; utra tere kinare jab caravan humara* ('O water of the river Ganges, thou remembers the day when our torrent flooded thy valleys ...'). Over the centuries the outsider may have made the land his own, but Tagore is silent about the fruits of his presence.[72] This is an instance of the prevalent cultural prejudices of the upper-caste Bengali elite.[73]

Behind Chattopadhyay's and Chaudhuri's wishing to have very little to do with Muslims even on a social, everyday basis were deeper issues of identity. As a social group that took to European ways, educated Hindu Bengalis based their lifework on either the formula of a synthesis of Hindu and European currents or refashioned and revisited the past glory, to which they constantly harked back with nostalgia and misplaced loyalty, of a predominantly Hindu past. The 'awakened' in Bengal also happened to be almost exclusively Hindu by origin.[74] Hence literary histories rarely talked of Muslim literatures; Bengal *sahitya* tended not to disturb the boundaries of the social identity of the *bhadralok*;[75] reform

[70] 'The Way to Unity', 1923, in Das, *The English Writings of Rabindranath Tagore*, Vol. 3, p. 461.

[71] Rabindranath Tagore, quoted in Somnath Zutshi, 'Women, Nation and the Outsider in Hindi Cinema', in Alok Bhalla and Sudhir Chandra (eds), *Indian Responses to Colonialism in the 19th Century* (New Delhi, 1993), p. 111.

[72] Ibid., p. 112.

[73] Partha Chatterjee, *Nationalist Thought and the Colonial World: A Derivative Discourse* (New Delhi, 1987), p. 77.

[74] Sarkar, *Bengal Renaissance*, p. 155.

[75] Datta, 'Bangla Sahitya and the Vicissitudes of Bengali Identity', p. 223.

movements largely concerned themselves with specifically Hindu issues such as sati, female infanticide and widow remarriage; even the 'terrorist' or revolutionary outfits excluded Muslims from membership. Indeed, Bengal's dominant classes, having built rational structures to defend their economic and social supremacy, moulded modern Bengali literature and the fine arts in a manner which offended Muslim sensibilities on many points.[76]

Pursuit of reason was part of the Brahmanical high culture, exemplified in *Gift to the Monotheists* by Rammohun Roy (1772–1833), written in Persian with an Introduction in Arabic. Ordinarily, though, Islamic thought and various ideological trends among Muslims did not touch the arc of Bengali consciousness. Even for Bhudeb Mukhopadhyay whose liberalism was surpassed only by that of Rammohun Roy, Muslims were the 'foster children' of Mother India.[77] Their mentalities and those of the low-caste cultivating communities were cast in a mould sharply distinct from the expanding world consciousness of the educated high castes and their mannered artificialities.[78] If the Muslims, with their blunt ways, desired to enter the cultural world of the latter, they could do so only as an 'external proletariat' and after giving up their values and traditions. In this way, the new nineteenth-century Indian/Bengali culture built a perimeter of its own and banished specifically the Muslim elements beyond the pale.[79] Hence the history of the nation could accommodate Islam only as a foreign element, domesticated by shearing its own lineages of a classical past.[80] As Surendranath Banerjea (1848–1925), a Congress stalwart, noted: 'Our surroundings being what they are, and what they have been for generations, every Hindu has in him a strong conservative bias.... Scratch a Hindu and you will find him conservative.'[81]

The point is overstated; yet the cleavage in consciousness had explosive long-term implications for Hindu–Muslim relations in Bengal and elsewhere.[82] The domination of the Congress by Hindu bhadralok,

[76] Introduction, Ray, *Mind Body and Society*, p. 29.

[77] Sen, *Hindu Revivalism in Bengal*, p. 173.

[78] Ibid., p. 29.

[79] Chaudhuri, *Autobiography*, pp. 226–7.

[80] Chatterjee, *Nation and Its Fragments*, p. 74.

[81] Surendranath Banerjea, *A Nation in the Making: Being the Reminiscences of Fifty Years of Public Life* (Calcutta, 1963), p. 367, cited in Chatterjee, *Bengal Divided*, p. 158.

[82] Ray, *Mind, Body and Society*, p. 19.

their equivocation over liberal, secularist principles, and, from the time
of partition, their recurrent appeals to Hindu symbolism, all served to
convince the Muslims that Congress rule would lead to a Hindu regime.[83]
This wrought havoc and gave to the Muslim League the confidence to
woo the inarticulate masses in the name of Islam. The League, having
survived lazily on the margins of national politics until 1937,[84] did not
otherwise possess the energy to create or galvanize its constituency.
Moreover, it received stimulus from the Congress's failure to strike a
balance between its class interests and the aspirations of the Muslim poor.
To quote J.H. Broomfield:

If history united the Bengali Muslim community, so too did its enmity towards the
Hindu *bhadralok*. In search of an object of denunciation the community politician
did not, like the nationalist, have to resort to the remote and relatively unfamiliar
figures of the British raj. He had an excellent target for attack in that dominant Hindu
minority that supplied the landholders and their agents, the moneylenders, the
lawyers, the tax collectors and other government officials with whom every Bengali
Muslim, rural or urban, was forced to have dealings. To charge this group with tyranny
and to call for united backing to break its power was a sure way to arouse popular
enthusiasm. And if anger ran to violence, it was the privileged Hindu minority that
was likely to be hurt most seriously.[85]

The remarkable quality of national identity which distinguishes it from
other identities, and also its essential quality, is that it guarantees status
with dignity to every member of whatever is defined as a polity or society.[86]
If systems are meant to help realize popular aspirations and if
representative institutions prove to be no longer useful for that purpose,
then individuals and groups look elsewhere for other instruments and
better alternatives. Muslim groups across the board had ignored the
League until the 1937 elections, but force of circumstances led them to
change course. As the years rolled by, the Congress high command too
seemed prepared to pay the price of partition to strengthen its hold over
Unitary India, and the Bengal Congress campaigned successfully for the

[83] J.H. Broomfield, *Elite Conflict in a Plural Society: Twentieth-century Bengal* (Bombay,
1968), p. 327.
[84] In the 1937 elections, the League won 108 out of 482 seats. Of the 73,19,445
Muslim voters, only 3,21,722 voted for the League candidates.
[85] Broomfield, *Elite Conflict in a Plural Society*, p. 328.
[86] Liah Greenfield, 'Transcending the Nation's Worth', *Daedalus*, Summer 1993, p. 49.

vivisection of its province along communal lines.[87] G.D. Birla (1894–1983), who financed Congress activities, told one of Gandhi's confidants in July 1942: 'You know my views about Pakistan. I am in favour of separation, and I do not think it is impracticable or against the interests of Hindus or of India.'[88]

As an exponent of contemporary tendencies, the historian often exercises a direct influence on ideas, conditions, and events. This applies to Bankim Chandra Chattopadhyay and Nirad Chaudhuri as well, even though, strictly speaking, they were not historians. Intellectual circles took them very seriously indeed, and the sham logic they presented somehow touched a deep spring of the Bengali Hindu consciousness. Chaudhuri's insidious thesis on the 'gigantic catastrophe of Hindu–Muslim discord' casts a spell over the RSS (Rashtriya Swyam Sevak Sangh)-infested groups and has had the effect, whether intended or not, of weakening an otherwise pluralist society.

The brand of nationalism or patriotism Bankim Chandra and Chaudhuri produced desired neither to attract the majority Muslim population nor to counter the Hinduized and Islamized perspectives. Reciting the noblest of lines from the famous *Gitanjali*, 'Awake my mind by the sacred shore of India's sea of humanity', was an easy matter but striking a chord with Muslim peasants in Malda or Mymensingh involved much more than idle rhetoric. As time passed, certain identifiable Muslim groups became restless with their fluctuating fortunes under colonial rule. A few became increasingly susceptible to the growing currents of Islamization, a process initiated by Haji Shariatullah (1781–1820), founder of the Faraizi movement, and carried forward by his son

[87] Chatterji, *Bengal Divided*, p. 267. Bengal's partition on 14–15 August 1947 brought relief to all, except a few idealists who dreamt of a United Bengal. But the province still retained a large Muslim population, and its relations with other communities, notably the Hindu refugees from East Pakistan, were strained. After decades of embittered Hindu–Muslim relations, the picture changed when the Left Front government occupied office. Although the Muslims have fared poorly since then, the Left Front government's commitment to protecting their lives and property is comforting. In Bengal, neither Hindutva nor Islamism has struck a chord. One of the reasons is the long-lived left and democratic movements. Kolkata's academic institutions, though Bengali-centric, are staffed mostly by scholars with a secular worldview. At best, the Bharatiya Janata Party (BJP) can appeal to the migrant communities from Bangladesh's depressed areas.

[88] Cited in Sumit Sarkar, 'Popular Movements and National Leadership 1945–47', *Economic and Political Weekly*, Annual Number, 1982, p. 679.

Haji Muhsin, alias Dudu Mian (1819–62).[89] In rural Bengal, in particular, the upward mobility of the underprivileged strengthened the process of Islamization. Even the quest for 'identity' was closely related to their social aspirations.[90]

In urban areas Muslim groups heeded the exhortation of the publicist-politician, who had gained a fresh lease of life when the Hindu–Muslim entente collapsed after non-cooperation. Soon, they were part of a wider struggle, in which caste and community groups were also involved, for a share in resources and patronage. Soon enough, these trends led to the sharpening of Hindu–Muslim antipathies. Rabindranath Tagore had attributed the Hindu–Muslim schism very substantially to Muslim under-representation in jobs and honours. Real unity of hearts could not be accomplished, he had suggested as far back as 1908, without overcoming such disparity.[91] The statesmen of the 1930s and 1940s had not prepared a blueprint for overcoming differences. They mouthed slogans that invariably fell on deaf years.

'AN INTELLECTUAL CATASTROPHE OF THE FIRST ORDER'

> Islam is in its origins an Arab religion. Everyone not an Arab who is a Muslim is a convert. Islam is not simply a matter of conscience or private belief. It makes imperial demands. A convert's world view alters. His holy places are in Arab lands; his sacred language is Arabic. His idea of history alters. He rejects his own; he becomes, whether he likes it or not, a part of the Arab story. The convert has to turn away from everything that is his. The disturbance for societies is immense, and even after a thousand years can remain unresolved; the turning away has to be done again and again. People develop fantasies about who and what they are; and in the Islam of converted countries there is an element of neurosis and nihilism. These countries can be easily set on the boil.
> —V.S. Naipaul, *Beyond Belief: Islamic Excursions among the Converted People*, p. 1

In this section I come to the more general reflections to which the works of Chaudhuri and Naipaul as a whole give rise by moving into the

[89] It was characterized by the denunciation of 'Hindu' superstitious and polytheistic beliefs.

[90] Rafiuddin Ahmed, *The Bengali Muslims 1871–1906: A Quest for Identity* (New Delhi, 1981), p. 116.

[91] Quoted in Sarkar, *Bengal Renaissance*, p. 176.

contested terrain of stereotyped notions that have stayed, despite changing times, with writers, poets, journalists, filmmakers, and publicists; in the final section, I briefly consider the self-image and self-perception of a community that has had to carry the burden of history, and, after 1947, carve out a place for itself in a multi-cultural and multi-religious society. One can only delineate some aspects of this great challenge, an ongoing one, for the minorities to avail of the opportunities and for the democratic processes to accommodate them within the given spaces. We focus on the Muslims simply because they faced a far more serious challenge after 1947 than any other community; others, notably the Sikhs who were cruelly displaced from the large tracts in Western Punjab and yet they could look to a secure future in the new land to which they had migrated under such harrowing circumstances.

One of the many overseas-based writers who routinely fulminate against Islam and the Muslims is none other than Sir Vidiadhar Naipaul. His ancestors left India in the early 1880s as indentured labourers for the sugar estates of Guyana and Trinidad. He returned to India to publish *An Area of Darkness*, advertised as 'tender, lyrical, [and] explosive'. Thereafter, he chronicled the histories of a wounded civilization and a million mutinies in India. In between, he aimed salvos at Islam not once but twice, in laboured projects. He seems to wholly subscribe to the views of Samuel P. Huntington (b. 1927), a controversial American political scientist, who earned his reputation by arguing that the New World Order is based on patterns of conflict and cooperation founded on cultural distinctions and identifications—the clash of civilizations theory. He therefore talks of 'the indigestibility of Muslims' and their propensity towards violent conflict, which makes them threatening. Naipaul too warns readers of Islamic 'parasitism' and the menace of Islam and thereby supports the Orientalist belief that Islam as a coherent, transnational, monolithic force has been engaged in a unilinear confrontational relationship with the West. His essentialist reading of history allows him to sustain the myth of an inherent hostility between two antagonistic sides.

Perhaps he should have made himself more familiar with the views of C. Snouck Hurgronje (1857–1936) who wrote convincingly about Islam as a living and changing reality, what Muslims mean by it is constantly changing because of the particular circumstances of time and place. He insisted that if non-Muslims wish to understand Islam, they must study it in its historical reality, without value judgements about what it ought to be.[92] The sense of Islam as something more than words in texts, as something living in individual Muslims, however, does not emerge from Naipaul's writings.

His is an analysis of a person ignorant of the nuances of Islam and unacquainted with the languages of the people he speaks to. He records and assesses only what he sees and hears from his interpreters.[93] In the most literal sense, he found the cultures indecipherable, for he could not transliterate the Arabic alphabet.[94] He had known Muslims all his life in Trinidad, but knew little of Islam. Its doctrine did not interest him; 'it didn't seem worth inquiring into; and over the years, in spite of travel, I had added little to the knowledge gathered in my Trinidad childhood.'[95] He continued to subscribe to the illogical mistrust of Muslims he had been taught as a child: a particular greybeard Muslim, described in An Area of Darkness, came to embody 'every sort of threat'. Much like Nirad Chaudhuri, Naipaul's encounters with Muslims 'are suffused with a sense of youthful bigotries'.[96] There is, then, a diametrical difference between his empathy for Brahmanical Hindus and his experience of Muslims as opaque.[97] The nature of his upbringing may, therefore, explain the uneasy relationship with Aziz, Naipaul's personal servant for the six months of his sojourn in India, and Sadeq, his first interpreter in Iran. It may also explain Naipaul's ignorance of Islamic theology and his lack of grounding in history and sociological and political theory.[98]

Among the Believers: The Islamic Journey is permeated with the sentiment that Islam is hostile and aggressive towards the advanced and 'civilized' West, and that Muslim societies are, by comparison with the West, rigid, authoritarian, and uncreative.[99] He therefore insists that Islam sanctifies rage—rage about the faith, political rage.[100] In Jakarta, Indonesia, he runs into Imamuddin who confirms him in the stereotype.

[92] Hourani, Islam in European Thought, pp. 42–3.
[93] Suman Gupta, V.S. Naipaul (Plymouth, 1999), p. 76.
[94] Rob Nixon, London Calling: V.S. Naipaul, Postcolonial Mandarin (Oxford, 1992), p. 145.
[95] Naipaul, Among the Believers: The Islamic Journey (New Delhi, 1981), pp. 15–16.
[96] Nixon, London Calling, p. 146.
[97] Sudha Rai, V.S. Naipaul: A Study in Expatriate Sensibility (New Delhi, 1982), p. 16.
[98] Naipaul, Among the Believers, p. 76.
[99] Outlook, 8 June 1998.
[100] Naipaul, Among the Believers, p. 354.

In Teheran, Behzad leaves him convinced that, 'now in Islamic countries there would be the Behzads who, in an inversion of Islamic passions, would have a vision of society cleansed and purified, a society of believers.'[101] Both Iran and Pakistan, 'a fragmented country, economically stagnant, despotically ruled, with its gifted people close to hysteria',[102] remind him of the power of religion and the hollowness of secular cults.

In most of the description, otherwise nicely woven into a coherent story, there is hardly any reference to the debilitating legacy of colonial rule either in Iran or Indonesia. The civilized, innovative, and technologically advanced West stands out as a vibrant symbol of progress and modernity, whereas the Muslim societies he encounters, despite their varying experiences and trajectories, are destructive, inert, and resentful of the West. With Naipaul relegating colonialism and imperial subjugation of Muslim societies to the background, the West appears an open, generous, and universal civilization. In fact, it is the West that is consistently portrayed as exploited by lesser societies resentful of its benign, or at worst natural, creativity: 'Indeed, Naipaul is so decided in his distribution of moral and cultural worth between the cultures of anarchic rage and the "universal civilization" that he ends up demonizing Islam as routinely as the most battle-minded of his Islamic interlocutors demonize the West.'[103]

Beyond Belief: Islamic Excursions among the Converted People (1998), chooses Islamic bad faith as its theme, portraying 'the same primitive, rudimentary, unsatisfactory and reductive thesis' that the Muslims, having been converted from Hinduism, must experience the ignominy of all converted people.[104] In *India: A Million Mutinies* (1990), the 1857 revolt is regarded as the last flare-up of Muslim energy until the agitation for a separate Muslim homeland. So far so good. But when Naipaul finds the Lucknow bazaars expressing the faith of the book and the mosque, for example Aminabad, a crowded marketplace, serving the faith,[105] it becomes too much to swallow.

Two years after *A Million Mutinies*, Naipaul defends the destruction of the Babri Masjid by calling it 'an act of historical balancing'.[106]

---

[101] Ibid., p. 399.
[102] Ibid., p. 82.
[103] Nixon, *London Calling,*, p. 149.
[104] Edward Said, in *Outlook*, 30 October 2001.
[105] V.S. Naipaul, *India: A Million Mutinies* (New Delhi, 1990), p. 356.
[106] 'I would call it an act of historical balancing. The mosque built by Babur in

'Ayodhya,' he rationalizes, 'was a sort of passion. ... Any passion has to be encouraged. I always support actions coming out of passion as these reflect creativity.' Whose passion? Of those Muslims who, despite the bitterness since December 1992, still weave the garlands used in the temple and produce everything necessary for dressing the icons preparatory to worship?[107]

It is noteworthy that the fraternity of poets and writers to which Naipaul belongs strongly contests not only his reading of the calamitous effects of Islam,[108] but also his virtual justification of vandalism in the name of religion. The best examples are Sardar Jafri and Kaifi Azmi, two senior Urdu poets, who used secular rather than religious vocabulary to delineate the tragic impact of the demolition of the Babri Masjid and its aftermath:

> *Manaya jaayega jashn-e masarrat soone khandaroan mein*
> *Andheri raat mein roshan charagh-e-chashme-e-tar honge.*
>
> *Jo yeh tabeer hogi Hind ke dereena khawabon ki*
> *To phir Hindustan hoga na uske deedawar honge.*
>
> Orgies of joy among desolate ruins
> Glimmer of tear-rimmed eyes in the black night
>
> If these be the meaning of our ancient dreams
> Then the land and its seers will be gone.

Ayodhya was meant as an act of contempt. Babur was no lover of India. I think it is universally accepted that Babur despised India, the Indian people and their faith.' *Outlook*, 30 October 2001.

[107] Ashis Nandy, Shikha Trivedy, Shail Mayaram, and Achyut Yagnik, *The Ramjanmabhumi Movement and Fear of the Self* (New Delhi, 1995), p. 2.

[108] *Outlook*, 27 February 2004. 'Fractured past is too polite a way to describe India's calamitous millennium. The millennium began with the Muslim invasions and the grinding down of the Hindu-Buddhist culture of the north. This is such a big and bad event that people still have to find polite, destiny-defying ways of speaking about it. In art books and history books, people write of the Muslims "arriving" in India, as though the Muslims came on a tourist bus and went away again.' Again, the Muslim invasion had 'a calamitous effect on converted peoples. To be converted you have to destroy your past, destroy your history. You have to stamp on it, you have to say "my ancestral culture does not exist, it doesn't matter".' He claimed what he called 'this abolition of the self demanded by Muslims' as being 'worse than the similar colonial abolition of identity'.

There is no place for such sentiments in Naipaul's jaundiced views. To him, Hindu militancy is a necessary corrective to the past,[109] a creative force. He therefore rejects the possibility of Islam, a religion of fixed laws, working out reconciliation with other religions in the subcontinent.[110] This is, in short, the clash of civilizations theory. In sharp contrast, Mohammed Mujeeb had written:

Unless we have decided in our own minds that medieval Indian history is not the history of the Indian people, we must courageously examine our present criteria of judgement and develop a perspective on persons, policies and events of the past that will enable us to understand and forgive and to obtain a clear vision of the past and the future.[111]

Given a choice, Naipaul would give voice to the 'defeated people', not the poor or the downtrodden but the *Hindus* living in *Hindu India*. Among the many choices available in India with its bewildering variety, he talks of reviving memories of temples being destroyed, of Hindus being forcibly converted to Islam, and of Sikh gurus being mercilessly executed by the Mughals. He rubbishes what goes in the name of assimilation, and suggests that the name of Mahatma Gandhi (1869–1948) be dropped from the history syllabus. Even though Indians use the very idea of 'Gandhi to turn dirt and backwardness into much-loved deities', the Mahatma, according to Naipaul, has no worthwhile message for this generation. The *Hind Swaraj*, which Gandhi himself translated from Gujarati into English, 'is so nonsensical that it would curl the hair of even the most devoted admirer'; the title especially moves him to scorn.[112] The fact is, as a social scientist points out,

[109] Interview with Tarun Tejpal, *Outlook*, 23 March 1998.
[110] Ibid.
[111] Mohammad Mujeeb, 'Approach to the Study of Medieval Indian History', in Special Issue on Professor Mohammad Mujeeb, *Islam and the Modern Age*, vol. 34, nos. 3–4, August–October 2003.
[112] 'Gandhi shouldn't be considered as laying down a prescription for anything. He was uneducated and never a thinker. He is an historical figure. He came at a particular moment; he turned all his drawbacks into religion; and he used religion to awaken the country in a way that none of the educated leaders could have done. He has absolutely no message today. People talk too much about Gandhi and study him too little. His first book, *Hind Swaraj*, written at white heat in two weeks in 1909, is so nonsensical it would curl the hair of even the most devoted admirer. I don't know Indians who actually read Gandhi. They take him as some vague idea of a great redeeming holiness and they are free

Hind Swaraj is the seed from which the tree of Gandhian thought has grown to its full stature. For those interested in Gandhi's thought in a general way, it is the right place to start, for it is here that he presents his basic ideas in their proper relationship to one another.[113]

Naipaul's exposition is clumsy, naïve, and, if taken seriously, potentially dangerous. He is as ill informed about India as Huntington is about the world outside the Western hemisphere. He talks of a fractured past solely in terms of Muslim invasions and conveniently forgets the grinding down of the Buddhist-Jain culture during the period of Brahmanical revival. He fumes and frets even though a fringe element alone celebrates the vandalism of the early Islamists who were driven more by the desire to establish the might of an evangelical Islam than to deface Hindu places of worship. With anger, remorse, and bitterness becoming a substitute for serious study and analysis, Naipaul's plan for India's salvation collapses like a pack of cards. Hence the devastating denunciation of his *Beyond Belief* by Edward Said:

Somewhere along the way Naipaul, in my opinion, himself suffered a serious intellectual accident. His obsession with Islam caused him somehow to stop thinking, to become instead a kind of mental suicide compelled to repeat the same formula over and over. This is what I would call an intellectual catastrophe of the first order.

The pity of it is that so much is now lost on Naipaul. His writing has become repetitive and uninteresting. His gifts have been squandered. He can no longer make sense. He lives on his great reputation which has gulled his reviewers into thinking that they are still dealing with a great writer, whereas he has become a ghost. The greater pity is that Naipaul's latest book on Islam will be considered a major interpretation of a great religion, and more Muslims will suffer and be insulted. And the gap between them and the West will increase and deepen. No one will benefit except the publishers who will probably sell a lot of books, and Naipual, who will make a lot of money.[114]

---

to ignore the practical side—Gandhi the hater of dirt, the hater of public defecation. That last is still very much an Indian sport. In fact, the Gandhian idea of piety and a very holy poverty is used now to excuse the dirt of the cities, the shoddiness of the architecture. By some inversion, Indians have used the very idea of Gandhi to turn dirt and backwardness into much-loved deities.'

[113] M.K. Gandhi, *Hind Swaraj and Other Writings*. Edited by Anthony J. Parel (New Delhi, 2004 reprint), p. xiii.

[114] *Outlook*, 30 October 2001. See also the analysis in Gupta, *V.S. Naipaul*, Chapter 8.

IMAGING THE BELEAGUERED

Na gul-e naghma hun na parda-e saaz
Mein hun apni shikast ki awaz

I am no melody; I am no lute;
I am the sound of my own breaking heart.[115]

—Asadullah Khan Ghalib (1797–1869)

The Muslim hardly figures in academic discourse, except when the conversation veers around poetry, music, cuisine, or Awadh's feudal culture. The Urdu tune is played before audiences in Delhi and Uttar Pradesh, the two important regions where Hindi bigots and Hindu chauvinists have emasculated the language. Poets, in search of government patronage, knock at the doorsteps of cultural czars and academies to sell their poetry for a pittance. They do the same in the West with better rewards. These are undeniable truths. The following lines from Anita Desai's *In Custody* reflect not just the anguish of a weak, gasping Urdu poet, but the story of Urdu language and literature.

'Urdu poetry?' he finally sighed, turning a little to one side, towards Deven although not actually addressing himself to a person, merely to a direction, it seemed. 'How can there be Urdu poetry when there is no Urdu language left? It is dead, finished. The defeat of the Moghuls by the British threw a noose over its head, and the defeat of the British by the Hindi-wallahs tightened it. So now you see its corpse lying here, waiting to be buried.' He tapped his chest with one finger.

'No, sir, please don't talk like that,' Deven said eagerly, perspiration breaking out on his upper lip and making it glisten. 'We will never allow that to happen. That is why Murad is publishing his journal. And the printing press where it is published is for printing Urdu books, sir. They are getting large orders even today. And my college— it is only a small college, a private college outside Delhi—but it has a department of Urdu—'

'Do you teach there?' A wrinkled eyelid moved, like a turtle's and a small, quick eye peered out at Deven as if at a tasty fly.

Deven shrank back in apology. 'No, sir, I teach in—in the Hindi department. I took my degree in Hindi because—'

But the poet was not listening. He was laughing and spitting as he laughed because he did it so rustily and unwillingly. Phlegm flew. 'You see,' he croaked, 'what did I tell

---

[115] Ralph Russell, *The Pursuit of Urdu Literature: A Select History* (London, 1992), p. 16.

you? Those Congress-wallahs have set up Hindi on top as our ruler. You are its slave. Perhaps a spy even if you don't know it, sent to the universities to destroy whatever remains of Urdu, hunt it out and kill it. And you tell me it is for an Urdu magazine you wish to interview me. If so, why are you teaching Hindi?' he suddenly roared, fixing Deven with that small, turtle-lidded eye that had now become lethal, a bullet.

'I studied Urdu, sir, as a boy, in Lucknow. My father, he was a schoolteacher, a scholar, and a lover of Urdu poetry. He taught me the language. But he died. He died and my mother brought me to Delhi to live with her relations here. I was sent to the nearest school, a Hindi-medium school, sir,' Deven stumbled through the explanation. 'I took my degree in Hindi, sir, and now I am temporary lecturer in Lala Ram Lal College at Mirpore. It is my living, sir. You see I am a married man, a family man. But I still remember my lessons in Urdu, how my father taught me, how he used to read poetry to me. If it were not for the need to earn a living, I would—I would—' should he tell him his aspirations, scribbled down on pieces of paper and hidden between the leaves of his books?

'Oh, earning a living?' mocked the old man as Deven struggled visibly with his diffidence. 'Earning a living comes first, does it? Why not trade in rice and oil if it is a living you want to earn?'

Crushed, Deven's shoulders sagged. 'I am—only a teacher, sir,' he murmured, 'and must teach to support my family. But poetry—Urdu—these are—one needs, I need to serve them to show my appreciation. I cannot serve them as you do—'

'You don't look fit to serve anyone, let alone the muse of Urdu,' the old man retorted, his voice gaining strength from indignation. Or perhaps he was wider awake now; he sounded upright even if he was still reclining. 'Sit down,' he commanded. 'There, on that stool. Bring it closer to me first. Close. Here, at my side. Now sit. It seems you have been sent here to torment me, to show me, let me know the worst.' He rolled out the syllables, in a lapidarian voice, as if he were inscribing an epitaph. 'I am prepared for suffering. Through suffering, I shall atone for my sins.' He groaned. 'Many, many sins,' and shifted on the wooden bed as if in pain.[116]

In the essay *India's History* (1902) Rabindranath Tagore had asked: 'Do "decorated mausoleums" or "stone masjids" constitute the "history of India"?' The fact is that all of us respect the innovative genius that has given us memorable buildings. Such genius must not be curbed, and must be left free to innovate. Our cities offer, after all, space to diverse and multiple cultural and religious traditions to prosper. Thus the Muslim inhabitants of the sacred Hindu places do not detach themselves from Kashi and Ayodhya, the temple town situated on the bank of the river

[116] Anita Desai, *In Custody* (New Delhi, 1994), pp. 42–4.

Saryu. When Ayodhya, some six miles from Faizabad in eastern UP, became an important pilgrimage centre in the eighteenth century, it was as much due to the activities of the Ramanandi *sadhus* as to the patronage of the Awadh *nawabs*. Nawab Safdarjang (1739–54), the *diwan*, built and repaired several temples, and donated land for building a temple on what is known as the Hanumangarhi. Muslim officials doled out gifts for rituals performed by Hindu priests.[117]

While major monuments like the Taj Mahal, Humayun's Tomb, and the Qutub Minar are looked after, most medieval structures suffer appalling neglect.[118] This is an outcome of both the apathy towards their culture and history that characterizes South Asians as well as a deliberate religious targeting. Our founding fathers were aware of the significance of heritage and the necessity of conservation. Unlike leaders like Jawaharlal and Maulana Azad who creatively engaged with the past and inspired in citizens a sense of that past through the most democratic means possible, political parties today are much less interested in providing a sane and healthy stimulus to conservation.

Generally speaking, 'Muslim' histories are shunned and 'Muslim' figures are disregarded intentionally, though even saffronized textbooks may find a place for Akbar or Dara Shikoh. 'In estimating the greatness of a great mind,' Mujeeb wrote in his short biography of Akbar, 'we have ourselves to be as imaginative and large-hearted as we can.'[119] We have not shown such large-heartedness. Some time back, Karnataka was the battle ground for an acrimonious debate centred on Tipu Sultan, one of the key figures in the mythological and historiographical constructions of the subcontinent. Early in 1990, the BJP (Bharatiya Janata Party) sought a court injunction to prevent the screening of a television serial entitled, *The Sword of Tipu Sultan*. The complainants argued that the series presented Tipu sympathetically as a secular ruler, rather than the fanatical Muslim persecutor of Hindus they imagined him to be. *Sangh*

[117] Peter van der Veer, 'God Must be Liberated! A Hindu Liberation Movement in Ayodhya', *Modern Asian Studies*, vol. 21, no. 2, 1987, p. 287, and also his 'The Concept of the Ideal Brahman as an Ideological Construct', in Gunter D. Southeimer and Herman Kulke (eds), *Hinduism Reconsidered* (Delhi, 1989), pp. 71–7.

[118] Sunil Kumar, *The Present in Delhi's Past* (New Delhi, 2002); Rakhshanda Jalil, *Invisible City: The Hidden Monuments of Delhi* (New Delhi, 2008).

[119] Mohammad Mujeeb, *Akbar* (New Delhi, 1969), p. 66; and *The Indian Muslims* (London, 1967), pp. 264–5.

parivar activists aired the same arguments to decry the state-sponsored celebrations to mark 200 years of Tipu's martyrdom. So the battle lines were drawn between those who insisted that the 'Tiger of Mysore' was a martyr to the cause of Independence and those deriding him as a tyrant and Muslim bigot.

Whatever the motivation behind the polarized sentiments, there is no denying that the Mysore ruler employed a large number of Hindus in high offices, sanctioned generous grants of rent-free land to temples, patronized pilgrimage sites, including the great *math* at Sringeri, and wrote to its Swami to pray for his success in war against 'the hostile armies that have marched against our country and are harassing our subjects'. Indeed, Tipu extended patronage to construct the massive temple at Sibi. His gesture gives the lie to the notion that Hindus, solely because they were Hindus, suffered discrimination or persecution at his hands.[120] Prior to 1860 there was no identifiable 'Hindu', 'Sikh', or 'Islamic' identity that could be abstracted from the particular circumstances of individual events or specific societies; Tipu's attitude appears to confirm this.

At the same time, there is no reason to elevate Tipu to the ranks of a Sufi or place him on a nationalistic pedestal. His territorial ambitions, rather than any nationalistic sentiment, led him to forge alliances with the French against the British. He was doubtless generous towards the Hindus, but that does not make him 'liberal' or 'secular' in an age when these expressions made little or no sense. A dispassionate analysis is required to place Tipu in the context of the turbulent decades of the eighteenth century in the south and the subcontinent generally. People often speak of 'the verdict of history' and 'the philosophy of history'. According to G.P. Gooch (1873–1968), the Cambridge-educated British historian, there is no agreed verdict, only individual verdicts, no agreed philosophy, only a welter of conflicting ideologies. We are yet to evolve a methodology that can establish a final view on events and people in history.

Moving to 'modern India', Syed Ahmad Khan (1817–1898), probably one of the most enlightened public figures of his time, is portrayed as wicked and threatening because of his aversion to the Congress. No such strictures are passed against rajas, zamindars, and some social reformers

---

[120] Mohibbul Hasan, *History of Tipu Sultan* (Calcutta, 1971); Kate Brittlebank, *Tipu Sultan's Search for Legitimacy* (New Delhi, 1997); C.A. Bayly, *Indian Society and the Making of the British Empire* (New Delhi, 1987).

who spewed venom against the same organization. In Delhi, major public places such as Kashmiri Gate's sprawling bus terminal, innumerable parks, roads, and stadia are often named after feudal chieftains and not Hakim Ajmal Khan (1863–1928) and Dr Mukhtar Ahmad Ansari (1880–1936), fine examples of India's composite traditions and devoted nationalists. The indifference, or is it a stubborn refusal, to take cognizance of Muslim luminaries, does not end here. Not even an alley in the old city is named after Delhi's renaissance figures—Maulvi Nazir Ahmad (1831–1912), the Urdu novelist, and Maulvi Mohammad Zakaullah (1832–1910), the historian. The memory of Mirza Mohammad Ismail (1883–1959), the Dewan of Mysore (1936 to May 1941) who conceived and executed the Brindavan Garden and other public projects, is all but faded. Such lives are commemorated either by a few 'Muslim' institutions or placed in a separate domain of enquiry, distinct and removed from mainstream narratives. As Sunil Kumar puts it in *The Present in Delhi's Pasts*,

the process of renaming sites after an individual from Indian history was an expansive moment marked by considerable diversity in the selection of heroes: Asoka and Teen Murti, Aurangzeb and Shivaji were all accommodated within Delhi. In the post-independence xenophobic mood of searching for an indigenous identity and self-reliance, the historical lineage of the Indian nation had to erase the memory of 'foreigners' who had subverted the country's independence.

With their milling crowds, Delhi's older sections form part of an alien landscape. The Juma Masjid and Karim's spicy kebabs belong to the 'other'. The Maulana Azad Medical College on Bahadur Shah Zafar Marg marks the 'border' between the 'modern' and a quasi medieval world; if one is generous, the borderline may be extended up to the turning for the Juma Masjid. Occasionally, requiems are sung to Delhi's culture, now lost. Hence re-enacting *The Last Mushaira of Delhi* by Farhatullah Beg (1884–1947) would draw Delhi's elite to the India International Centre. Often a public outcry over the appalling state of Ghalib's house in Ballimaran is heard, but the less sympathetic voices treat the world beyond the Delhi Gate or the Khooni Darwaza as *dar al-harb* (land of war) in a *dar al-aman* (land of peace). Nirad Chaudhuri, a self-proclaimed child of the enlightenment, adds proudly: 'Whenever in the streets of Delhi I see a Muslim woman in a *burqa* ... I apostrophize

her mentally: "Sister! You are the symbol of your community in India."
The entire body of the Muslims is under a black veil.'[121]

The construction of stereotypes is dealt with in Urdu and Hindi short
stories of, for example, Ismat Chughtai (1911–91), Punni Singh (b. 1939),
and Abdul Bismillah (b. 1949). In 'Kafir', the inherited prejudice of the
unthinking child narrator comes to the fore in the form of her belief that
all Hindus will go to hell; in 'The Infidel Parrot', the apparently sympathetic
and otherwise perceptive narrator, without a trace of self-consciousness,
laps up the prevailing stereotype that Muslims are natural polygamists
and practitioners of other attendant vices; in 'Guest is God', the attitude
of an otherwise hospitable Hindu couple changes dramatically when they
discover their guest to be a Muslim and not a Brahmin.[122] There is, however,
a yawning gap between such passages and the reality of life as lived by a
Muslim man or woman!

In no case does the gap yawn more widely than when Hindi cinema
depicts images of the good life associated with medieval rulers, a model
of decadence and a stereotype of cultivated leisure: 'All of the above
were derived from a part-fantasized vision of nawabi Lucknow, which
was nostalgically remembered as the last bastion of a beleaguered
Islamicite culture, the culture of the Urdu-speaking elite.'[123] At one time
Hindus and Muslims, either as twins or brothers in the family, were a
recurring motif in several films and Muslim characters were routinely
shown as 'normal', so to speak. Communal harmony became a kind of
signature in a large number of films during the 1950s and 1960s.[124] In
later decades, these trends were not wholly reversed but a more dominant
trend constructed Muslim identity from a majoritarian perspective;
indeed, the Muslims represent the other as defined by the majoritarian
us. Treated as an undifferentiated mass, they emerge increasingly as
stereotypes represented by acceptable and well-defined signs of speech,
appearance, dress, and social and religious practice.[125] Only a few, notably

[121] Chaudhuri, *The Continent of Circe*, p. 235.

[122] Hasan and Asaduddin, *Image and Representation*, p. 13.

[123] Mukul Kesavan, 'Urdu, Awadh and the Tawaif: The Islamicite Roots of Hindi
Cinema', in Zoya Hasan (ed.), *Forging Identities: Gender, Communities and the State in
India* (New Delhi, 1994), p. 251.

[124] Shyam Benegal, 'Secularism and Popular Indian Cinema', in A.D. Needham and
Rajeshwari Sunder Rajan (eds), *The Crisis of Secularism in India* (New Delhi, 2007),
pp. 230, 231.

[125] Fareed Kazmi, 'Muslim Socials and the Female Protagonist: Seeing a Dominant

M.S. Sathyu, Shyam Benegal, and Mahesh Bhatt, tread a different path. *Dhoka* by Bhatt, for example, carries the resonance of our times. It is the story of an Indian Muslim policeman who deals squarely with the wrath of the Hindu and Muslim communities.

Noorel Mecklai's doctoral dissertation shows the continuity in the construction and representation of the Muslim image in Bollywood, as also the nexus between the film industry, criminal underworld, crime, and rise of Hindutva politics. The dissertation concludes on a poignant note: 'Films post 1980 portray Muslims as villainous and capable of wanton violence. Earlier films critique their practices, personal relationships and often portray them as wealthy through ill-gotten means. All these characterizations exclude them as worthy citizens of the nation.'[126] This view is surely reinforced by the oft-repeated cliché about the extra-territorial loyalties of Muslims. 'Shameful' is how Khalid Mohamed, the film critic, describes the offensive dialogue in the recent film *Bheja Fry*—'*Yahan ki khaate ho aur wahan* [Pakistan] *ki gaate ho*' (you eat here but sing their praises). That, too, over a cricket match!

To contextualize this response, one must bear in mind the response to Dilip Kumar receiving the Nishan-e Imtiaz Award in Pakistan in March 1998. Even before leaving for Islamabad, the Shiv Sena questioned his loyalty to his country. He became yet another victim of the gaping wound that partition had inflicted on the peoples of the once undivided subcontinent.[127]

In *Covering Islam*, Edward Said examines 'how the media and experts determine how we see the rest of the world' by looking at US media coverage of the siege of their embassy in Iran in 1981. Texts written after Said's work have a discursive consistency in identifying the same derogatory themes and topics associated with Islam.[128] In India, along

---

Discourse at Work', in Needham and Sunder Rajan, *The Crisis of Secularism*, p. 239. And the comment: 'In the name of patriotism, our films are littered with anti-Muslim dialogues, and the portrayal of Indian Muslims is restricted to a man wearing a namaz topi, chewing paan and doing no good to his nation.' Rana Siddiqui, 'Riding on Terror?' *Hindu*, 24 August 2007.

[126] Noorel-nissa Sultanali Mecklai, 'Abrogated Identity: Muslim Representation in Hindi Popular Cinema' (Unpublished Ph.D. thesis, Edith Cowan University, Western Australia, 2006).

[127] Bunny Reuben, *Dilip Kumar: Star Legend of Indian Cinema* (New Delhi, 2005 impression), p. 459.

[128] Edward Said, *Covering Islam, How the Media and the Experts Determine How We*

with legitimizing popular misconceptions,[129] the print and electronic media shore up a Hindu public sphere through their ideological support in framing a militarized Hindu nationalism.[130]

Newspapers in the 1960s and 1970s had their share of journalists who had inherited the prejudices of the pre-partition generation. Girilal Jain, editor of The Times of India from 1978 to 1988, emerged as one of the few opinionated 'intellectual' journalists. In many ways, he is a perfect example of Hindu nationalism. But because he was a famous journalist, he was rarely criticized as a reactionary opposed to the liberal creed. A bitter no-holds-barred Muslim baiter, he approached Muslim societies from his own idiosyncratic perspective rather than from their own rich setting of ideas and strivings. For example, his considered opinion was that, unlike the Hindus, Muslims proved incapable of engaging in 'self-renewal' even under the stimulus provided by British rule. 'Only the triumph of Hindutva can help to create,' according to him, 'a milieu which obliges them to try and overcome the inertia of tradition reinforced by the ulama.'[131]

There are many other instances in his writings of the demagogic kind that convey the impression of Hindu/Indian civilization being undermined by the Muslim rulers. The grandeur of the nineteenth-century reform movements in Bengal and Maharashtra was an article of faith with Girilal Jain, and he looked for identical trends in Indian Islam. He did not possess the scholarly training or skill to 'discover' the liberal trends. He very simplistically believed that while 'the emerging Hindu elite linked itself with dominant Western civilization and adopted the road to modernity and progress, Muslims turned their gaze towards a past incapable of being restored.'[132] 'Those gods that always fail,' wrote

---

See the Rest of the World (New York, 1981); see also, Elizabeth Poole, Media Representation of British Muslims: Reporting Islam (London, 2002) on how knowledge of Islam is constructed and circulated.

[129] Sabina Kidwai, 'Images and Representations of Muslim Women in the Media, 1990–2001', in Zoya Hasan and Ritu Menon (eds), In a Minority: Essays on Muslim Women in India (New Delhi, 2005), p. 392.

[130] Rita Manchanda, 'Militarized Hindu Nationalism and the Mass Media: Shaping a Hindutva Public Discourse', in John McGuire and Ian Copland (eds), Hindu Nationalism and Governance (New Delhi, 2007); Victoria L. Farmer, 'Mass Media: Images, Mobilization, and Communalism', in Ludden, Contesting the Nation.

[131] Girilal Jain, The Hindu Phenomenon (Delhi, 1994), p. 107.

[132] The Times of India, 16 March 1993.

Edward Said, 'demand from the intellectual in the end a kind of absolute certainty and a total, seamless view of reality that recognizes only disciples or enemies.'[133]

Jain's writings showed no appreciation of Muslim societies, past or present. Like Nirad Chaudhuri and Naipaul, he was unaware of the historical situations in which certain deductions made from the Quran were no longer relevant; Syed Ahmad Khan and Maulana Azad had repudiated them long ago. Ghalib despised the *ulama* for claiming special and providential wisdom for themselves and their friends; Akbar Allahabadi (1846–1921), the poet, ridiculed the type of casuistry practised by them; progressive writers kept lamenting that 'power' rested in their flowing gowns to hide the wickedness of tyranny.

Several of Girilal Jain's contemporaries, without being specialists on the Muslims, wrote with infinitely greater sympathy and comprehension.[134] They consciously cultivated a distinctly secular point of view which had grown out of a reaction against partition. Whether out of pragmatic cynicism or from conviction, they saw secularism as the only cure for the real or imagined evils of democracy. Their approaches varied, but they were inspired by Jawaharlal Nehru's commitment to liberal thinking and rational thought. The secular constitution, moreover, moulded their ways of thinking, and more than once they saw Independence as a great revolution which closed one epoch and inaugurated a new one. Frank Moraes, a sombre realist, wrote that the Prime Minister 'stands apart from and above his immediate colleagues, his main communion with the country being through its vast masses, with whom he loves to mingle and talk.'[135] Inder Malhotra, once editor of *The Times of India*, has recently written: 'India is a better place because Nehru lived, and no matter how long the babies born on the diamond jubilee of Independence live, they will not see the like of him.'[136] These men prized Nehru's courage, ingenuity, good taste, and independence of spirit.

Pieter Geyl reminded us that the historian should be interested in his subject for its own sake, he should try to get in touch with things as

[133] Edward W. Said, *Representations of the Intellectual* (New York, 1996), p. 121.

[134] Ajit Bhattacharjee, Pran Chopra, Shyam Lal, Inder Malhotra, Frank Moraes, Manohar Mulgaokar, Kuldip Nayyar, M. Chalapathi Rau, S. Nihal Singh, Khushwant Singh, and B.G. Verghese.

[135] Frank Moraes, *Jawaharlal Nehru: A Biography* (New York, 1956), p. 478.

[136] Inder Malhotra, 'Nehru's Luminous Legacy', in Ira Pande (ed.), *India 60* (New Delhi, 2007), p. 32.

they were, the people and the vicissitudes of their fortunes should mean something to him in themselves.[137] One runs into another kind of problem with Arun Shourie: that of differentiating between the author-journalist and a politician having occupied a ministerial berth in a BJP-led coalition government.[138] In his case the problem is compounded by ambition and self-interest being laced with idealism.

As a master polemicist, Shourie is a victim of his own 'system'. He reveals his prejudices in the deadly seriousness with which he accumulates *fatawa* or documents from the National Archives of India to relentlessly demonize Muslims, Christians, Dalits, and Communists.[139] Thus his conclusion that Indian civilization experienced decline owing to Muslim rule and a surfeit of religious intolerance and other evils is the thesis fixed and determined beforehand. 'For centuries,' he observes, 'wherever Islam actually ruled it had been sacrilegious and traitorous to study, develop or propagate what had been the very essence of the life of the people.'[140] He is clearly unaware of Al-Beruni (973–1048), Amir Khusrau (1256–1325), 'Parrot of India', Malik Mohammad Jaisi (d. after 1570), Abul Fazl (1551–1602), Raskhan, Abdur Rahim Khan-e Khankhanan (1556–1627), Dara Shikoh (1615–59), and the other poets and writers who wrote paeans to Hindu gods and goddesses or translated Sanskrit texts into Persian.[141]

On the destruction of the Babri Masjid, Shourie stated: 'The hand that destroyed the mosque was of course that of the persons who had gathered there. But that hand was impelled by all our familiar

[137] Pieter Geyl, *Debates with Historians* (The Hague, 1955), p. 201.

[138] The Bharatiya Jana Sangh was founded in 1951. Its enterprise was to convert politics from disputes about party programmes into a great battle for the cultural heart of the nation, a battle in which those who believed in the corporate integrity of the Hindu community would be aligned against the forces of Islam. Thus secularism was regarded as a euphemism for the policy of Muslim appeasement. 'The Muslim menace has increased a hundredfold,' wrote M.S. Golwalkar 'after the creation of Pakistan.' 'Even today,' he continued, 'Muslims, whether in high positions of the government or outside, participate in rabidly anti-national conferences.'

[139] Mitsuhiro Kondo, 'Hindu Nationalists and Their Critique of Monotheism: The Relationship between Nation, Religion, and Violence', in Mushirul Hasan and Nariaki Nakazato (eds), *The Unfinished Agenda: Nation-Building in South Asia* (Delhi, 2001); Jacques Waardenburg (ed.), *Muslim Perceptions of Other Religions: A Historical Survey* (New York, 1999), Chapter 3.

[140] Arun Shourie, *A Secular Agenda* (New Delhi, 1993), p. 19.

[141] Annemarie Schimmel, *Islam in the Subcontinent* (Leiden, 1980), p. 1.

perversities.'[142] The allusion to the 'secularists' here seems so fantastic that it could hardly have been seriously put forward. Most of Shourie's prodigious and carefully marshalled 'facts' and 'figures' sustain the crooked logic he employs and the inherent contradictions, the maze of inconsistencies, and the poor quality of 'historical' writing.

Scholarship should not be designed or even trimmed to serve some non-scholarly purpose, whether religious or national or ideological. Journalists, like the rest of humankind, are entitled to their beliefs but these should not distort—even if they inspire—their scholarship. One assumes that the task of a print journalist is not to define words but to discover reality. Arun Shourie, a vocal champion of Western democracy and senior minister in the NDA (National Democratic Alliance), remained studiously silent during the anti-Muslim pogrom in Gujarat. This 'error' was more than a fortuitous lapse. It was connected with the fundamental aspects of his attitude towards the minorities in general. With his silence went the moral certitude which had justified him in his assertion that truth and right should prevail, and, if necessary, impose themselves by force.

Some object to Arnold Toynbee's conception of what a historical fact really is, what it is worth, and what can be done with it.[143] One cannot help applying this to the work of Shourie, author of numerous 'history' books, who uses historical facts selectively to reinforce his ideological predilections.[144]

The BJP's electoral success in 1991 brought to the fore more outspoken commentators: Swapan Dasgupta and Chandan Mitra. Educated in British universities, they have met all remonstrances and all criticisms, not with argument or persuasion, but with a flat appeal to Hindutva. In their writings and television appearances, they criticize Article 370 in Kashmir routinely and insist on a uniform civil code.[145] They believe in

---

[142] Arun Shourie, *Indian Controversies: Essays on Religion in Politics* (New Delhi, 1993), p. 9.

[143] Geyl, *Debates with Historians*, p. 166.

[144] See, for example, the concluding paragraphs in his *Worshipping False Gods: Ambedkar, and the Facts Which Have Been Erased* (New Delhi, 1997), pp. 638–9.

[145] The said Article preserves the autonomy of the state of Jammu and Kashmir. The provision of a uniform civil code exists in the Directives of State Policy, but has not been put in practice owing to the opposition of the religious minorities, especially the Muslims. See Shourie, *Secular Agenda*, pp. 122–37.

the eternal conflict between the Hindus and Muslims as an article of faith. The only difference between them and Nirad Chaudhuri is that the latter's conclusions were based on a hand-me-down observation of Indian history, whereas Swapan Dasgupta, with his Trotskyite background, and Chandan Mitra, armed with a D. Phil degree from Oxford, draw largely upon their imaginations, arguing in the abstract and making deductions from the dogmatic propositions of M.S. Golwalkar (1906–73), the high priest of the RSS.[146] It is therefore easy to question their method, premises, conclusions—everything. For all that, they had their share in paving the way for their short-lived triumph.

The English novelist Thomas Hardy (1840–1928), quoting St Jerome, declared in his Explanatory Note to *Tess* that 'if an offence comes out of the truth, better is it that the offence comes than that the truth be concealed.'[147] For writers who subscribe to this view, the 11 September attacks on the World Trade Centre and the 'terrorist' violence, notably the attack on the Parliament building in New Delhi on 13 December 2001, has aided the conflation of Islam with terrorism. Although Muslim terrorists enacting violence against the putative Hindu nation state is a necessary construct for the RSS and BJP's discourses around the need to protect the nation from its Muslim enemies, the post 9/11 global developments have shaped their violent campaign against the 'enemy within'.[148]

But not all in the media, past and present, are similarly inclined. For them, the Constitution is still the gospel and Nehru the man who tried to realize its ideals. Saner voices have explained the idea behind 'Unity

[146] Swapan Dasgupta (*India Today*, 18 September 2000) advised India's Muslims not to retreat 'into fundamental ghettos sustained by foreign funding'. Assuming that the criterion for nationhood is determined by loyalty to the BJP, he expected them 'to forge an expedient working relationship' with that party. Without referring to the historical roots of their estrangement, he warns them of 'the grim consequences of a contrived alienation'. In his customary acerbic tone, the columnist chided the *mullahs* as well as the modernists for their deep-rooted aversion to the BJP. The vehemence of his vituperation reaches its crescendo when petty Muslim politicians in that party are compared with Azad, Abdul Ghaffar Khan, and Rafi Ahmed Kidwai (1894–1954). This is adding insult to injury.

[147] Ralph Russell, 'Aziz Ahmad, South Asia, Islam and Urdu', in Milton Israel and N.K. Wagle (eds), *Islamic Society: Essays in Honour of Professor Aziz Ahmad* (New Delhi, 1983), p. 67.

[148] Paula Chakravarty and Srinivas Lankala, 'Media, Terror and Islam: The Shifting Landscape and Culture Talk in India', in Amrita Basu and Sripu Roy (eds), *Violence and Democracy in India* (Calcutta, 2007), p. 176.

in Diversity' fully, provided instances and cases of different castes and communities living together harmoniously, and returned to the fundamental ideas on secular democracy. Editors and correspondents have shielded from attack the secular Nehruvian institutional and ideological framework.[149]

The list from the print media is long and impressive, led by Ajit Bhattacharya, former editor and columnist, Praful Bidwai, columnist, Pran Chopra, editor of *The Statesman* for long years, Harish Khare, Resident Editor of *The Hindu*, Kuldip Nayyar, an ardent champion of Indo-Pakistan peace, N. Ram, editor of *The Hindu* and *Frontline*, Vir Sanghvi of *Hindustan Times*, Vinod Mehta of *Outlook*, Dilip Padgaonkar, formerly editor of *The Times of India*, and Malini Parthasarathy, formerly editor of *The Hindu*. *Outlook* exposed the complicity of the police in the massacres at certain places in Gujarat, while Rajdeep Sardesai, then in NDTV (New Delhi Television), brought out the secular liberal traditions of media institutions. An issue that requires deep probing is whether or not 'communalism' and 'secularism' coalesce, in the everyday practice of reporting, into a double-headed, inadvertently Hindu, nationalism.[150]

Ideally, secular institutions should have presented not only the complexities of history but also resisted its reduction to simplistic religious classification to fit narrow partisan ends of the present. Our centres of excellence have not done enough to include some consideration of the history of Islam into the curriculum and suggest possibilities for more interdisciplinary collaborations. Teachers teach medieval Indian history without knowing Persian; its knowledge would have made the major texts available and created the maturity to understand that the relationship between history and contemporaneous conflicts need not be mechanical.

Urdu's virtual extinction has deepened the crisis in the scholarly world. West Asia is not a part of the history curriculum in the prestigious Jawaharlal Nehru University in New Delhi; scholarship on this region and on Central Asia is woefully inadequate; Islamic history, a specialized subject in Calcutta University, is not often taught by qualified Arabic-, Persian-, or Urdu-proficient teachers; Islamic studies, the preserve of the Aligarh Muslim University or the Jamia Millia Islamia, is reduced to Sunni theology; the Iran Society in Calcutta languishes; and readers at

---

[149] Ibid., p. 193.
[150] Ibid.

the Khuda Bakhsh Library in Patna, the Maulana Azad Library in Aligarh, and the Raza Library in Rampur (UP) have been reduced to a handful. Put briefly, graduate students have no incentive to discover the 'Muslim' past. As a result, they are willy-nilly pushed into joining research and teaching centres overseas. Whether it is the lure of the crisp US dollar or the search for a secure and vibrant academic enclave, the brain drain is, in every sense of the word, a case of our loss being the gain of others.

CONCLUSION

In my earlier works, I have detailed how the images of Islam and of Muslims were selectively appropriated by the ulama–publicist combine to extract concessions from the British government. The ulama, in particular, heightened insecurity and insularity among their co-religionists but did little to improve their well-being in this world. The Muslim apologists adopted everything they could from the West but critiqued Western culture and civilization. Mohammad Mujeeb sagely remarked, 'The inconsistency between condemning Western civilization in principle and accepting it in practice was noted but ignored.'[151]

To scholars like Mujeeb the choices were simple enough: if Islam is suspended between adjustment to ongoing change and resistance to the needed accommodation, Muslims, to make the most of their potential, would be required to shun obscurantism and take their distinct values and proud and tolerant culture into the mainstream of political life. They could no longer subscribe to the infallibility of established dogma; instead, they would be expected to awaken once more the spirit of conscientious objection to prejudice, shake off the shackles of the past, and create a social order conducive to the dignity of the common man and woman.

G.E. Von Gruenbaum criticized the failure of the Muslim world, 'so eminently conscious of its individuality, to achieve, and largely even to attempt, an analysis of the fundamentals of its civilization.'[152] I have, likewise, elsewhere described the intellectual apathy at the Aligarh Muslim University and the Jamia Millia Islamia, the two major centres

---

[151] Mujeeb, *Islamic Influence*, p. 99.
[152] G.E. Gruenbaum, *Islam* (London, 1955), p. 185.

of Western learning in north India.[153] To set the record straight, it must be reiterated that sections of the Muslim urban literati have made their own history at least as much as others have made it for them and the reality is that they have not done it very well. The interface between certain kinds of Western writings and certain kinds of Islamic ones, and their resurfacing in various forms of subsequent articulations, is something that neither Edward Said's diktat nor the idea of 'colonial discourse' can ever accommodate.

New schools of research, interpretation, and reconstruction of Muslim history and thought did emerge, but they remained confined to certain cities, such as Lahore or qasbas in UP and Bihar, the princely states of Bhopal and Hyderabad, and Calcutta and Dacca in Bengal. For the most part they produced cautious pedagogues instead of bold thinkers. Their scholars were predisposed towards an urban milieu, looking with some contempt on the rural hinterland and thinking of the city as the stronghold of faith in the face of the threat from Western education and the missionaries. A small group held its ground at the Delhi College before the 1857 Revolt, but the picture was different elsewhere. Aligarh's MAO College, for example, sought above all to induce in students a spirit of servility to the rulers. Its founder Syed Ahmad Khan saw that education and intellectual training could be used for purely materialistic ends, but his approach did not equip many of his students to distinguish between rational knowledge and belief. Education merely deepened the social conflict instead of healing it. Reformers like Syed Ahmad Khan had been inspired by an exalted commitment to the qaum (community) but the motives of many of his colleagues were ridden with factional- and self-interest. Maulana Azad too could not overcome the difficulties he encountered, for fellow Muslims tried 'his spirit sorely, with their ready surrender to populist passion, their incapacity for the perspectives he desired for them, their proneness to mass hysteria and their inability to perceive, as they saw it, their true destiny.'[154]

[153] Introduction to David Lelyveld, *Aligarh's First Generation: Muslim Solidarity in British India* (Princeton, NJ, 1978), pp. xxviii–xxx, and Mushirul Hasan (ed.), *Islam and Indian Nationalism: Reflections on Maulana Abul Kalam Azad* (New Delhi, 2001 reprint), pp. 1–3.

[154] Kenneth Cragg, *The Pen and the Faith: Eight Modern Muslim Writers and the Quran* (Delhi, 1988), p. 15.

The intelligentsia creates mirrors through which we see ourselves and windows through which reality is perceived. These mirrors and windows define the boundaries of ideas and institutions. The intelligentsia's role, both as creators of a cultural outlook and the product of the milieu, is central to my view of what happened in South Asia generally and among certain Muslim groups in particular. In the following chapters I will analyse the reception of various ideas and examine how they were, in turn, affected by institutional changes, political movements, and popular aspirations.

3

Let Colour Fill the Flowers, Let Breeze of Early Spring Blow[*]

Cheen-o-Arab humara; Hindostan humara; Muslim hain hum; watan hai sara jahan humara.
China and Arabia are ours, India is ours; we are Muslims; the entire universe is ours.

—Iqbal

There was in India now that didn't exist 200 years before: a central will, a central intellect, a national idea.
—V.S. Naipaul, *India: A Million Mutinies Now*, p. 518

Having composed several poems imbued with patriotic fervour, Iqbal, the 'Poet of the East', abandoned nationalism. *'Jo pairahan uska hai woh mazhab ka kafan hai'* ('The nation's garment is religion's shroud'), he wrote.[1] By this time, of course, the Indian National Congress, a vibrant symbol of nationalism, had got off to a good start and, during its early years, comparatively little was said in official circles about the imminent danger to the Raj. Soon, however, apprehension and concern became the dominant mood. The Viceroy Dufferin (1862–1902) felt that the

[*] The line is from Faiz Ahmed Faiz.
[1] The lines from Iqbal are taken from Ralph Russell, *The Pursuit of Urdu Literature: A Select History* (London: 1992), pp. 179, 180, 181.

Congress was out to promote countrywide disaffection. He condemned the vanity and presumption of its leaders and their ideological pretensions.

In the late 1960s and 1970s, students of modern India experienced the historian's denial of the element of ideology in nationalism. They saw that new approaches, including those resting on sociological theories, shifted the paradigms and the search for new answers. They found the political historian analysing political structures and events with the aid of a political vocabulary provided by Lewis Namier (1888–1960), the historian of George III, King of Great Britain and Ireland (1760–1820), and eighteenth century thought.[2]

Today, of course, the Congress of the 1880s and 1890s is seen as a striking testimony to the inventiveness, the creative power, and the eclectic spirit of its founders. It constituted a considerable element of strength in the anti-colonial struggle that reached new heights following the Bolshevik Revolution, and as a powerful vehicle for articulating popular aspirations. Indeed, the events of the last quarter of the nineteenth century gave a fresh edge and stimulus to the earlier politics of the Associations and, in some cases, a new revolutionary content.

In the 1960s, Anil Seal, the doyen of the 'Cambridge school', drew upon the histories of social strife to postulate that the Congress-led movement was not inspired by the prompting of any class demand or as a consequence of sharp economic changes. Ignoring the dynamism of social processes, he preferred to identify and focus on the keen internal rivalries between caste and caste, community and community, not between class and class. In the three coastal presidencies, in particular, he found the newly formed elite locked in a bitter power struggle to

---

[2] Arnold J. Toynbee (1889–1974) assessed Namier in the following manner: 'Lewis Namier had two virtues that are great in themselves and are cardinal for the study of human affairs. He had insight and he had courage. Lewis saw that, in this field of study, the problem is to demythologize our language by describing things in terms of the human realities; he saw that, if we are to solve this semantic problem, we have also to solve the operational problem of coping with inordinate quantities, and he worked out a plan of campaign. He decided to start operations from the side of the realities. He would make a survey of the acts, thoughts, and feelings of the individual human beings involved in the transactions that he was studying. This survey was to be so exact, minute, and extensive that it would embrace the sum total of the realities and would thus make the mythological travesty of these realities superfluous. When he had made his plan, he had the courage to put it into action. This was an act of faith; for he was relying on his own human intellectual powers alone, without aid, either supernatural or technological.' Arnold J. Toynbee, *Acquaintances* (London, 1967), p. 80.

conserve or improve the position of their prescriptive groups: caste and community. For Seal, their politics was characterized by self-interest rather than altruism.

Some years later, Seal modified his argument to underline the race for influence, status, and resources as deciding political choices at the local level. He suggested that in pursuing these aims, patrons regimented their clients into factions, which jockeyed for positions. Rather than partnerships between fellows, these were usually associations of bigwigs and followers. He talked of vertical rather than horizontal alliances. More frequently, Hindus worked with Muslims, and Brahmins were hand-in-glove with non-Brahmins; and notables organized their dependants as supporters, commissioned professional men as spokesmen, and turned government servants into aides. In the everyday decisions of life, the social dockets devised by the administrator and adopted by the historian had little meaning.

The poet Iqbal was conscious of the diversities in society and the resultant caste, regional, and community-based conflicts: 'The various caste units and religious units in India have shown no inclination to sink their respective individualities in a larger whole.'[3] Rabindranath wrote in a similar strain. But they still envisaged a 'nation', not necessarily unified but tranquil, cohesive, and harmonious. 'Nationalism' is an extraordinary phenomenon, and both Iqbal and Rabindranath Tagore contested its contemporary meanings. Yet, on close reflection, they saw 'nationalism' emerging as a powerful sentiment, a means to creating new spaces for cultural interactions, and a vehicle to fostering ties that could be utilized for the creation of an inexhaustible creative future. Moreover, Gandhi was willing to build upon the contradiction between the nationalism which entered India as an imperial category and the nationalism which sprang out of democratic aspirations, hoping that the latter would some day supersede the former.[4]

Ideologies are subject to incessant shifts and changes, but Seal found no trace of ideology in late-nineteenth-century India. Looking more closely at his political opinions that gave rise to bitter, stormy, and protracted disputations, the very idea of nation becomes problematic. In so shapeless, so jumbled a bundle of societies, India was no more than

[3] Sharifuddin Pirzada (ed.), *Foundations of Pakistan: All-India Muslim League Documents: 1906–1947* (Karachi, 1970), vol. 2, p. 157.

[4] Ashis Nandy, *The Illegitimacy of Nationalism* (New Delhi, 1994) p. 77.

a graveyard of old nationalities with new nationalisms struggling to be born. Thus it made no sense to Seal to write about a movement grounded in common aims, led by men with similar backgrounds, and recruited from widening groups with compatible interests. Consequently, he dismisses the patriotic sentiments that came to the fore in the popular commotions over the Ilbert Bill.[5] In general, the Congress-led movement appears to him like a ramshackle coalition throughout its long career. Its unity was illusory, its power as hollow as that of the imperial authority it was challenging; its history was the rivalry between Indian and Indian, its relationship with imperialism that of the mutual clinging of two unseemly men of straw.[6] For these reasons, Seal concluded that modern Indian history cannot be organized around the notions of imperialism and nationalism. Though serious-minded historians reacted strongly to it, *The Emergence of Indian Nationalism* had enormous influence.

This is just an outline of the background to the debates in the 1960s and 1970s. Few would deny that colonialism roused the spirit of resistance and the traditions of freedom and of dignity that were very much alive in late-nineteenth-century India. Gandhi, who experienced an inhuman regime and its savagery in South Africa, creatively harnessed these traditions for the realization of Swaraj. In *Hind Swaraj*, based on the South African experience, he provided not only an alternative to violence but also expressed his boundless faith in the people.

Although historians on South Asia in Cambridge differed among themselves, Anil Seal's ideas have been carried forward by Francis Robinson, who has promoted his mentor's ideas in his doctoral dissertation, though his later works mark a sharp break from his first book. This is borne out by his debate with Paul Brass.

Paul Brass, the American political scientist, talked of the ideology of Muslim separateness flowing not out of the objective differences between Hindus and Muslims but out of the uses made of those differences through a conscious process of symbol selection. According to him, Muslim leaders in north India in the late nineteenth century did not recognize a common destiny with the Hindus because they saw themselves in danger of losing

[5] The Ilbert Bill, introduced by Ripon on 2 February 1883, enabled Indian judges to try European British subjects on criminal charges. It led to an 'Anglo-Indian Mutiny'.

[6] Anil Seal, 'Imperialism and Nationalism in India', *Modern Asian Studies*, 3, 1973, p. 321.

their privileges as a dominant community. So they emphasized a special sense of history incompatible with Hindu aspirations and a myth of Muslim decline into backwardness. For Brass, Muslims organized on the basis of their faith in politics, it was because the community's elites perceived it to be the most effective way of keeping or maintaining political power in their own hands.[7]

In this framework, communalism becomes more of a construct, a public face which masked economic agendas. Even the professed concern for the welfare of courtesans became an issue to be bandied about in a power struggle between the communalized Hindu and Muslim factions in the Banaras Municipal Board and made the courtesans more the victims of social reform than its beneficiaries.[8] Robinson argued against this, saying that in Uttar Pradesh (UP) as a whole, many Muslims and Hindus had more in common with each other than with their co-religionists.[9]

As an exponent of the 'instrumentalist' approach, Brass laid stress on the elites being separate from their societies and their cultural traditions. They manipulate in order to choose within their cultural framework at will and according to their political interests. Their own culturally-determined preferences and beliefs do not matter; they are constrained only by the cultures of the groups they hope to lead. Thus the Hindu–Muslim differences in UP were less important in creating Muslim solidarity than 'the subject process of symbol manipulation and myth creation'.[10] Indeed, it was only through social mobilization that the differences could be communicated and stressed to the mass of Muslims.

Questioning the myth of Muslim backwardness in UP complicated the simplistic theories on Muslim nationalism. Added to such theories are invaluable insights into the popular mentalities that informed public conduct in public arenas, including the ways sentiments and myths shaped the lives of ethnic groups.[11] Sandra B. Frietag, for one, traced religious conflict during the period 1880–1930 in terms of the boundaries of local practice during festivals and their becoming abstracted to a new

[7] Paul R. Brass, *Religion, Language and Politics in Northern India* (Cambridge, 1974).

[8] Martin Gaenzle and Jorg Gengnagel (eds), *Visualizing Space in Benares: Images, Maps and the Praxis of Representation* (Wiesbaden, 2006), p. 337.

[9] Francis Robinson, *Separatism among Indian Muslims: The Politics of the United Provinces' Muslims, 1860–1923* (Cambridge, 1974), p. 33.

[10] Brass, *Religion, Language and Politics in Northern India*, pp. 177–8.

[11] Sajal Basu, *Communalism, Ethnicity and State Politics* (Jaipur, 2000).

form of group identity in which affiliation, not practice, justified the strife.[12]

In sharp contrast, Robinson traces the influence of Islamic ideas on the elites in the United Provinces (now called, Uttar Pradesh). According to him, the continuing power of these ideas suggests the balance of the argument to be tilted in favour of the primordialists.[13] This is by no means a novel position. W.C. Smith had suggested long ago that an independent political community as the arena of religious activity was part of the very genius of Islam.[14] Many writers have since backed this view, asserting that the determination to maintain a distinct political identity was throughout the basic factor in Muslim thinking.[15] This does not hold any more in the light of the varied social, political, and ideological contexts through which Muslim identity has been, and is being, constantly created and recreated.

In this view, what goes by the name of 'distinct political identity' has been no more than the elites jockeying for position and masquerading as community spokesmen. Religion is used as an obfuscating cover for one's less than honourable—indeed entirely unreligious—motives and the community as a tool, a convenient instrument, for securing benefits from the government that created both a caste and a community consciousness. Thus Hasan Manzar (b. 1934), Pakistan's well-known Urdu writer, underscores their great potential for division and disruption.[16] In the case of writers from at least a dozen languages, neither the forms nor the lives they portray derive from a supposedly homogeneous and unbroken tradition. Instead, they throw into sharp relief the multicultural reality of Muslim societies in the local cultures. Whether it is the Muslim in Kashmir (Padma Sachdeva's 'Where Has my Gulla Gone') or the story

[12] Sandria B. Frietag, *Collective Action and Community. Public Arenas and the Emergence of Communalism in North India* (Berkeley, 1989).

[13] Francis Robinson, 'Nation Formation: The Brass Thesis and Muslim Separatism', and Reply by Paul Brass, *Journal of Commonwealth and Comparative Politics*, vol. 15, no. 3, November 1977, pp. 215–34; Francis Robinson, 'Islam and Muslim Separatism', in Mushirul Hasan (ed.), *Communal and Pan-Islamic Trends in Colonial India* (New Delhi, 1985 revised and enlarged edition), p. 375.

[14] W.C. Smith, *Islam in Modern History* (Princeton, NJ, 1957), p. 211.

[15] J.H. Broomfield, *Elite Conflict in a Plural Society: Twentieth-century Bengal* (Bombay, 1968), p. 327; Farzana Shaikh, *Community and Consensus in Islam: Muslim Representation in Colonial India 1860–1947* (Cambridge, 1989).

[16] Hasan Manzar, *A Requiem for the Earth: Selected Stories* (Karachi, 1998), p. xii.

of Muslim life in coastal Karnataka ('Nimbus'), or the tale of the Muslim woman in Ismat Chughtai's writings, the stories unravel different aspects of Muslim lives.

In *Separatism among Indian Muslims*, Robinson traces the anxieties of the Urdu-speaking elites in a province with a substantial Muslim minority, analyses the data on the differential impact of the administrative and bureaucratic changes ushered in by colonial rule in some towns of west UP and the Doab, and tracks the career of Muslim organizations working their way through the imperial system. The British assumed that the Muslims were separate and distinct, a potential danger to the Raj, and an important conservative force. All these notions contributed to the belief that they deserved special treatment.[17] And then the *ulama* burst on to the public platform, the masses were overwhelmed by pan-Islamic fury, Gandhi jumped into the fray, and a new anti-colonial-cum-religious ideology reigned supreme. Soon the winds of political change in Turkey struck at the roots of the Khilafat edifice.[18] The Khalifa's fate caused not a ripple of protest among the masses. The abolition of the Khilafat too was taken calmly; the prevailing mood was one of apathy rather than anger.[19] Though functionaries perpetuated the myth of the pervasive influence of pan-Islamism, overseas writers visiting India, including the Turkish author Halide Edib, insisted that during World War I,

the Muslem-Indian allegiance to England during the Great War demolished a strong historical myth—it showed that political Pan-Islamism was a mere bogey. The attachment of the Indian Muslem to the interests of his country was a greater reality

[17] Robinson, *Separatism among Indian Muslims*, pp. 164–5.

[18] Among Sunni Muslims, who formed an overwhelming majority of the Muslim population, the Sultan of Turkey was the *Amir al-Mu'minin* (Commander of the Faithful) and the protector of the Holy Places. The Khilafat, transferred to Salim I of the House of Ottoman in 1517, was the viceroyalty of the Prophet of Islam, ordained by Divine Law for the perpetuation of Islam and the continued observance of its *sharia* (Islamic law). The Khalifa, derived from the word *khalafa* (to leave behind), was both the religious head of the Sunnis as well as the ruler of an independent kingdom.

[19] On 21 November 1922, the Turkish National Assembly at Ankara decided to separate the Khilafat from the Sultanate. And since the maintenance of the temporal power of the Khalifa was one of the main objects of the Khilafat movement, this action by a purely Muslim body completely took the wind out of its sails. In March 1924, the final blow was struck by Mustafa Kamal Pasha who abolished the Khilafat and expelled the Khalifa from Turkish territory.

than his solidarity with Muslims outside India. When there was a choice between the interests of India and their religious sentiment, the choice went to the interests of India. Had England given Dominion Status to India, the writer believes that the Khilafat agitation would have remained in the sentimental field only. It would be useful for the Western Powers with Muslem colonies to realize this point clearly; there is still a more or less common outlook on life among Muslems, but there is also a distinct sense of nationhood separate from their religious life. The Indian Muslem would resent an Afghan-Muslem domination and fight it.[20]

So were the Indian Muslims a nation? They were not. But being Muslims under British imperial rule did give them some common experience. Is that why they grouped together? Robinson's answer is that it was the threat of becoming backward, rather than backwardness itself, which encouraged UP Muslims to organize themselves separately. Even Muslim revivalism, a 'defence mechanism' to counter Hindu resurgence, was more the creation than the creator of politics of the UP Muslim landed and service elites.[21]

The east Doab and Awadh on the one hand, and western UP and the Doab, on the other, were different from each other in more ways than one. In the former region, connections based on landed rather than communitarian interests worked. So that the towns were largely unaffected by the cow-protection riots: its public figures, especially those with a degree of sagacity, 'made sure that cows were kept in their byres and not allowed to foul the path of politics'.[22] In western UP and the Doab, the dominant alignments tended to be based on commerce, largely a Hindu affair, and Hindu businessmen were among the foremost supporters of Hindu revivalism.

Separatism among Indian Muslims is a work of scholarship, based on patient research. It contains a wealth of general information on the background of political and social actors, and the author has a great capacity for coining striking phrases. He is at home in the world of facts and people and happenings, picturing a world of accidents, conjunctures, and curious juxtapositions of events. But the flaw is his assumption that public men were entirely motivated by 'the loaves and fishes of political

[20] Halide Edib, *Inside India*. With an introduction and notes by Mushirul Hasan (New Delhi, 2002), p. 213.
[21] Robinson, *Separatism among Indian Muslims*, p. 347.
[22] Ibid., pp. 79–80.

office and administrative place'. He carries his disregard of ideology to
the point of cynically portraying the Khilafat movement and caricaturing
Mohamed Ali (1878–1931) and Shaukat Ali (1873–1938) as power-
hungry brokers.[23] At times they appear to be thieves organizing pan-
Islamic ventures in order to be able to lay their hands on the Khilafat
Fund. While my own estimate of Mohamed Ali and his younger brother
is less than complimentary,[24] they were nonetheless spokespersons for
popular passions and prejudices.[25] What prompted their associates to
select them for the part they played in pan-Islamic and nationalist politics
was the aura of fame that clung to them from their student days, their
remarkable success as editors of *Comrade* and *Hamdard*, and their
popularity with the public. The description of Bernard Shaw by the
English philosopher-mathematician, Bertrand Russell (1872–1970) that
as an iconoclast he was admirable, but as an icon rather less, may well
be applied to Mohamed Ali.

Mohamed Ali's *My Life: A Fragment* is an important personal statement
on how some educated Muslims lived through the turbulent decades
following the death of Syed Ahmad Khan in 1898.[26] Its importance is
enhanced by the absence of a similar text written by any other leading
actor of the period. Moreover, while *My Life* is an individual's intellectual

[23] Mushirul Hasan, *Nationalism and Communal Politics in India, 1916–1928* (New
Delhi, 1979), p. 133.

[24] Mushirul Hasan, 'Mohamed Ali's Quest for Identity in Colonial India', in Mushirul
Hasan (ed.), *Islam, Communities and the Nation* (New Delhi, 1998), pp. 93–4.

[25] 'He has wit and emotional appeal. He has also the physique which would dominate
any public gathering. He is a very big man in every sense, and this has been responsible
for his nickname, "Big Brother". He has a flowing beard, a shock of picturesque grey hair,
and eyes which twinkle like those of a mischievous boy. His dress is suggestive of the
vagueness of his politics. He wears a long shirt over tight Indian trousers and leggings;
and a loose Arab Mashlak (mantle) with a Turkish Kalpak (fur cap) in the fashion of
about sixteen years ago. His attire is reminiscent of a combination of Indian, Muslim,
Arab and Turk; in a word, it is a reflection of Pan-Islamism, which though lacking
political reality will, I believe, never die out entirely. Maulana Shaukat Ali has a young
and pretty English wife. In caricatures he is represented as a big baby to whom the King
gives a pretty doll so as to keep him quiet. There are always stories about his quick
retorts. The last was this: A highly placed English official said to him in regard to his wife:
"I hear that you bully your wife." Shaukat Ali answered, looking at the wife of the
Englishman: "Your Excellency is in a position to know which bullies which."' Edib, *Inside
India*, p. 157.

[26] Mohamed Ali, *My Life: A Fragment: An Autobiographical Sketch of Maulana Mohamed
Ali*, edited by Mushirul Hasan (New Delhi, 1999).

and spiritual journey, and his inner self-awareness of Islam, it also reveals how some Muslims constructed their identity in a colonial context. With scholars analysing the complexity of communitarian identities, one must pay due regard to Mohamed Ali's reflection on a society that was being gradually transformed by far-reaching political and administrative changes.

Reading *Separatism among Indian Muslims*, the gap between the events constructed and described and the apparent reasons for them is at once evident. Why were so many people swayed by the Ali brothers' rhetoric? How did they prevail upon Gandhi and the Congress to back the Khilafat? Why did the ulama fall in line with the Ali brothers? The answers do not always emerge from Robinson's story. Just as we go back to the cultural and ideological underpinnings of the Khilafat movement to discover what the fuss was all about, we need to turn to Ansari, leader of an All-India Medical Mission to Constantionople during the Balkan War, for a different reason. Why did the man who led the mission for the sick and wounded in Turkey in 1912 wake up to the dangers inherent in the pan-Islamic doctrines he and others had until then accepted because they seemed to form part of their religion's glorious heritage?[27]

It is not as if Robinson collected facts arbitrarily, assembled them haphazardly, and accepted them passively. His major conclusions, however, rest on official records and intelligence reports, and on the assessment of bureaucrats who were detached from the people and who preferred to stay in the heights of the imperial system. Lastly, his assigning labels to individuals and groups or slotting them into neat categories such as 'Young Party'/'Old Party' does not adequately convey the complexities of a world of shifting loyalties and alignments. One has to look at Mohamed Ali's letters written between 1928 and 1930 to see how he was driven into the camp of the conservatives by fear mingled with rage and aggression, fear of the majority, fear of 'Hindu Raj', and fear of Hindu domination.

[27] He wrote: 'I feel that the Indian Muslims should understand that their perspective was faulty. They have a tendency, as have all those who are isolated, to identify not only their beliefs but also manners and customs with the prescriptions of their faith. Religion and social life are no doubt inseparable, and a society that overlooks the religious element is sure to drift from one vicious whirlpool to another. But the position of a society which lacks the judgment to distinguish between conservatism and stagnation is equally insecure.' Introduction to Halide Edib, *The Conflict of East and West in Turkey* (Delhi, 1935), p. 6.

These fears surfaced as the road to separatism became accessible by 1922–3. Various changes were underway. One of them was the victory of Madan Mohan Malaviya (1861–1946), financed by G.D. Birla, in the elections to the UP Assembly. This disappointed Motilal Nehru, a key player in UP politics. The Malaviya–Lala (with Lajpat Rai, 1865–1928) combine, he wrote to his son Jawaharlal, was busy trying to capture the Congress.[28] The Swaraj Party, an outcome of the bitter controversy in the Congress rank and file, had fought on a non-communal plank in the 1923 elections and won thirty-one seats. Three years later, it was down to sixteen members. This was largely because its Muslim support had declined. Eleven Muslims had been nominated and four returned in 1923; in 1926, only six were nominated and one returned. Of the original eleven, only the member for Bareilly and Shahjahanpur-cum-Moradabad was re-nominated. Not only had Muslim enthusiasm for the Swarajists dwindled, but they had also drifted towards overtly communal organizations such as the *tabligh* and *tanzim*. Elsewhere, the picture was the same. In February 1923, the All India Shuddhi Sabha started its 'purification campaign' at Agra. In the same year, V.D. Savarkar (1883–1966) published an anti-Muslim, anti-Christian tract entitled *Who is a Hindu?* That year, C.R. Das (1870–1925), Motilal Nehru, Sarojini Naidu (1869–1946), Ajmal Khan, and Maulana Azad visited the Punjab. They saw with disbelief the deterioration in Hindu–Muslim relations. They felt that the masses had been exploited by interested persons to serve selfish ends.[29] While others brokered pacts and unity conferences, Gandhi, anguished by the rise in communal temperature across the country, saw salvation only in deep-seated and long-term inter-community peace and understanding.

David Page, the Oxford historian, examined the consolidation of political interests around communitarian questions.[30] He shows how the Punjabi Muslims worked against a responsible government at the centre and extracted, under the terms of the Communal Award (1932), a major concession—control of their own province under the new constitution. He profiled Fazl-i Husain (1877–1936), the architect of the Punjab

[28] Motilal to Jawaharlal, 2 December 1926, in Jawaharlal Nehru, *A Bunch of Old Letters* (New Delhi, 1958), p. 52.

[29] Cited in Hasan, *Communal and Pan-Islamic Trends*, p. 274.

[30] This is a revised version of what appeared in my Introduction to *The Partition Omnibus* (New Delhi, 2002), pp. xxxiii–xxxiv.

Unionist Party, to indicate how his successors led 'Muslim India' in the complex constitutional arrangements that resulted in the Government of India Act of 1935, and how their perspective mattered during the fateful negotiations of the 1940s.

David Page makes sense of the nitty-gritty of power politics and of imperial policies and their impact on shifting loyalties and changing political alignments. Their very nature leads him to dwell on Hindu–Muslim antagonism, a shattering spectacle as rioters resorted to arson and killing at the slightest pretext. This is the mood, sombre and piquant, in which Page describes the prelude to partition.

Page does not regard Hindu–Muslim strife as a spontaneous outburst but points to the government's reformist zeal as creating the situation and the spirit for communitarian claims to be advanced by a 'minority' and contested by the 'majority'. He concedes that well-established traditions of Muslim political thought and socio-economic disparities shaped communal consciousness in the localities, but 'if these streams of thought and consciousness fed into the river of all-India politics, the Imperial system was like a series of dams, diverting the waters to left and right to suit its own purpose. Structures may not tell the whole story but they tell an important part of it'.

'What we see today,' Sumit Sarkar stated in his 1980 S.G. Deuskar Lecture, 'are the beginnings of an Indian participation in a worldwide trend of history-writing, associated with imaginative use of a wider range of sources, along with a certain distrust or cynicism about more-or-less bureaucratically-organized and outwardly successful movements.'[31] Gyanendra Pandey, a contemporary of David Page at Oxford, exposed the fragile rural base of the Congress,[32] and the limits of its campaigns in relation to the *kisans* (peasants) and Muslims. These factors, according to him, led to a process of self-mobilization by the peasants, a feature of many of the most famous mass demonstrations of the 1920s and 1930s.[33] The Congress also alienated the Muslims between the Non-Cooperation

[31] Sumit Sarkar, *Popular Movements and 'Middle Class' Leadership in Late Colonial India: Perspectives and Problems of a 'History from Below'* (Calcutta, 1983), p. 1.

[32] Gyanendra Pandey, 'A Rural Base for Congress: The United Provinces, 1920–40', in D.A. Low (ed.), *Congress and the Raj: Facets of the Indian Struggle 1917–47* (London, 1977), pp. 199–225.

[33] Gyanendra Pandey, *The Ascendancy of the Congress in Uttar Pradesh 1926–34: A Study in Imperfect Mobilization* (New Delhi, 1978), p. 213.

movement of 1920–2 and the Civil Disobedience campaigns of 1930–3, and this, according to Pandey, remained a constant factor thereafter.[34] This is an untenable proposition, for the Muslim presence in Civil Disobedience was by no means inconsiderable.[35] Moreover, a few years later they responded positively to the Congress-led Muslim Mass Contact Campaign of March 1937.[36]

'Histories from below' have not been particularly interested in identity issues, but Gyanendra Pandey's work stands as an exception. He has written insightfully on the cow as a symbol of sectarian strife in the Bhojpur region (1888–1917),[37] on a *qasba* in the nineteenth century,[38] and on the different conceptions of nationalism/communalism that sought to establish a hierarchy of cultures among the cultures of India and to assign to one or another a primary place in fashioning the future of the society.[39] In his view the assumption of Hindu–Muslim antagonism became a guiding principle in colonial sociology and administrative practice. For him, the British constructed a 'communalist' narrative to interpret the disconnected and highly divergent events with which they were confronted. Such a narrative is characterized by

an emptying out of all history—in terms of the specific variations of time, place, class, issue—from the political experience of the people, and the identification of religion, or the religious community, as the moving force of all Indian politics. The communal riot narrative served to substantiate this reading of history.[40]

[34] Ibid., p. 205.

[35] See Mushirul Hasan, *A Nationalist Conscience: M.A. Ansari, the Congress and the Raj* (New Delhi, 1987), pp. 182–4.

[36] The idea, as propounded by Jawaharlal Nehru, was to approach the Muslims not as a collective fraternity but as a segment of an impoverished population. The principal motivation was to convince them that they did constitute a nation, and that their fortunes were not bound up with those their Muslim brethren per se but with fellow artisans, peasants, and workers in other communities.

[37] See Gyanendra Pandey, 'Rallying Round the Cow: Sectarian Strife in the Bhojpuri Region, c. 1888–1917', in Ranajit Guha (ed.), *Subaltern Studies II: Writings on South Asian History and Society* (New Delhi, 1983), pp. 60–129.

[38] Gyanendra Pandey, 'Encounters and Calamities': The History of a North Indian Qasba in the Nineteenth Century', in Guha, *Subaltern Studies II*, pp. 231–70.

[39] Gyanendra Pandey, *The Construction of Communalism in Colonial North India* (New Delhi, 1990), p. 261.

[40] Gyanendra Pandey, 'The Colonial Construction of "Communalism": British Writings on Banaras in the Nineteenth Century', in Ranajit Guha (ed.), *Subaltern Studies VI: Writings on South Asian History and Society* (New Delhi, 1989), p. 132.

An apt illustration is the first recorded major riot in Banaras in 1809. The colonial accounts gave it a cause and the cause a name, that is fanaticism/irrationality, thus emptying it of all other significance. They undertook this exercise to describe the 'native' character, establish the population's perverse nature, and reinforce theories on the fundamental antagonism between Hindus and Muslims.[41]

Gyanendra Pandey and his colleagues are inspired by Ranajit Guha, who revived some of the ideas of the Marxists and made a dent in conventional beliefs. He provided a section of the intellectual elite, educated mostly in Oxbridge, with a *Weltanschauung* wholly consistent with the opening statement in *Subaltern Studies I*. Taken as a whole, though, they did not contribute much to the arguments on communalism that the West was beginning to evince interest in. Although about the only thing the subaltern historians had in common was the downplaying of nationalism, they have inspired a line of reasoning that has gained a fairly large following in academia.

In the 1980s and 1990s, 'liberal' histories replaced the magisterial works of the earlier decades and carried the entire process of historical study from the general to the particular and from the abstract to the concrete. They are commendable works for the information they contain and often for the interpretations they offer. David Gilmartin and Ian Talbot traversed Punjab's fertile terrain to reveal vital aspects of its polity and society, and furnish proof on the interconnection between religion and politics;[42] Sarah Ansari showed the influence of the *pirs* of Sind in swinging the support of the province's Muslims in favour of the demand for Pakistan; Bidyut Chakrabarty, Joya Chatterjee, Suranjan Das, Taj ul-Islam Hashmi, Tazeen Murshid, Harun-or-Rashid, Rajat Kanta Ray, and Yunus Samad, all historians of Bengal, subjected a number of areas and periods of history to the scrutiny of theoretical presuppositions; R.F. Miller and S.F. Dale produced insightful books on the Mapillas of Malabar;[43] on Islam south of the Vindhyas, Susan Bayly traced the evolution of a

---

[41] Ibid., p. 109.

[42] See also Ian Talbot and Gurharpal Singh (eds), *Region and Partition: Bengal, Punjab and the Partition of the Subcontinent* (New Delhi, 1999); Bidyut Chakrabarty, *The Partition of Bengal and Assam 1932–1947* (New Delhi, 2004).

[43] S.F. Dale, *Islamic Society on the South Asian Frontier: The Mappilas of Malabar 1498–1922* (Oxford, 1980); R.E. Miller, *Mapila Muslims of Kerala: A Study of Islamic Trends* (New Delhi, 1992, rev. edn.).

tradition of worship marked by a striking capacity to accommodate itself to indigenous patterns of faith and worship, and the sharing of beliefs and practices built up into a dynamic and expansive religious system;[44] the same perspective informed the writings of K.N. Panikkar, a Marxist historian.[45] As an example of this, one could recall the incident where the guru Sivabhinava Narasimhabharati (the guru of Sringeri *matha* from 1899 to 1912), who found a *panja* in the river in Sringeri, a pilgrimage town in north-western Karnataka, gave it to the Muslim elders, saying, 'You do worship for this, and the *matha* will meet the full expenses of the ten-day celebration [*sic*] of Muharram.' The matha also helped during the ten-day Muharram celebrations by sending four men to hold the *pallaki* (palanquin) and giving kerosene lights in the days without electricity.[46]

Although Marxist historiography had taken firm root in the 1930s and 1940s, it dominated the Indian intellectual landscape only after the end of British rule. Following D.D. Kosambi (1907–66), historians studied, without a strong narrative of political events and without recognizing religion as a marker of social and economic identity, class formations, social structures, and agrarian economies. Leaving aside for the moment the flaws in their suppositions and arguments, they challenged many of the colonial and nationalist shibboleths that had robbed historical studies of their depth and vibrancy. As Alfred Cobban remarked in the context of writings on the French Revolution: 'If one source of the strength of Marxism is the satisfaction it can give to the human desire for a purpose to justify and provide an end for the life of the human animal, another is its appearance of providing a scientific statement of the laws of social development.'[47]

The early Marxist historians were influenced by the writings of Rajni Palme Dutt (1896–1974) and M.N. Roy, who had a large following among Muslims in the émigré Communist Party of India in Tashkent. Shaukat Usmani (b. 1901), Ghulam Hussain, and Muzaffar Ahmad (1889–1973) were his principal contacts in the early 1920s in the groups at five

[44] Susan Bayly, *Saints, Goddesses and Kings: Muslims and Christians in South Indian Society 1700–1900* (Cambridge, 1990), pp. 13–14.

[45] For example, his *Colonialism, Culture and Resistance* (New Delhi, 2007).

[46] Leela Prasad, *Ethics in Everyday Hindu Life: Narration and Tradition in a South Indian Town* (New Delhi, 2007), p. 36.

[47] Alfred Cobban, *The Social Interpretation of the French Revolution* (Cambridge, 1964), p. 11.

'communist centres' in India.[48] All firmly believed that the materialistic conception of history alone could produce both progressive and objective history. In *India Today and Tomorrow*, R.P. Dutt tried to analyse the communal problem in terms of the socio-economic rivalry which affected the middle class. Again and again, he noted, what was reported as communal strife concealed a struggle of Muslim peasants against Hindu landlords, Muslim debtors against Hindu moneylenders, or Hindu workers against Pathan strike-breakers.[49]

Whatever their strength, Marxist scholars avoided discussing the role of religion and did not dwell much on communalism. They were mostly guided by Jawaharlal Nehru who traced the communal problem to a lag in modernization among Hindus and Muslims; and because their arguments did not go beyond imperial machinations in keeping the two communities apart, they could not recognize identity issues and the circumstances creating communitarian consciousness. Thus Bipan Chandra thought that communalism had no objective reality: if anything, it symbolized 'a distorted or perverse reflection of reality'. Without a 'real conflict' between communities, the use of religion as a vehicle of political organization and mobilization was an aspect of 'false consciousness'.[50] 'Objective' or not, 'real' or not, the fact is that Muslim groups desired to carve out their own sphere of influence on the grounds that their community numbered 70 million and was far more homogenous than any other people in India. 'Indeed,' announced Iqbal in December 1930, 'the Muslims of India are the only Indian people who can fitly be described as a nation in the modern sense of the word.'[51]

The Sikhs and the Hindus in the Punjab too wished to carve out their spheres of influence in the impending federal structure. The Hindus of Sind resisted the demand to separate Sind from the Bombay Presidency simply to maintain their dominance in a Muslim-majority region.[52] While one agrees with Bipan Chandra that communalism was not the 'logical and inevitable product of India's historical development',[53] this does not imply the absence of a 'real conflict'.

[48] Sibnarayan Ray (ed.), *Selected Works of M. N. Roy*, vol. 4 (New Delhi, 1997), p. 364.
[49] R.P. Dutt, *India Today and Tomorrow* (Delhi, 1955), pp. 227, 229.
[50] Bipan Chandra, *Communalism in Modern India* (New Delhi, 1984), p. 23.
[51] Pirzada, *Foundations of Pakistan*, vol. 1, p. 169.
[52] See Mushirul Hasan, 'The Communal Divide: A Study of the Delhi Proposals', in Hasan, *Communal and Pan-Islamic Trends*, pp. 281–301.
[53] Chandra, *Communalism in Modern India*, p. 25.

The first generation of writers in Pakistan contested the Marxian framework and, predictably, the 'nationalist perspective'. This was a necessary precondition for rationalizing the birth of the new nation. However, this exercise ran into rough weather in 1971 when linguistic nationalism triumphed over the two-nation theory and Pakistan and Bangladesh went their separate ways. After that, there were no entreaties for unity and no mention of Pakistan and Bangladesh coming together or working out a confederation plan. Islam, a cementing force in the 1940s, lost its validity in the new political arrangements being worked out in Lahore and Dhaka.

With Pakistan's national fabric torn apart and the legitimacy of Islamic nationhood exposed by the army brutalities on fellow Muslims, it was time to strike a discordant note in the existing discourses. Some time back, Yunus Samad, a Bangladesh-born political scientist, traced the gap between Muslim nationalism and ethnicity, the emergence of 'centrifugal forces' in reaction to efforts at centralization, and the growing influence of the military-bureaucratic oligarchy.[54] Another Bangladesh-born scholar, Farzana Shaikh, turned to the factors sustaining the politics of Muslim representation. One of them is the awareness of the ideal of Muslim brotherhood, a belief in the superiority of Muslim culture and recognition of the belief that Muslims ought to live under Muslim governments.[55] The other is the body of assumptions concerning the community's pivotal role, its exclusive claim to individual allegiance, the nature of political consensus, and the organization of power in society.[56] The notion of 'Muslimness', an elementary condition of legitimate political power, constituted for Muslims over the ages the ultimate test of representative status and political legitimacy. Indeed, it sustained the Muslim League's political development.[57]

Peter Robb, having rejected the instrumentalist explanation of Muslim separatism, contends that a 'Muslim' constituency already existed to which separatists and secularists had to appeal, and that communalism and pan-Islamism rested on a long-standing sense of community (as also among Hindus), reinforced by actual movement and contacts, which

[54] Yunus Samad, A Nation in Turmoil: Nationalism and Ethnicity in Pakistan, 1937–1958 (New Delhi, 1995).

[55] Farzana Shaikh, Community and Consensus in Islam, p. 230.

[56] Ibid., p. 233.

[57] Ibid., pp. 233–6.

complemented or transcended the syncretic regional elements.[58] This formulation is close to Farzana Shaikh's thesis, though its long-term implications are not the same. The 'pre-history' of communalism is an invention, as much as the assertion that Muslim political interests had already been cogently enunciated well before the Government of India Act of 1935. Nobody had done so except for some splinter groups; not even Jinnah. It was all very well to trace the historical evolution of an imaginary community as an antithesis to the Congress thesis of 'unity in diversity' and to underline the distinct historical character of the Muslim community to use the leverage thus acquired to bargain with the government for separate electorates, weightages, and representation. But there was nobody to reach out to for the consolidation of Muslim-centric interests. The results of election to the provincial assemblies demonstrated that a Muslim constituency did not even exist in 1937. Even after securing 'deliverance' from the Congress Ministries in 1939, Jinnah dithered as province after province mounted pressure for a share in the pie.

Put briefly, a decidedly elitist discourse should not be seen as reflective of Indian Muslims or their so-called communal consciousness. Nor can the politics of Muslim identity be reduced to a mere rationalization of normative Islamic discourse. There is much variation even within this elitist discourse, not all of which focused on electoral representation, and still greater evidence of Muslim willingness to differ from rather than defer to the consensus of the community, however construed, in the rough and tumble of practical politics.[59] Indeed, the puzzle over identity in South Asia has been more complex and nuanced than admitted by the protagonists of the two-nation theory or the practitioners of a historiography based on binary opposition between secular and religious nationalism.[60]

The complexity of Muslim identities becomes even more pointed when issues regarding appropriation, self-images, and representation are problematized.[61] Identities have seldom been unified; in British India,

[58] Peter Robb, *Liberalism, Modernity, and the Nation* (New Delhi, 2007), Chapters 'Muslim Identity and Separatism in India: The Significance of M.A. Ansari' and 'The Impact of British Rule on a Religious Community: Reflections on the Trial of Maulvi Ahmadullah of Patna in 1865', pp. 167–8, 225.

[59] Sugata Bose and Ayesha Jalal (eds), *Nationalism, Democracy and Development* (New Delhi, 1997), p. 80.

[60] Ibid., p. 103.

[61] On this point, see, Maulana Hussain Ahmad Madani, *Composite Nationalism and*

they were not only multiple but also invariably fractured owing to the working of an inherently disruptive colonial system. Hence it has not been easy to capture them on a single axis. The career of the Kidwais of Barabanki district, an influential family in Awadh, shows how history throws open some paths and closes off others, how identities are layered, fluid, situationally negotiated constructs, and not neatly tied to places in an unproblematic way. Official identifications in the census reified or solidified identities, but the 'identity' of the Kidwais was multilayered. They, accordingly, created meanings that shaped their lives. [62]

It is imperative to shed some light on the everyday life of such families and to ask: Is it the case that their lives are led differently because of the overriding impact of the *sharia*, or is it that they had a more inclusive profile that made it difficult to measure religious commitments on a scale that would embrace multiple identities? One ponders such matters that transcend territorial boundaries. If, as Herbert Butterfield pointed out, history can serve any practical purpose, it is to remind us of those complications that undermine our certainties, and to show that all our judgements are merely relative to time and circumstance.[63]

Increasingly, scholars question the validity of analytical dyads like Shia and Sunni, Sufi and ulama, and 'Great Tradition' and 'Small Tradition', and refer to the complex ways in which each group defines itself in relation to the other as well the larger community (*ummah*).[64] Studying the everyday experience of sharing and interaction by the Meos in Mewat one is struck by identities being articulated, developed, and revised in multiple sites, ways, and locations. Despite erosion and attack, the 'universe of coexistence' shows resilience and holds in check 'boundary-making enterprises'.[65] On the other hand, syncretic cultural ideas and

---

Islam, translated by Mohammad Anwer Hussain and Hasan Imam (New Delhi, 2005), pp. 135–6.

[62] Mushirul Hasan, *From Pluralism to Separatism: Qasbas in Colonial Awadh* (New Delhi, 2004).

[63] Herbert Butterfield, *The Whig Interpretation of History* (London, 1921; Pelican Books 1973), p. 58.

[64] Vernon James Schubel, *Religious Performance in Contemporary Islam: Shia Devotional Rituals in South Asia* (South Carolina, 1993), pp. 159–60.

[65] 'Despite the extensive evidence of sectarian contention during this period, there has also been something strange and inexplicable going on at the interface of the cultural encounter. This is a phenomenon that the historical record hardly recognizes and sociological theory is hard put to explain. Western philosophy and disciplinary traditions,

associated liminal identities in Alwar and the shrine in Pirana bring in
the process of purification and homogenization. This is not all. The
movement from living together harmoniously to division of the sacred
space of *dargah/samadhi* entailed the rewriting/reinventing of history.[66]

What occurs in Alwar and Pirana happened in Lucknow and Allahabad,
the two major sites of the creative fusion of religions and cultures. Yet,
owing to identities being subject to a radical historicization and being
constructed across different intersecting sites, discourses, and practices,
we see Shia–Sunni tension developing in one city and Hindu–Muslim
rioting taking place in the other.[67] Once, the Ram Lila festivities in
Allahabad were an open-air affair and Muslims too swelled the crowds,
and there was joy and light-heartedness. But all this changed owing to

---

in any case, prioritize binarism given their emphasis on monadic selfhood, incommensurable
identities, and boundaries around cultural isolates. But human agency subverts boundaries
at the most unexpected sites: say the realm of desire as in the passion of a Sindhi girl for
a Muslim painter; Colonel Dixon's marriage with Bibi, a Merat Muslim woman; Gibson's
willing of his property to his gardener; in the friendship and close professional relationship
that grew between Hakim Nizamuddin and the Vaidya Ramachandran Vyas as the latter
tried to convert mercury into gold in his quest for alchemy and was isolated by other
practitioners of Ayurveda; in the collaborative ventures of civil society and crime.
The incommensurability of communities and identities, therefore, requires to be
sustained by high energy levels of ideological intervention, to override the universes of
coexistence and encounter that are constantly eroding and subverting boundary-making
enterprises.' Shail Mayaram, 'Living Together: Ajmer as a Paradigm for the (South) Asian
City', in Mushirul Hasan and Asim Roy (eds), *Living Together Separately: Cultural India
in History and Politics* (New Delhi, 2005), pp. 169–70.

[66] Ian Copland, 'Islam and the Moral Economy', and Dominique-Sila Khan and Zawahir
Moir, 'Co-existence and Communalism', in Asim Roy (ed.), *Islam in History and Politics:
Perspective from South Asia* (New Delhi, 2006), p. 150.

[67] Mushirul Hasan, 'Traditional Rites and Contested Meanings: Sectarian Strife in
Colonial Lucknow', in Violette Graff (ed.), *Memories of a City* (New Delhi, 1997), pp.
114–35. Note the following: 'The Shia–Sunni conflict is at once a struggle for the soul of
Islam—a great war of competing theologies and conceptions of sacred history—and a
manifestation of the kind of tribal wars of ethnicities and identities, so seemingly archaic
at times, yet so surprisingly vital, with which humanity has become wearily familiar. Faith
and identity converge in this conflict, and their combined power goes a long way toward
explaining why, despite the periods of coexistence, the struggle has lasted so long and
retains such urgency and significance. It is not just a hoary religious dispute, a fossilized
set piece from the early years of Islam's unfolding, but a contemporary clash of identities.
Theological and historical disagreements fuel it, but so do today's concerns with power,
subjugation, freedom, and equality, not to mention regional conflicts and foreign intrigues.
It is, paradoxically, a very old, very modern conflict.' Vali Nasr, *The Shia Revival: How
Conflicts within Islam Will Shape the Future* (New York, 2006), p. 20.

recurring disputes. 'Surely,' Jawaharlal Nehru bemoaned, 'religion and the spirit of religion have much to answer for. What kill joys they have been.'[68]

In the short-story 'Refugee', Debesh Roy provides, almost with black humour, a very complete picture of the construction of identity that followed partition. He constructs the identities of Anima and Satyabrata in several differing histories, each of which is plausible, in legal parlance. They appear at the local police station to prove their identities. But the uppermost questions in their minds were how they were going to do it, and what really was the 'truth' of their identity?

Prafulla Roy's 'Infiltration' also deals with the fluid identities marked as refugee/migrant/infiltrator, all of which serve as fodder for vote-bank politics.

A few hours later, while he walked back through the stone-strewn way to their vagabond living with Shaukat, there was this one thought recurring in Farid's mind. At the time of the British they were Indians, then Pakistani, after that Bangladeshi. Because of elections, 40 years later they found a new identity. Now they are again Indians.

Walking as if his mind was far away, Farid *salaamed* the elections a thousand times in his heart.[69]

'DIVIDE ET IMPERA'

> If progress consists in the individual taking a broader view of what constitutes politics, our communalists as well as our Government have deliberately and consistently aimed at the opposite of this—the narrowing of the view.
>
> —Jawaharlal Nehru, *An Autobiography*, p. 472

It is increasingly fashionable to be non-ideological and apolitical in a post-modern intellectual world. Nationalism, secularism, and pluralism, ideals cherished and upheld by the Indian people, have been sought to be divested of their intrinsic worth.[70] One of the casualties of this

---

[68] Jawaharlal Nehru, *An Autobiography* (London, 1936), p. 141.

[69] Bashabi Fraser (ed.), *Bengal Partition Stories: An Unclosed Chapter* (London, 2006), p. 540.

[70] Sucheta Mahajan, *Independence and Partition: The Erosion of Colonial Power in India* (New Delhi, 2000), p. 18.

approach is the neglect of the study of the role of colonial structures in creating religious and caste solidarities. There was a time when the nationalist historians agreed that the government stoked the fires of communal unrest by colluding with feudal, semi-feudal, and reactionary elements.[71] There was a time when Nehru's view gained currency: 'Of course, there was thwarting of us, deliberate and persistent thwarting, by the Government and their allies. Of course, British governments in the past and the present have based their policy on creating divisions in our ranks.'[72] Today, when economic and political conflicts have been reduced to stereotypes, not many appreciate the full acuteness or complexities of using communalism as an acceptable corrective to nationalist zeal.[73]

Peter Hardy felt that British policy should be acquitted of deep Machiavellian cunning.[74] Francis Robinson conceded that the British played the main part in establishing a separate Muslim identity in Indian politics but felt that they did not intend to do so: 'There was no deliberate attempt to foster communal hostility; indeed the aim was to avoid it.'[75] In another work, he states that the British did privilege religious identities, but warns against the tendency to regard the British as the only agency to sharpen distinctions between Muslims and non-Muslims by privileging the Muslims. He brings into focus the current of reform which sought to revitalize Muslim life from the early nineteenth century to the present.[76]

Adam Smith (1723–90) thought that 'Great Britain derives nothing but loss from the dominion which she assumes over her colonies'; the Indian people, on the other hand, suffered immeasurably owing to high prices and to various forms of colonial exploitation during World War I. In 1919–20, the bulk of the nation was united as never before; the social and intellectual discipline Gandhi provided accelerated this process.

[71] For example, K.B. Krishna, The Problem of Minorities or Communal Representation in India (London, 1939), and Asoka Mehta and Achyut Patwardhan, The Communal Triangle in India (Allahabad, 1942).

[72] Nehru, An Autobiography, p. 136.

[73] David Page, Prelude to Partition in The Partition Omnibus (New Delhi, 2002), p. 91. The following section is based on my Nationalism and Communal Politics in India, pp. 244–7.

[74] Peter Hardy, The Muslims of British India (Cambridge, 1972), p. 163.

[75] Robinson, Separatism among Indian Muslims, pp. 131–2, 348–9.

[76] Francis Robinson, Islam, South Asia, and the West (New Delhi, 2007), pp. 126–7.

Nobody realized this better than the government; and nothing illuminates its sense of panic and lack of tact more than the recourse to repressive measures. During the Rowlatt Satyagraha and the ill-fated Khilafat–Non-Cooperation movements,[77] an embattled government pinned its hope on the continuing rise of the Hindu–Muslim animosity. Some analysts suggested that Britain fuelled pan-Islamism so that the Muslims would dissipate their power of action by lip sympathy with the world of Islam. Iqbal told one of his interlocutors that the British desired that his co-religionists should 'not be practical but theoretical'.[78] Later, during the Round Table Conference, officials mixed quite happily together in the London social round, whereas in India they used clandestine means to organize Muslim opposition to the Civil Disobedience movement by telling Muslims to conduct local campaigns and financing itinerant preachers. Shaukat Ali, once a fervent anti-colonialist, rubbed shoulders with the British. In so doing, he dug his own grave.

The official version of the Communal Award of 1932 was that Ramsay MacDonald (1866–1937), the British Prime Minister, acted with great propriety after the Congress and the League failed to hammer out their differences. It was the way the Conservatives and the Liberals wanted it, and there is proof that the Award was especially designed to provoke the Congress. And provoked they were, but only the section led by Madan Mohan Malaviya.

During the 1940s, England oscillated between coercion and concession in its efforts to secure Congress's support for World War II. At that stage, the government harnessed the political energies inherent in the communal question. Various pressure groups rose and fell without achieving the League's spectacular success. Into this organization, then, poured the energy of all those supporters of ideals, such as the Jamaat-e Islami, and determined promoters of interests.

---

[77] The Rowlatt Committee recommended that the government should have powers to make arbitrary arrests and inflict summary punishments for the suppression of revolutionary activities in certain parts of the country. Accordingly, a Bill was introduced in the Imperial Legislative Council in February 1919 and was passed in the teeth of opposition from all the Indian members. On 24 February Gandhi informed the Viceroy of his decision to launch satyagraha against the Rowlatt Act. Two days later, he urged his countrymen to join the satyagraha. On 6 April, *hartal* was observed in different parts of the country.

[78] Quoted in Muhammad Sadiq, *A History of Urdu Literature* (New Delhi, 1995, 2nd edition), p. 464.

In Bengal, the divide and rule policy was put into operation to break the stranglehold of the Swarajists and to drive a wedge amongst its supporters. An attempt to sow the seeds of dissension was first made in March 1924, when a Muslim councillor from Malda sought to corner C.R. Das by insisting on the implementation of certain provisions of the Bengal Pact. Das foiled the move. Then, when the House rejected the demand for ministerial salaries the official and non-official blocs were thrown in to prop up the shaky ministries.

In Punjab, the well-entrenched landed and commercial classes constrained the administration's options in augmenting its support base. It was easy to play up one sectional group against the other and to take advantage of the controversies that bedevilled the ministry of Fazl-i Husain (1877–1936), who was elected to the legislative council in 1920 and appointed minister of education in 1921 and 1924. But in a province where the lines of cleavage were not always defined communally this strategy could only be partially successful. So, besides inducting community-oriented groups into positions of power, Edward Maclagan (1864–1932) and his successor, Malcolm Hailey (1872–1969), relied heavily upon the 'agriculturists' and their chosen leaders, Fazl-i Husain and Chhotu Ram (1881–1941), against the urban-based trading and commercial classes.

Hailey did not undervalue Muslim support but warned against making wholesale concessions to them. When the Swarajists lost ground, he wooed the urban Hindus to hold 'the balance between the parties'. To have carried on with the old arrangement would have meant that the Hindu party as such was to be permanently excluded; it would have driven them back to opposition and ultimately to Swaraj.[79] This rethinking on Hailey's part adversely affected the fortunes of the Unionists, especially its Muslim constituents. Their adversaries vetoed the Registration of Moneylenders Bill and obstructed the passage of the Land Revenue [Amendment] Bill. This led to Fazl-i Husain's wings being clipped. Ultimately his arch-rivals occupied the ministerial berth while he moved to the reserved half of the government. In this way, Hailey played his cards well to successfully split the legislative council into communal blocs.

[79] Hailey to Alexander Muddiman, January 1927, F. No. 1O(A), Hailey Papers, quoted in my *Nationalism and Communal Politics in India*, p. 246.

Yet, in the last resort, Hailey had to throw his weight behind the Muslim bloc. After moving from Lahore to Lucknow, he advised the viceroy on Muslim representation at the Round Table Conference, and sought assurances on the preservation of Muslim rights so that a 'moderately satisfactory' tilt towards the Muslims would keep them on the government's side and there would be far less tendency on their part to drift into opposition. But this sophisticated jugglery could not obscure Hailey's real designs.[80] Examining his role in Punjab (1927–8), Hailey's biographer endorses the view that British rule aided the growth of communalism. Hailey, in particular, did not attempt to solve the communal riddle: 'Instead, he watched its dynamics closely and, in pursuit of his first priority—the success of British policy—he did his best to capitalize on it.'[81]

Ian Talbot insists that British officials were 'anxious to limit communal violence rather than to risk encouraging it by dividing and ruling'.[82] Penderel Moon (1905–87), the civil servant, testifies that the Punjab holocaust could not be avoided without a Sikh–Muslim settlement, and that 'by the time Lord Mountbatten arrived in India it was far too late to save the situation'.[83] H.V. Hodson (1906–99) made similar assertions.[84] However, there is little reason to subscribe to their thesis; Sudhir Ghosh, a young executive from the Tata firm, rightly told Stafford Cripps; 'If the Governor-General and the Governor say that this kind of killing and barbarity [following the Direct Action Day] is inevitable in the present circumstances of our country, I look upon that argument as an excuse put forward by men who have failed to do their duty.'[85]

According to Moon, 'You couldn't prevent [the Hindu–Muslim conflict], but you might if you were sufficiently prompt and on the spot at the time, prevent it from assuming a very serious form.' There is sufficient evidence to prove the culpability of those who exercised

[80] Ibid., pp. 245–6.

[81] John W. Cell, *Hailey: A Study in British Imperialism, 1872–1969* (Cambridge, 1992), p. 154.

[82] Ian Talbot, *Punjab and the Raj 1849–1947* (Delhi, 1988), p. 4.

[83] Penderel Moon, *Divide and Quit* (New Delhi, 1988), pp. 296–7. For a different point of view, see Raghuvendra Tanwar, *Reporting the Partition of Punjab 1947: Press, Public and Other Opinions* (New Delhi, 1996).

[84] H.V. Hodson, *The Great Divide: Britain-India-Pakistan* (Karachi, 1977 edn), pp. 402–7.

[85] Quoted in Charles Allen (ed.), *Plain Tales from the Raj* (London, 1975), p. 246.

authority in perpetuating violence. Thus Hukam Chand, resident magistrate and chief election administrator in Khushwant Singh's novel *Train to Pakistan* (1954) is not free from communal and anti-Muslim feeling. Moreover, the administrators were not prepared to risk British lives. Quickening their retreat from civil society, they sought the safety of their bungalows and cantonments. While large parts of urban areas in the Punjab, UP, and Bengal were aflame, they played cricket, listened to music, and read Rudyard Kipling. While trainloads of refugees were being butchered, the small boundary force in the Punjab, for the most part, stayed in the barracks.

The retreat of the British administration, once the source of Curzonian pride, was an act of abject surrender to the forces of violence. Viceroy Wavell (1883–1950) wrote later that the administration lost nearly all power to control events and was simply running on the momentum of its previous prestige. The death count made it abundantly clear that the people, rather than the administrators, had paid a heavy price for the law-and-order machinery breaking down. After 1947, the Congress government faced a civil-war-like situation; it had to clear up the debris of death and destruction.

Existing ethnic rivalries and religious cleavages had facilitated India's colonization. After the 1857 Revolt, the colonial government proceeded on the assumption that Hindu–Muslim clashes were a foregone conclusion, a view British historians of India invented and perpetuated. Officials then constructed their categories to differentiate one community from the other and created spaces for each in their system. After 1857, in particular, the colonial state could not wait complacently for the enemy to strike. In what was then perceived as enemy territory, the government courted reliable friends and dependable allies to provide a counterweight to its inveterate enemies. The Simla Deputation (1 October 1906) was, at least on the strength of Mohamed Ali's testimony, a 'command performance'. Peter Hardy remarked:

To expect them (the British) to encourage the ideals and growth of non-communal nationalism and thus to hasten their own demise as the rulers of India, with all that would mean for the British political and economic position in the world, was to expect a degree not merely of altruism but also of prophetic insight out of the world of the history of governments.[86]

[86] Hardy, *Muslims of British India*, p. 164.

During the first decade of the twentieth century, the government buttressed the privileges of the few Muslims at the top and protected the welfare of the many in the middle rung. The plant of responsible government, fed by some radical sympathizers in London, and watered by the Indian nationalists, brought no comfort to the government. So the idea of separate electorates was conceived to encourage the familiar inter-community struggles and people's representatives confronting lieutenant-governors and their privileged cliques of nominated local worthies on the basis of religion. As David Page put it:

In the consolidation of political interests around communal issues, the Imperial power played an important role. By treating the Muslims as a separate group, it divided them from other Indians. By granting them separate electorates, it institutionalized that division. This was one of the most crucial factors in the development of communal politics. Muslim politicians did not have to appeal to Muslims. This made it very difficult for a genuine nationalism to emerge.[87]

And again.

With each stage of devolution, Indian was set against Indian, caste against caste, community against community. But as each area of government and administration was ceded to Indian control, it was followed by demands for more concessions. Ultimately, even the Raj's closest allies were only allies for a purpose. In 1947, the Raj withdrew, ceding its dominant position to those who had triumphed in the electoral arena. But the final act of devolution was also a final act of division.[88]

We need to open up the long forgotten debate on the British-invented religious/communitarian categories and their translation into institutional arrangements. 'To ignore it', Nehru noted, 'and not to provide against it is in itself a mistake in one's thought.'[89]

SCREENING SOCIAL REFORMS

The reasonable man adapts himself to the world: the unreasonable one persists in trying to adapt the world to himself. Therefore all progress depends on the unreasonable man.
—Bernard Shaw, *Prefaces by Bernard Shaw*, p. 193

[87] Page, *Prelude to Partition*, p. 260.
[88] Ibid., p. 264.
[89] Nehru, *An Autobiography*, p. 136.

> The claim of the present generation of Muslim liberals to reinterpret
> the foundational legal principles, in the light of their own experience
> and the altered conditions of social life, is, in my opinion, perfectly
> justified … . Each generation should be permitted to solve its own
> problems.
>
> —Mohammad Iqbal, *The Reconstruction of Religious Thought*
> *in Islam*, p. 168

Criticism of social conditions, in the sense of an indignant awareness of
shortcomings allied to a desire to remedy them, is hardly to be found in
the colonial system.[90] The imperial policies themselves stemmed from a
broad strategy of checking change, repelling attacks against radicalism,
and curbing the influence of the traditional Muslim groups beyond their
own self-defined boundaries. After 1857, conservative state action
restrained the tide of rapid change, preserved the old landmarks, and
healed divisions. The imperial claim to social reconstruction in the
Victorian image appeared to be a discarded project. No wonder the
government usually backed the traditionalist interpretation of the sharia.
To give one example, the courts' rulings very often worked to deny
women access to property even though the Quran asserts that women
are entitled to inherit a portion of a parent's or husband's wealth. Like
the courts, the political arm of the Raj did not pursue a consistent policy
with regard to women's property rights. This suited the theologians, who
ignored women's property rights. In sum, if a mark of modern society was
improvement in women's rights, then neither the administrative nor the
legal arms of the Anglo-Indian government were engines of
modernization. What they gave to women with one hand, they often
took away with the other.[91]

The government made concession after concession to the *muftis*,
mujtahids, and *maulvis*. Even before 1857, it had fought shy of modifying
Muslim criminal law even when some of its features were demonstrably
not suited to the notions of justice entertained by the British themselves.[92]
Not only was there a dual court system, but Hindu and Muslim criminal

[90] This section is based on my essay 'Living Plurally: Muslim Intellectuals in the
Nineteenth Century' (forthcoming).

[91] Gregory C. Kozlowski, 'Muslim Women and the Control of Property in North
India', *The Indian Economic and Social History Review*, vol. 24, no. 2, 1987, p. 181.

[92] M.P. Jain, 'Challenges of Indian Legal System', in K.L. Raman, 'Utilitarianism and
the Criminal Law in Colonial India', *Modern Asian Studies*, vol. 18, no. 4, 1994, p. 746.

law continued to operate, albeit often without British participation or permission.[93] In this rather complex process, officials sanctified the men of religion, while secular intellectuals, public figures, and other Westernized elites encountered exclusion and denial of recognition. Indeed, they either ignored their concerns on the presumption that they were uninfluential and unrepresentative, or glided imperceptibly into the assertion that they were not quite attuned to the so-called Muslim/Islamic way of life. As in the case of specific themes of social reform, such as widow immolation, so also in relation to the growing liberal opinion, they secured 'an insistence on their own view by ignoring, marginalizing, domesticating, and exceptionalizing whatever did not accord with their presumptions'.[94] This profoundly impacted liberal processes as well as the secular nationalist projects.

In the end, colonial perceptions of where the liberal intelligentsia stood influenced the government's strategy towards the Muslims. Soon enough, public discourse was polarized, as evident from Syed Ahmad Khan's torturous reform career, between various perspectives. Liberals and modernists of all hues felt inhibited fighting their battles on an enlightened plank, because the government narrowed their platform and their stature within its structures. Some pressed on regardless, as evident from the path of various progressive literary movements from the 1920s onwards; others joined revolutionary movements. Meanwhile, the Communist Party of India acknowledged, in the late 1930s, and ultimately yielded to, the growing demand for cultural self-determination in terms of a Muslim collective identity. This was, of course, a fatal mistake.

In a more general way, the Muslim public in the 1930s and 1940s had only one choice: to shore up the variegated Islamist groups who claimed to be the protectors and authentic interpreters of the Islamic codes. They received strength from Iqbal, who talked of keeping the faith thriving in his poem 'Hindi-e Islam' and dismissed all thought of Islam's emancipation in the subcontinent.

[93] David Skuy, 'Macaulay and the Indian Penal Code of 1862: The Myth of the Inherent Superiority and Modernity of the English Legal System in the Nineteenth Century', *Modern Asian Studies*, vol. 32, no. 3, 1998, p. 522.

[94] Lata Mani, *Contentious Traditions: The Debate on Sati in Colonial India* (New Delhi, 1998), p. 193.

Mulla ko jo hain Hind me sajde ki ijazat
Nadaan ye sumajhta hai ke Islam hai azad.

Just because in India the mullah has the right to prayer-prostration
The naive mullah thinks that Islam is free.[95]

As the decades rolled on, more and more reformers conceded the high religious ground to their opponents, especially on women's education, property rights, and *purdah*. This opposition emanated not so much from traditional thinkers as from those steeped in modern learning.

Thus the failure of Muslim modernism lies as much in colonial mentalities that retarded the flowering of liberal thought as in the orthodoxy's resistance to reform and innovation. This is probably what Shibli (1857–1914), the *alim* at Lucknow's Nadwat al-ulama, meant while apostrophizing his community as 'blind' in the lifetime of Syed Ahmad Khan and his own.[96] Blind or not, large sections of it were ill-equipped to value or promote democratic aspirations of the kind that became so central to the powerful reformist currents engendered by the Brahmo Samaj in Bengal and Arya Samaj in Punjab. We can see what this has meant to the lives of the Muslim communities in the subcontinent in the twenty-first century.

[95] Victor Kiernan (ed.), *Poems from Iqbal* (Lahore, 1999 edition), pp. 172–3.
[96] Shibli to Abdul Majid Daryabadi, 15 November 1913, *Makatib-i Shibli*, vol. 1 (Azamgarh, 1924), p. 292.

4

Questioning Civilizational
Fault Lines

Are there any common historical antecedents which the Hindus and
Muslims can be said to share together as matters of pride or as matters
of sorrow…. So far as this aspect of their relationship is concerned,
they have been just two armed battalions warring against each other.
There was no common cycle of participation for a common
achievement. Their past is a past of mutual destruction—a past of
mutual animosities, both in the political as well as in the religious fields.
—B.R. Ambedkar, *Pakistan or Partition of India*, pp.17–8

So, while kings quarrelled and destroyed each other, silent forces in
India worked ceaselessly for a synthesis, in order that the people of
India might live harmoniously together and devote their energies
jointly to progress and betterment. In the course of centuries they
achieved considerable success.
—Jawaharlal Nehru, *Glimpses of World History*, p. 253

Two observations from two leading public figures: one voicing the
aspirations of Dalits and the other articulating the vision of a multicultural and multireligious society. They reflect one of the many
paradoxes of modern Indian history. What does one make of B.R.
Ambedkar (1891–1956) asserting, in 1940, that 'the political and religious
antagonisms divide the Hindus and the Musalmans far more deeply than

the so-called common things are able to bind them together,'[1] and then taking such a leading part in framing free India's secular constitution? What is disconcerting is that the champion of the lower castes, some of whom embraced Buddhism, a religion famous for its ecumenical spirit, cites Bhai Parmanand (1876–1947), a well-known Muslim baiter, to endorse the 'two-nation' theory.

Even before Ambedkar had come into the public limelight, he found an unusual ally in Iqbal, who had composed many delightful patriotic songs,[2] calling his land of birth a garden inhabited by people who were members of a *qaum* (nation), with the two circles of Islam and *watan* (country) intersecting and at several places coalescing into a coherent whole. But after much soul searching in the late-1920s, the author of 'Himala', the first poem in *Bang-e Dara, Hindustani Bacchon ka Qaumi Geet* (National Anthem of Indian Children) and the 'Tarana-e Hindi' (Anthem of India) discovered the civilizational fault lines upon which he would base the notion of a separate land of the future. Speaking at the Muslim League session in 1930, he urged his co-religionists to achieve complete organization and unity of will and purpose, both in their interest as a community and in the interest of India as a whole. He did not envisage a separate Muslim state but talked of Punjab, the North West Frontier Province, Sind, and Baluchistan being amalgamated into a single state *within the body politic of India*. He referred to autonomous states being formed, obviously not all-Muslim, based on the unity of language, race, history, religion, and identity of interests. Though Iqbal is noted for his diffused poetical utterances, this demand was nowhere near to the polemical two-nation theory expounded by Jinnah in March 1940. Did the 'Poet of the East' not write in his diary of 1910: 'Nations are born in the hearts of poets, they prosper and die in the hands of politicians'?[3]

Iqbal's turnaround can be attributed to a number of factors. One of them could well be the post-1922 pessimism engendered by the low ebb in inter-community relations. Hence the call for 'an independent line

---

[1] B.R. Ambedkar, *Pakistan or Partition of India* (Bombay, 1945), p. 17. See also Anupama Rao, 'Ambedkar and the Politics of Minority: A Reading', in Dipesh Chakrabarty, Rochona Majumdar, and Andrew Sartori (eds), *From the Colonial to the Postcolonial* (New Delhi, 2007), pp. 143–5, 152.

[2] For example, '*Sare jahan se acha Hindostan humara*' (Our India is the best country in the world).

[3] Quoted in Annemarie Schimmel, *Islam in the Indian Subcontinent* (Lieden, 1980), p. 226.

of action to cope with the present crisis'. The other was his dissatisfaction with the Congress criteria of nationhood and his own philosophical disposition towards a conception of Muslim community. One lesson he had learnt from the history of the Muslims was this: 'At critical moments in their history it is Islam that has saved Muslims and not *vice-versa*.'[4] So that the Muslims had to focus their vision on Islam and seek inspiration from the ever-vitalizing ideas embodied in it. He concluded with the appeal:

Rise above sectional interests and private ambitions, and learn to determine the value of your individual and collective action, however directed on material ends, in the light of the ideal which you are supposed to represent. Pass from matter to spirit. Matter is diversity; spirit is light, life and unity.[5]

Iqbal's use of Islamic images, symbols, and metaphors galvanized his followers to accomplish Pakistan. His populism provided a grand ideology, a phantasmagoria in which some Muslims could find their image. He offered a romantic egalitarian vision to nurture, a vision shimmering with an idealized recall of the past. He inspired faith, pride, and confidence in the Islamic heritage. Instead of the dry ritualized dogma of the theologians, he emphasized Islam's social dynamism, an Islam that had created equality between the rich and the poor, Arab and non-Arab. In a situation where the Muslim middle classes lived in colonial subjection and in competition with others, Iqbal's eloquent poetry inspired a new sense of dignity.

When asked, 'Why do you Pakistanis make so much of Iqbal?' Aziz Ahmad replied, 'Because he made us feel good.' Like many off-the-cuff remarks, this stated the truth of a kind less commonly and less openly expressed in academic writings.[6]

In this chapter I stay with the conflicting points raised by Ambedkar and Jawaharlal Nehru by comparing and contrasting not them but two writers from much the same social backgrounds but who arrive at different conclusions. I draw, first of all, upon Aziz Ahmad. Educated in Hyderabad (Deccan) and London, he taught English at the Osmania

---

[4] Sharifuddin Pirzada (ed.), *Foundations of Pakistan: All India Muslim League Documents: 1906–1947* (Karachi, 1970), vol. 1, p. 171.

[5] Ibid.

[6] Ralph Russell, *The Pursuit of Urdu Literature: A Select History* (London, 1992), p. 186.

University before leaving for Pakistan. Thereafter, he joined the School of Oriental Studies in London until 1962 before moving to the Department of Islamic Studies, University of Toronto. Colleagues knew him as a man of letters, whose Urdu novels and poetry, as in the case of his historical scholarship, reflected both sensitive understanding of his own culture and a breadth of knowledge and vision which helped and encouraged the uninitiated to appreciate and understand.[7] He stood out as a man who united a thorough knowledge and critical appreciation of his native traditions with the ability to view them through a truly modern lens and to a considerable extent to write frankly about what he saw and what he concluded.[8] A skilful synthesizer of information and knowledge, Aziz Ahmad reached out to Western audiences whose interest in South Asia was rekindled by the 'discovery' of an ancient culture and civilization.

Besides his short stories and novels, Aziz Ahmad's three major works in English are: *Islamic Culture in the Indian Environment* (1964), *An Intellectual History of Islam in India* (1969), and *Islamic Modernism in India and Pakistan, 1857–1964* (1967). With G.E. Von Grunebaum, he put together selections from significant literature and documents that hold a mirror to modern Islamic self-consciousness, self-statement, and self-definition in the subcontinent.[9] The scope of *Islamic Modernism in India and Pakistan* is 'to place in the hands of the western Islamist or student of international affairs a handbook of religious and political thought, as faithfully as possible'.[10] His analysis, sharp and illuminating as it is, however, does not go far enough and does not take into account all the factors that went into the making of a distinctly *Indian* Islam. For one, he scarcely covered the Marxian writings, notably those by W.C. Smith, and other nuanced interpretations of medieval and modern Indian history. He discerned 'the alternating and simultaneous processes of mutual attraction and repulsion',[11] but not the strength of the amalgamation of different religions, cultures, or schools of thought, that is composite trends. Indeed, he tailored his narrative to rationalize the idea of 'Pakistan' and

[7] Milton Israel and N.K. Wagle (eds), *Islamic Society: Essays in Honour of Professor Aziz Ahmad* (New Delhi, 1983), p. vi.

[8] Ralph Russell, 'Aziz Ahmad, South Asia, Islam, and Urdu', in ibid., p. 66.

[9] Aziz Ahmad and G.E. Von Grunebaum (eds), *Muslim Self-statement in India and Pakistan 1857–1968* (Wiesbaden, 1970), p. 1.

[10] Aziz Ahmad, *Islamic Modernism in India and Pakistan 1885–1964* (New Delhi, 1967), p. xi.

[11] Ibid., p. vii.

did not, consequently, question its contestation in many quarters, Hindu and Muslim. He assumed that Pakistan's creation and survival bore testimony to the relevance and legitimacy of the two-nation theory. Without questioning the validity of this thesis or casting any doubt over the status of Pakistan as an independent nation state, one is still entitled to ask certain basic questions about the tortuous journey that led to partition, to Hindu–Muslim violence, and to India–Pakistan hostilities.

Ralph Russell has criticized *Islamic Modernism in India and Pakistan* for Ahmad's implied definition of 'Muslim' as one who is a Muslim believer instead of using Smith's definition of a Muslim as 'any person who calls himself a Muslim'. It is a 'definition' which has the advantage of adapting to a variety of contents and historical situations, including the traditional ones.[12] Further, Aziz Ahmad ignored the fact that nearly all modern Muslim thought has, amongst other features, a political aim that transcends the bounds of modern Muslim *religious* thought. Russell argued:

It is not to belittle the religious thinkers to acknowledge that they too shared a political aim; while on the other hand insufficient stress upon that aim makes impossible an adequate treatment of the enormously important figure of Jinnah, who, though he too may have been a Muslim in the sense of Aziz Ahmad's implied definition of the term, certainly sought the solution to Muslim problems not in a reinterpretation of traditional Muslim doctrine but in the study of modern politics. All of this Aziz Ahmad knew very well, and it was for diplomatic reasons that he refrained from making it clear that he knew it.[13]

Muslim cultural and intellectual life in the nineteenth and twentieth centuries has been profiled by some other writers, apart from Aziz Ahmad and W.C. Smith, benefiting from the scholarship of Aligarh- and Allahabad-based historians. A lot more names, not just of professional historians but other social scientists as well, can be thrown into the ring. For example, the editor to the proceedings of a conference held at Simla in May 1967 underlined:

The movement of thought and ideas in contemporary Islam is important not only because there is a substantial portion of its population professing the religion, but also

---

[12] Fredrick Jameson, *Archaeologies of the Future: The Desire Called Utopia and Other Science Fictions* (London, 2007), p. 398.

[13] Russell, 'Aziz Ahmad, South Asia, Islam, and Urdu', pp. 67–8.

because of the establishment of Pakistan on two nation theory based on religion. The recent happenings in Bangladesh have rather demolished the theoretical foundations of the Pakistan state.[14]

The stream of scholarship flowed in different directions. I next take up the work of Mohammad Mujeeb, author of numerous books in English and Urdu. He worked for the Jamia Millia Islamia from 1926 to 1973, the last twenty-five years as its Vice-Chancellor. Inspired by Nehru's *The Discovery of India*, he published *World History: Our Heritage* in 1960. *Educational and Traditional Values* appeared a few years later. But Mujeeb's magnum opus is, undoubtedly, *The Indian Muslims*. It has force and unity, its breadth of view is impressive, and its content incredibly learned. Because of its firm roots in knowledge and scholarship, the book will long retain a special place in historical literature unaffected by changing trends.

Mujeeb was a professional historian, although with him we are not really in the sphere of the university. *The Indian Muslims* is in line with the long and varied tradition of broad and liberal historical interests maintained by Mohammad Habib (1889–1971), his elder brother at Aligarh. He offered a reappraisal of Sultan Mahmud of Ghazni (r. 999–1030), the iconoclast, and edited major nineteenth-century texts.[15] 'A brilliant tour de force, *The Indian Muslims* is unequalled by any work on the highly important theme of the intellectual and cultural life of the Muslims in the medieval and modern history of India. It is a major work of reinterpretation and synthesis, skilfully constructed and engagingly written.'[16]

Mujeeb illumined his history with a conscious and rational set of values, applying a genuinely scientific and creative approach to the historical method and avoiding a capricious selection of sources. Seeking autonomy in compiling and transmitting to schoolchildren an understanding of the pre-colonial Indian past, he exalted history for its search for the objective truth about the past. A historian cannot, therefore, be political propagandist; his function is simply to state and interpret the facts without allowing his own prejudices to influence the discussion of his theme or warp his judgment. Indeed, as Nehru wrote to Indira Gandhi from prison in the early 1930s, 'We have today to march

[14] S.T. Lokhandwala (ed.), *India and Contemporary Islam* (Simla, 1971), p. xv.

[15] See K.A. Nizami (ed.), *Collected Works of Professor Mohammad Habib*, vol. 2 (Delhi, 1981).

[16] V.N. Datta, in *Islam and the Modern Age*, vol. 34, August–October 2003, p. 21.

the same way and work for a synthesis of all that is good. But this time it must be on surer foundation. It must be based on freedom and social equality, and it must fit in with a better world order. Only then will it endure.'[17] These words made good sense to Mujeeb and he said:

How can a Hindu put himself in the place of a Muslim or a Sikh or a Christian? How can the minister of a ruling party put himself in the place of one who is opposed to him? How can someone who is rich and contented imagine himself in the position of a man who is starving because he can find no work? It is not easy. But if we do not try to understand one another, there will be conflicts. We shall all be unhappy, and our country will be poor and weak.[18]

Instead of a dogmatic reconstruction of the Muslim past subscribing to religious emotion and theological dogma, Mujeeeb underlined the absence of high standards of social equality, women's rights, and just inheritance. He pleaded for action in accordance with the precepts of public good, and wanted Muslims to promote fundamental equality—or equity—reasoned in the best of Islamic traditions. Otherwise, he feared, they would remain an isolated static unit in one of the most dynamic centuries.

Works on theology and jurisprudence compiled outside India had to change to suit India. Mujeeb asked: Why is the *sharia* sacrosanct? To him, the jumble of beliefs and practices, and customs revealed that Muslims did not follow the sharia as such but these practices and customs, and to some extent, even their beliefs which eventually became the divine law of Islam.[19] Without predicting their return to it in the new spirit, he invoked the truth of the Quranic verse: 'God does not change the condition of a people unless they change it themselves.'[20] Mujeeb furthermore endorsed the principle of a uniform civil code but not without the necessary integration of the different communities through judicial decisions and practical government measures. He introduced a cautionary note:

We cannot at one and the same time proudly proclaim the diversity of our cultural life and propose a uniform personal law for all citizens. It has also to be remembered

---

[17] Jawaharlal Nehru, *Glimpses of World History*, (London, 1939), p. 253.
[18] Mohammad Mujeeb, *Akbar* (New Delhi, 1969), pp. 1–2.
[19] Mohammad Mujeeb, *Islamic Influence on Indian Society* (Meerut, 1972), p. 90.
[20] Ibid., p. 99.

that laws should be made when they are needed and not only for theoretical satisfaction. The protest of the Muslims in 1962–63, when it appeared—perhaps without sufficient cause—that a uniform legal code was being contemplated by the government is understandable, because there was no obvious and impelling reason that this should be done. And about the most tactless thing that could be said in this context was that Parliament was supreme and could make any laws it chose.[21]

It is difficult to think of anyone more erudite and more independent in his thinking.

Born into an educated family and brought up in Awadh's composite milieu, Mujeeb studied at Lucknow's Loreto Convent, a Roman Catholic school, and Dehradun's Cambridge Preparatory School. Here Principal Robert Talbot Dalby taught him English, Latin, Mathematics, Physical Geography, and the Bible. He read the *Bhagwadgita* as well as several books of Annie Besant (1847–1933) and other theosophists. In 1922, he graduated from Oxford's New College. Afterwards, he tried his hand at painting and music in Germany. This experience would have harnessed his aesthetic sense and it enabled him to appreciate in later years the finest and most elaborate combination of sculpture and architecture in the Konark temple, the Hoysalesvara temple in Halebid, and the Dilwara temples in Mount Abu. He found the multiplicity of forms and ornamental motifs staggering.[22]

Mujeeb's genuine passions were for history and literature, and he would gladly spend all his time in studying them. His natural intellectual inclination, this far, was towards men of enlightenment. William Shakespeare (1564–1616) introduced him to 'the music of words, the cadence of sentences, the sheer emotional delight of dramatic expression'; Mirza Abu Taleb Khan (1752–1806), the late eighteenth-century Awadh traveller, opened to him the creativity of Europe as well as its more unpleasant features; Syed Ahmad Khan had a larger view of life than any of the purely religious leaders, and he was grateful to him for having given commonsense its rightful place in religious thought;[23] Ghalib, a poet of colonial modernity, gave man a new insight into his own nature and the nature of life. Mujeeb praised Ghalib's intellectual

[21] Ibid., p. 97.

[22] Mohammad Mujeeb, 'The Discovery of India', in *Islam and the Modern Age*, vol. 34, August–October 2003, p. 171.

[23] Mujeeb, *Islamic Influence on Indian Society*, p. 86.

adventure and courage in rejecting the 'conditions of existence which encroached upon freedom and dignity'.[24] Convinced that liberalism and faith in progress were requisites for producing great literature, he ridiculed orthodoxies.

Mujeeb admired Zakir Husain (1897–1969), a quintessential liberal, as no previous biographer had done. He commended his efforts to build the Jamia Millia Islamia, founded in Aligarh in October 1920, as 'an example of a determination rarely found among Muslims and of aspirations that many felt in their hearts without having the courage to strive for their fulfillment'.[25] When Zakir Husain accepted the Vice-Chancellorship of the Aligarh Muslim University even before Jamia Millia could adjust itself to conditions after Independence, he observed: 'The smaller sphere of activity provides opportunities for concentrated and persistent effort and can produce positive and definable results, while results in the larger sphere are often not enduring.'[26]

Mujeeb believed that it was high time for men of good sense and goodwill to intervene and to take politics out of the hands of self-seeking politicians of the Right and the woolly idealists of the Left. He therefore respected the gentlemanly ways of Dr Ansari and Ajmal Khan; he felt stimulated by Maulana Azad's exuberance for inter-religious unity; Gandhi's eloquent humanism harnessed his intellect to a moral purpose and thereby released tremendous energy.[27] Jamia Millia, a fruit of his endeavours, made the lives and activities of its teachers and students an embodiment of the ethical values of Islam.[28] But Mujeeb bemoaned that free India had set aside Gandhi's idea of reconstructing life on the basis of poverty and adopted instead a standard of affluence which had to be attained. In a line that has contemporary resonance, Mujeeb asked: 'How far we are in the right or whether we are in the right at all is something we are finding out now.'[29] The fact that mattered to him was that Gandhi managed to get his message across, a thought succinctly expressed by one of his favourite poets, Akbar Allahabadi, in the following three verses:

---

[24] Ibid., p. 160.
[25] See his *Dr. Zakir Husain, A Biography* (New Delhi, 1972), p. 74.
[26] Ibid., p. 78.
[27] See K.G. Saiyidain, in *Islam and the Modern Age*, vol. 36, August–November 2005.
[28] Mohammad Mujeeb, *Education and Traditional Values* (Meerut, 1965), p. 160.
[29] Mujeeb, *Islamic Influence on Indian Society*, p. 79.

In the age of Gandhi there is no need for foresight;
He who walks in a dust-storm shuts his eyes.

The torch of the East was running the risk of being extinguished by the
storm of the West,
We are assured of light because of Gandhi.

The Shaikh is welcome to think of Constantinople and Persia;
I would prefer to say: Victory to Gandhi.[30]

Mujeeb pinned his hopes on Nehru, the mainstay of the enlightened
Indian leadership, and desired fellow Muslims to identify themselves with
such persons who made democracy work in order to achieve social justice
and social welfare.[31] At the same time, they were obliged to obey a
government which allowed them full freedom. Loyalty, as something
higher than habitual obedience, was a virtue that all Indians, not the
Muslims alone, had to cultivate. They had to realize the moral stature
of the democratic state.[32]

LIVING WITH DIVERSITY

Har rang be bahaar ka asbat chahiye.

Each colour needs truthful expression of spring.
—Ghalib

Cultures and communities are not to be viewed as monolithic entities
and all cultural boundaries are porous enough to allow for a certain degree
of permissible interaction. While Islam presents the outward
characteristics of a well-organized system, one must not lose sight of, first
of all, the indeterminancy of social identity and, second, the importance
of the secular in the history of social life. Regional and local variations
in values and perceptions refute, once and for all, the essentialist view
of Islam in India.

Mujeeb found throughout India great differences of dogma, ritual,
and social practice partly because many Muslims carried with them into
their new faith Hindu principles and practices. He delineated the

[30] Muhammad Sadiq, A *History of Urdu Literature* (New Delhi, 1995), pp. 400–1.
[31] Mujeeb, *Education and Traditional Values*, pp. 147–51.
[32] Ibid., p. 71.

diversity of belief on the basis of samples from the *Imperial Gazetteer*, fixing
Delhi as the centre, and proceeding in different directions, one after
another. In another study he found the Meos continuing their practice
of exogamy after conversion, regarding cousin marriage as forbidden, even
though the sharia permits such marriages which had been the rule rather
than the exception among the generality of Muslims.[33]

The life of Muslims in 'all its aspects' is an intricate subject, specially
when one is dealing with Islam in India and the articulation of remarkable
social trends, political perspectives, and religious thought in the early
thirteenth century, a trend which eventually underpinned the nineteenth-
and twentieth-century religious and reformist tendencies. Mujeeb
unravelled these trends with skill. The core of *Indian Muslims* approaches
the changes in ideas, approaches, and practices from within and without.

Unlike Aziz Ahmad, I.H. Qureshi (b. 1986), and K.K. Aziz (b. 1896),
the foremost historians in Pakistan, Mujeeb did not regard 'Hindu' and
'Muslim' as self-explanatory terms, but suggested examining the structure
and character of the Hindu and Muslim communities in order to
comprehend not only beliefs and practices but also the dominant
attitudes and ideas.[34] He did not confuse the identity of the Muslims as
believers in Islam with their identity as a distinct body politic, as a nation,
which they never were and never wanted to be.[35] 'If I were an eighteenth
or early nineteenth century Muslim,' he stated, 'I could easily have
become that public nuisance called a reformer. I could have said, "Islam
is buried deep beneath Hindu influences, let us dig it out, clean it and
see what it really looks like!"'[36]

Mujeeb defines Muslims as *Indians* who call themselves Muslims, who
believe in the unity and fraternity of their brethren and who demonstrate
in practice that they act in accordance with this belief, however they
might differ in doctrine and observances.[37] He digs deep into history and
sociology to identify the various constituent elements of their religious,
political, and social life, and questions the fallacies arising out of the
identification of an entire community with some element of its belief or

[33] Mujeeb, *Islamic Influence on Indian Society*, p. 75; on the Meos, see Shail Mayaram,
Resisting Regimes: Myth, Memory and the Shaping of a Muslim Identity (Delhi, 1997).

[34] Mujeeb, *Islamic Influence on Indian Society*.

[35] Mohammad Mujeeb, *The Indian Muslims* (London, 1967), p. 23.

[36] Mujeeb, *Islamic Influence on Indian Society*, p. 11.

[37] Mujeeb, *Indian Muslims*, p. 23.

practice, with some political figures or military or political achievements, and with particular social forms and patterns of behaviour.[38] While uncovering diverse beliefs, social forms, ideas, and movements, he finds allegiance to Islam as the only common factor. The rest is nothing but a distinct body politic as opposed to a nation, which the Muslims never were and never wanted to be. Muslim society is a complex organism, containing within itself unhealthy tensions, and forces of growth, stability and decay.

Those who see Muslims in parts and fail to take into account the totality of their experience throughout the course of their history err in their judgement.[39] Generalizations about them are partial statements of the truth and are, consequently, misleading. As one who did not reduce history to a pattern of abstract concepts, Mujeeb views concrete facts in the light of their particular concrete circumstances. Peter Hardy, the British historian, agrees:

Excluded from the mosque and from eating with 'respectable' Muslims, Muslim sweepers in many parts of India would not have recognized themselves as members of a nation or indeed of a community devoted to the practice of social equality. In so far as village Muslims occasionally made offerings to local Hindu deities, they could not be said to be more monotheistic than their non-Muslim neighbours. In reality, the British began, in the eighteenth century, to rule over a Muslim community unified at best by a few common rituals and by the beliefs and aspirations of a majority—not the totality—of its scholars.[40]

The intellectual is 'an individual endowed with a faculty for representing, embodying, articulating a message, a view, an attitude, philosophy or opinion to, as well as for, a public'.[41] Mujeeb questions the ways in which educated Muslims see themselves. In the process, he finds them to be inspired by an idealization of themselves as the embodiment of religious truth. Time and again he finds their discourse resting on the colonial state privileging religious distinctions in society,[42] and, in the process, ignoring class, regional, and sectarian variations. Instead of self-

[38] Ibid., p. 554.
[39] Ibid., pp. 24, 554.
[40] Peter Hardy, The Muslims of British India (Cambridge, 1972), pp. 1–2.
[41] Edward W. Said, Representations of the Intellectual (New York, 1996), p. 11.
[42] On this point, see Ayesha Jalal, Self and Sovereignty: Individual and Community in South Asian Islam since 1850 (New Delhi, 2001).

introspection, for which there was sufficient justification, Ameer Ali (1849–1928) and Shibli Nomani, the two major authors of historical treatises, idealized individuals and dynasties, some of whom did not fulfil this- or other-worldly standards of good conduct (*Amal-e Salah*).

Rulers or pious men did not require testimonials, but Nomani, an otherwise wise man, did just that—strive to provide such testimonials. Such writers looked backward, always clutching at things which had already slipped away from them. Nehru wrote perceptively: 'It is not the beautiful that these people clutch at, but something that is seldom worth while and is often harmful.'[43] History thus came to acquire a new centrality in the concerns of the intelligentsia, for it became a principal 'way of talking about the collective self, and bringing it into existence'.[44]

Given their particularistic regional and local concerns, it was not easy for the ideologues to develop a pan-Indian perspective around social and economic affairs. Poets and novelists in Bengal, for example, were preoccupied with the purity of their racial pedigree to the exclusion of other subjects (most belonged to the *ashraf* or elite as opposed to the *ajlaf*, or local 'low-born'). Some even spurned Bengali, viewing it as a Hindu language. Mujeeb critiqued these trends:

The creative potentialities of belief were reduced even more by apologetics, whose appeal to sentiment increased with time. The modern Muslim's listlessness, his lethargy, his disregard for his own welfare, his betrayal of a great religious and cultural heritage was contrasted in eloquent terms with the faith, the energy, the splendour of earlier times. The Muslim was so carried away by the eloquence of the apologists that the achievements and the glories of the past came to life again, and the experience was so vivid and intense that the present was merged in the past, and the most spineless subject of the British Raj transformed himself in imagination into a conquering world force. Apologetics also generated a pride which made the Muslim look down on others, and if forced to face reality, he excused or even justified his own degradation by arguing that others were worse. Another aspect of apologetics derived from the resentment created by the judgements on Islam by Western orientalists. The beliefs and practices embodied in the *shariah* of Islam were not studied more deeply to refute unfavourable criticism, only everything Islamic came to be admired with greater fervour. The facts of history were forgotten, incidents not very significant in themselves

[43] Jawaharlal Nehru, *An Autobiography* (London, 1936), p. 471.
[44] Sudipta Kaviraj, *The Unhappy Consciousness: Bankimchandra Chattopadhyay and the Formation of Nationalist Discourse in India* (New Delhi, 1998), quoted in Sumit Sarkar, *Writing Social History* (New Delhi, 1997), p. 13.

were magnified into permanent characteristics. For instance, if Muhammad Tughlaq once appeared before a qazi to explain his conduct, or Jahangir had a bell put up in his palace which any person unjustly treated could come and ring, this was enough to characterize Muslim rulers as upright and just. I shall not multiply instances. Even a cursory examination will reveal that apologetics inculcated an approach to Islam and Muslim history that was completely unrealistic and distorted.[45]

Mujeeb underlined the historical weight of composite forces and their evolution only to conclude that there were far more convincing reasons for Hindus and Muslims to stay together than to stay apart. Even after the orgy of violence in Bihar in 1946–7, he saw Hindu women perform circumambulations and prostrations at the grave of a Sufi saint on the banks of the Ganga.[46] This was hardly a rare occurrence: in much of north and south India, Sufi centres stood as symbols of a shared past and visible signs of assimilation and pluralism.[47] This fact alone reinforced Mujeeb's trust in the wisdom of history. He echoed in large measure the sentiments of Urdu and Hindi writers and their portrayal of Hindu–Muslim amity in day-to-day living.

'The Holy Judges' and 'The Temple and the Mosque', two well-known stories by Munshi Premchand (1880–1936), depict the two communities sharing common cultural traits. A devout Muslim character like Miyan Chaudhary has a dip in the Ganga and is respectful of Hindu religious customs. Indeed, notwithstanding Premchand's complex responses to communalism and language chauvinism, he wrote 'Muktidham' (1924), 'Kshama' (1924), 'Mandir aur Masjid' (1925), and 'Himsa Paramo Dharm' (1926) at a time when Hindu–Muslim relations had reached their lowest ebb.

Like Premchand, Mujeeb saw future India as a land of plenty, where peace would prevail, and so the minorities would not be fearful of their status. On the occasion of Jamia's Golden Jubilee Celebration in October 1970, he declared: 'When it began to be said that Indians were not one nation but two, and the religious, cultural and ethical standards of these

[45] Mujeeb, *Islamic Influence on Indian Society*, p. 39.

[46] Muhammad Mujeeb, 'The Partition of India in Retrospect', in C.H. Philips and D.A. Wainright (eds), *The Partition of India: Policies and Perspectives* (London, 1970), p. 407.

[47] Jamal Malik and Helmut Reifeld (eds), *Religious Pluralism in South Asia and Europe* (New Delhi, 2005), p. 243.

two "nations" were basically different we continued to insist that true religion, true culture, true morality, created unity and not disunity.'[48]

'The intellectuals of the Jamia Millia Islamia are secularists and primarily concerned with establishment of cultural identity between Islam and Hinduism,' wrote Aziz Ahmad in *Islamic Modernism in India and Pakistan*. Mujeeb and Abid Husain exemplified these traditions. Sheila McDonough, the social historian, commented about the latter: 'There is a distinctive point of view in all his works, which, while undoubtedly individual, also emerges out of the long process of the experiences of common work, struggle, discussion, and unceasing mutual support which has characterized the group [in Jamia] with which he spent most of his life.'[49]

Abid Husain wrote a great deal in Urdu: *The Destiny of Indian Muslims* (1965), an English translation, was essentially a forecast of future possibilities. In *The National Culture of India* (1956), to which S. Radhakrishanan (1888–1975) the future President of the Republic wrote an eloquent foreword, he traced a common Hindu–Muslim culture to a Vedic base; through processes of challenge and response to Islam in medieval India, there developed a common Hindustani or Indian culture which disintegrated during the period of Mughal decline and was partly shattered and partly revived, fertilized, and enriched by the impact of Western civilization. He wrote that the new Indian nation which Akbar forged was based not on the community of religion but on the citizenship of the same state. He talked of the *Weltanschauung* of the modern educated classes of Hindus and Muslims. 'Looking at the concrete aspects of the cultural life of Hindus and Muslims,' he wrote, 'most of the common factors which had been partly the causes, partly the effect of the cultural synthesis which took place in the time of Akbar the Great, are still there, and new common ground has been created by the influences of the modern Western culture.'[50]

Abid Husain felt that educated Muslims should regard the coming age as the age of service and, leaving politics to those few persons who

[48] See Mushirul Hasan and Rakhshanda Jalil, *Partners in Freedom: Jamia Millia Islamia* (New Delhi, 2007).

[49] Sheila McDonough, 'The Spirit of Jamia Millia Islamia as Exemplified in the Writings of Syed Abid Husain', in Robert D. Baird (ed.), *Religion in Modern India* (New Delhi, 1981).

[50] S. Abid Husain, *The National Culture of India* (Bombay, 1961 revised edition), pp. 203, 206.

had the capacity for it, devote their attention, energies, and resources to religious and secular education and to other forms of social service. He observed: 'If they can hear the call of the present and profit by the experience of the past, they must begin the work of reconstructing their social life by strengthening the foundations which are certainly weak but, thank God, not rotten.' He was convinced that the future could be fathomed, for what prompt people to action, so he claimed, are their own particular interests. Thus striving for an increase in public welfare was not merely a prerequisite of progress; it was itself progress, a general and indispensable progress, because all that is Islamic is realized in this striving.

Ziya-ul-Hasan Faruqi (1925–96) and Mushirul Haq (d. 1990), also at Jamia, were influenced by Maulana Azad, always in their eyes the model of what a scholar should be, and Husain Ahmad Madani (1879–1957), both of whom recognized the significance of, and lent theological weight to, a political and social covenant with non-Muslims. In *The Deoband School and the Demand for Pakistan* (1963) by Faruqi and *Islam in Modern India, 1857–1947* (1970) by Mushirul Haq one finds implied approval of their thesis. Exposed to liberal and secularized discourses, they found, in the writings of Abid Husain and Mujeeb, a convergence of their own ideas that were otherwise close to 'traditional' rather than 'modern' thinking. It is therefore fair to stress their companionship that was due to circumstance, mutual regard, and cooperation in common tasks, in preparing a blueprint for Muslims in secular India.

In the political and social landscape, as we will see, the Jamia Millia Islamia obstinately tried to stitch together the sacred and the profane. But, as it discovered the hard way, the fabric was to come apart at the seams again and again. The next chapter examines why this was so.

5

Let a Thousand Flowers Bloom
Pre-history of Communalism?

Shub hui phir anjumam-e rakhshinda ka manzar khula,
Is takalluff se ke goya butkade ka dar khula.

The scene of the sparkling stars opened with the coming of the night
With such ceremony as if the door of the idol-house is opening.

—Ghalib

Historical scholarship in the 1970s and 1980s helped free, at least to some extent, the mind from sweeping generalizations and from tendentious exaggerations. The historian and the anthropologist placed cultural practices in their historical as well as socio-economic contexts, thereby establishing that culture and its manifestation are not immutable.[1] The foregoing chapters have described the manner in which diversity of cultures and voices has been assimilated and synthesized. They have argued, moreover, that being a Muslim is just one of several competing identities for an individual, and that there has never been a homogeneous 'Muslim India', whether in doctrine, custom, language, or political loyalty.

This chapter has a twofold objective. First, it traces the multiple influences on Muslims in places where they have adopted many social and cultural practices of pre-Islamic origin, and indicates the intersecting identities,

---

[1] Ravina Aggarwal, *Beyond Lines of Control: Performance and Politics on the Disputed Borders of Ladakh* (London, 2004).

such as caste, class, or religion, pulling group members in different directions. Second, it turns to social and cultural practices and their meanings and interpretations across different regions but also within each.[2] How did prominent Muslim intellectuals situate themselves in colonial India? How did they construct Islam? How did they understand themselves as Muslims and as Indians living in British India? What paths did they embark upon to negotiate with the government? How did they relate to the other religious and cultural traditions? In this chapter I endeavour to build a case for revisiting some of the forgotten themes and the existing interpretations.

'Kashmir', wrote Jahangir (r. 1605–27), 'is a garden of eternal spring, or an iron fort to a palace of kings—a delightful flowerbed, and a heart-expanding, heritage for dervishes.' By far the most important observation of the Mughal emperor was on the long tradition of religious tolerance and pluralism in Kashmir, starting with Syed Ali Hamdani (1313–80) and Sheikh Nuruddin (1376–1438) in the fourteenth century. In one tale, it is said that when a baby, Nuruddin, refused to take his mother's milk and would drink only from Lalla Deb (1320–89), the Kashmiri mystic. His tomb at Charan attracts thousands of people, both Hindu and Muslim, every year.

A century later, Sultan Zainul-Abidin (1420–70) exemplified a more civilized adherence to harmonious communal relations. According to Kalhana's *Rajatarangini*, he participated in Hindu religious festivals, visited Hindu shrines, and had the Sanskrit texts read to him. He banned cow slaughter and permitted those Brahmins who had become Muslim under duress to return to their former religion. English observers of the late nineteenth and early twentieth centuries in Kashmir found shared popular religious traditions especially in the countryside. Thus W. Lawrence referred to the 'delightful tolerance' between the followers of Islam and Hinduism.

Such fragments from Kashmir's history underline the hierarchical relationship between the scriptural and Rishi traditions; the latter may seem opposed to the former but is in fact encompassed by it.[3] Mohammad

---

[2] Mushirul Hasan, *From Pluralism to Separatism: Qasbas in Colonial Awadh* (New Delhi, 2004); *A Moral Reckoning: Muslim Intellectuals in Nineteenth-century Delhi* (New Delhi, 2005).

[3] T.N. Madan, in *Biblio*, July–August 2005, p. 23. For Zainul-Abidin, see Mohibbul Hasan, *Kashmir under the Sultans* (New Delhi, 2006 reprint).

Ishaq Khan believes that syncretism and the segmentation of Islamic beliefs and local practices was actually the beginning of a movement for realizing the ultimate, if not immediate, objectives of Islam at both the individual and social levels. He talks of Islamization as a process of Islamic acculturation in which individuals and groups gradually break their ties with traditional culture or religion and eventually follow a path that ends with their adherence to the *sharia*-bound structure of Islam. Syncretism or synthesis was not, according to him, the culmination of the Islamization process.[4]

Two recent books on Kashmir contest essentialist arguments on religion. Chitralekha Zutshi, the author of one of them, challenges a Kashmiri culture, history, and identity in terms of the concept of *Kashmiriyat*, a memory of the past 'refracted through rose-tinted glasses, in which Kashmir appears as a unique region where religious communities lived in harmony since time immemorial'.[5] It is not as if people did not cross one another's paths; they most certainly did. At the same time, the medieval and the post-medieval sources point to heterodoxy or a syncretism that essentially evolved as a mixture of Islam and the local Kashmiri identity.[6]

In the 1940s, Punjab was still in many ways a sleepy hollow where life moved at the slow pace of the feeble cab-horses drawing their two-wheel tongas; where young men could indulge in old carefree idle ways, with long hours of debate in coffee houses and moonlight picnics by the river Ravi.[7] Here, in this province of British India, Islam provided a repertoire of concepts and styles of authority that served to encompass potentially competing values, including the values of tribal kinship, within a common Islamic idiom. Sufism and the Bhakti stream intermingled and fermented among common people, helping to create a body of folk-poetry where the religious brotherhood of man blended with thoughts of social equality and deliverance from feudal bonds. As Victor Kiernan explained

---

[4] M. Ishaq Khan, *Kashmir's Transition to Islam: The Role of Muslim Rishis* (New Delhi, 1994). pp. 221–2.

[5] Chitralekha Zutshi, *Languages of Belonging: Islam, Regional Identity and the Making of Kashmir* (New Delhi, 2003), p. 2; Mridu Rai, *Hindu Rulers, Muslim Subjects: Islam, Rights, and the History of Kashmir* (New Delhi, 2004).

[6] Hasan, *Kashmir under the Sultans.*

[7] Faiz Ahmed Faiz, *Poems by Faiz.* Translated, with an Introduction and Notes by V.G. Kiernan (New Delhi, 1971), p. 21.

while locating Faiz in the context of Lahore and describing the affinity between Sufism and Bhakti:

Much of the mood and phraseology of Sufism, its catalogue of the 'states and stages' (hâl-o-maqâm) of the pilgrim soul, its vital relationship between the spiritual guide and his disciples, was taken over into poetry, and had a further existence there as part of the counterpoint of mask and symbol. When a poet did not picture himself seated in a court circle, it would often be the circle of disciples round their master that he conjured up. Nor were the two so far apart as might seem; mystics had often clothed their thoughts in verse, courtiers and even rulers might also be disciples; a divine Beloved could melt imperceptibly into an earthly one, an ideal feminine, an unattainable mistress who was also the wine-pourer at the never-ending feast, as uncertain, coy, and hard to please as Fortune, dispenser of life's never-ending deceptions.[8]

Prakash Tandon describes day-to-day living in a *mohallu* or locality in Gujrat, Punjab:

Our mohalla was mixed, and in both its squares there were Hindu and Muslim homes. Except for the burqa, with which the Muslim women veiled themselves when they went outside the mohalla, there was very little difference in the dress. The Hindu ghagra, the voluminous ankle-length skirt, had practically gone out by my time and only a few old women wore it. The women always wore salwar kameez. There was no social stratification in our mohallas, and amongst our neighbours there was a Muslim lawyer, a Hindu confectioner, a Muslim clerk in the municipality, and a Brahmin family. Boys and girls played together, and in the afternoon the women would take out their low stools and embroidery and sit on their tharas, talking and gossiping.[9]

Most Hindus and Sikhs accepted partition 'fatalistically'. They said to each other: 'We have lived under the Muslims before, then under the Sikhs and the British, and if we are now back under Muslim rule, so what? We shall manage somehow, as we have managed before. Nowadays governments are different, they give you some rights, they have to listen to the people!' Fortified by such arguments, people decided to stay where they were and face the change.

Munshi Lutfullah Khan (b. 1802) of Malwa—at the crossroads between northern India and the Deccan and between the western

---

[8] Ibid., p. 35

[9] Prakash Tandon, *Punjabi Saga 1857–2000: The Monumental Story of Five Generations of a Remarkable Punjabi Family* (New Delhi, 2003 Paperback edition), p. 90.

provinces and the seaports of Gujarat—provides instances of cross-community networks and composite practices extending to the central Indian tracts.[10] He mentions Hindus paying their respects at the shrine of Khwaja Muinuddin Chishti (1142–1236) at Ajmer, Mahadji Sindhia (1730–94) and Yashwant Rao Holkar, ruler of the Maratha dynasty of Indore from 1797 to 1811, annually sending an offering of money, and Daulat Rao Sindhia (1780–1827) repairing the edifices around. Elsewhere, he portrays a lived Islam in harmony with other religious and philosophical traditions. Hence, while explaining how devotees attribute the fulfilment of their hearts' desires to the miraculous powers of the Sufi, Lutfullah remarked pointedly, 'In such respects mankind are like a herd of sheep, one blindly follows another.' Without being 'secular' in the European sense, Lutfullah rose above doctrinaire Islam and respected composite practices at a time when religious tolerance was rarely acclaimed as a virtue. He talked of mutual respect between the followers of different faiths.

Rajaram, a priest, saved Lutfullah from being drowned in a pool. He performed this noble act because Mahadeva, his god, commanded him to do so. In return, Rajaram made Lutfullah prostrate before the deity. Islam does not sanction idol worship; yet Lutfullah not only bowed before the deity but touched the ground with his head. To those friends who maligned him as an 'infidel', he recited the following lines from Byron:

> Some kinder casuists are pleased to say,
> In nameless print, that I have no devotion;
> But set those persons down with me to pray,
> And you shall see who has the properest notion
> Of getting into heaven the shortest way,
> My altars are the mountains and the ocean,
> Earth, air, stars—all that springs from the great Whole
> Who hath produced and will receive the soul.

The incident with the priest raised serious doubts in Lutfullah's mind: 'I thought of Polytheism prevailing everywhere, and I argued with myself—if the Hindu shrines are stones, ours contain but dust and bones.

---

[10] References are drawn from Lutfullah, *Seamless Boundaries: Lutfullah's Narrative beyond East and West*. Edited, annotated, and with an Introduction by Mushirul Hasan (New Delhi, 2007). The autobiography was published in 1857.

To believe in one or the other, or believe or disbelieve in both, is a most puzzling question.' Likewise, doubts about Christianity assailed his mind. Until he was thirty years of age, he 'could not shake off such confused notions entirely'.

He described Hinduism as 'in its origin ... pure and sublime'. As one who regarded the Vedas as 'a sublime source of the genuine principles of Hinduism' that did not sanction *sati* and female infanticide, he concluded that the priests had led to 'immorality and corruption'. He admired temples, especially the ones in Dilwara that he saw in early 1832, and respected the austere Hindu and Jain devotees. He witnessed a great annual fair at the branch of a river and saw the 'beauties of the Hindu caste unveiled .... Some of them [were] no less graceful and charming than the nymphs of England'. The sati of a widow left him sad and dejected. 'Religions, pure in their origin, in course of time beget superstitions, which give birth to such results as we have just described,' he wrote philosophically. It is not very often that writers in early or mid-nineteenth century appraised Hinduism and its symbols with such understanding.

Lutfullah rejected certain Muslim practices. For example, he could not understand why Muslims practised circumcision, an 'antique Jewish ceremony', not sanctioned by the Quran. Besides he found that many Muslims neglected prayers (*namaz*) five times a day, fasting (*ramzan*), *zakat*, and pilgrimage.

In Bengal, Islam took many forms and assimilated values and symbols that did not necessarily conform to the Quranic precepts. This is clear from Rafiuddin Ahmed's work that looked at the new adjustments to life made by Bengali Muslims.[11] He focused, however, more on Islamization and its impact on the ground.[12] Although the big picture on Haji Shariat Allah and the 'Wahhabi' Movement is reasonably well known,[13] Ahmed brought to light the role of itinerant religious preachers

---

[11] David Gilmartin, 'Customary Law and Shariat in Punjab', in Katherine P. Ewing (ed.), *Shariat and Ambiguity in South Asian Islam* (New Delhi, 1988), p. 44; Rafiuddin Ahmed, 'Conflicts and Contradictions in Bengali Islam: Problems of Change and Adjustment', in Ewing, *Shariat and Ambiguity*, p. 115.

[12] Rafiuddin Ahmed, *The Bengali Muslims 1871–1906: A Quest for Identity* (New Delhi, 1981).

[13] Qeyamuddin Ahmad, *The Wahhabi Movement in India* (New Delhi, 1994; first edition, 1966).

and *mullah*s in sensitizing the rural Muslims to their Islamic rather than their local or national identity. He furnished invaluable information on *baha*s meetings and rural *anjumans*.

However, Ahmed, one suspects, read a little more than he should have in the religious tracts, mistaking religious rhetoric for expressions of genuine belief. Bengal's countryside until the 1920s was not getting more polarized or ready for an Islamist takeover. The Faraizis had not challenged the British as such, and their revolutionary views did not extend beyond disputing the *zamindars'* illegal claims for excess collections.[14] The *mujahidin*, mostly followers of Syed Ahmad Barelwi (1786–1831), produced familiar noises, but officials exaggerated their reach largely because they had little or no experience of dealing with a campaign imbued with religious fervour. Although W.W. Hunter's *The Indian Mussalmans* in 1871 created panic in the corridors of power, the Lieutenant Governor of the North-Western Provinces denounced exaggerated and misguided reports calculated to do mischief and create panic and alienation on both sides.[15] The fact is that just a tiny minority of the Muslim population at any time actively joined Barelwi or preached in favour of the purification of belief and custom.[16] By the closing years of the eighteenth century, educated Muslims were moving more and more towards integration with the imperial system and building bridges with their rulers.

Two examples would suffice: one from Awadh and the other from central India. Take the case of Mirza Abu Taleb Khan, one of the first among his community to journey to the West. Two points are noteworthy: first, Abu Taleb scarcely employed religious categories to unravel either Awadhi society or delineate the contours of Western polities, economies, and societies. In fact, he sharply criticized the Wahhabi movement that arose in response to the religious call (*dawa*) of Muhammad ibn-Wahhab (1703–92).[17] Moreover, he identified material factors in moulding attitudes and shaping the destiny of humankind. While comparing the

---

[14] Muin-ud-Din Ahmad Khan, *History of the Faraidi Movement in Bengal, 1818–1906* (Karachi, 1965), pp. 114–25.

[15] Quoted in S.A.A. Rizvi, 'The Breakdown of Traditional Society', in *The Cambridge History of Islam* (Cambridge, 1970), vol. 2, p. 81.

[16] Peter Hardy, *The Muslims of British India* (Cambridge, 1972), p. 59.

[17] On the Wahhabis, see Jacques Waardenburg, *Islam: Historical, Social and Political Perspectives* (Berlin, 2002), ch. 2.

ancien regime in France with Awadh, he foregrounded not only the growing disparities between various classes but also attributed the collapse of several worldwide empires to the exacerbation of class differentiation. In evaluating British society, however, he overstated the point by asserting that the difference between the comforts of the rich and the dismal conditions of the poor in England was much greater than in India.

Abu Taleb belonged to a declining aristocracy. So, like so many persons of his background, he made the best of the opportunities offered by the East India Company. He did not hesitate to work out a modus vivendi with the *firangis*. Nor did he face the dilemmas that were to afflict the post-1857 generations. On the contrary, he found the European political and cultural institutions to be consistent with Islamic laws. He acknowledged the imminence of change and adhered to his resolve, despite fears of being villified, of sharing his impressions of Europe with his countrymen. A scholar writes, not for himself, but for his readers. Abu Taleb hoped that his readers would take advantage of, and draw positive lessons from, many of 'the customs, inventions, sciences, and ordinances of Europe, the good effects of which are apparent in their countries, might with great advantage be imitated by Mohammedans'.

There is hidden tension in Abu Talib's thinking, but, on balance, he believed, as did eighteenth-century bourgeois liberals in Europe, that human society and individual man could be perfected by the application of reason and were destined to be so perfected by history.[18] In this respect, as also in other ways, he turned out to be a forerunner of the ideas of Syed Ahmad Khan, the major catalyst of social and educational reforms among Muslims in the last quarter of the nineteenth century. Although his legacy has endured, he did not find, in the way Syed Ahmad Khan did, a channel for promoting his ideas.

Munshi Lutfullah Khan, born on 4 November 1802, exactly half a century after Abu Taleb, was no different in his ideological orientation. His career offers a corrective to a generalized representation of an entire community being arrayed against the British. The fact is that his professional life, starting as a Persian teacher, was intertwined with British military men, including W.J. Eastwick, Assistant Resident in Sind and a person of immense personal charm. His contacts extended to

[18] E.J. Hobsbawm, *The Age of Revolution, 1789–1848* (Delhi, 1992), p. 286.

Mountstuart Elphinstone (1779–1859), the Governor of Bombay (1819–27) and the author of many books, including his *History of India* (1841), for which he was called the Tacitus of modern historians. The other important fact is that Lutfullah appreciated British rule and compared its blessings with the poor record of governance in the so-called independent states that had mushroomed in the twilight of the Mughals rule. Even before anyone at Daranagar, in Malwa, had set eyes on a Company representative, he had heard that the British did not deviate from the sacred book of the ancient law of Solomon, the son of David, in administering justice. This image, even if it was not true, not only stayed with Lutfullah but was suitably reinforced in England.

The British Enlightenment had a lasting impact on Lutfullah's mind and through him on other writers. He talks of justice, good government, and good laws. There is even a hint in his writings of changing laws according to circumstances. He persuaded the Biluchi Kamal Khan, chief of the Kahiri clan, to enter British service on the condition of non-interference with his religion. The chief had been told that the English would first take the country and then forcibly convert the people to Christianity:

I assured him that he need have no fear about that, and should not listen to the stories and fables fabricated by designing persons. I asked him if he had heard of any compulsory measures, towards persons of any religion, ever adopted by the English in India, where they had ruled now for the last one hundred years? In proof of their forbearance, I asked him to see the regiments of the army with his own eyes, in which he would find people of all castes following their own religions without any interference on the part of the Government; and lastly, I asked him what opinion he had of myself, who had been with the English more than twenty-two years. Hearing this, he put his index-fingers upon both his eyes, in token of his believing me with his heart and soul.[19]

Lutfullah unwittingly initiated the process of an Anglo-Muslim rapprochement and an inter-faith dialogue. All this was, of course, before the spread of communal ideologies. With the introduction of modern politics and the need to assert sectarian or communitarian identities, a great deal changed. For one, the slogans 'Muslim *ekta*' (solidarity) and 'one nation, one people, one culture' gained currency. The silver lining was that they struck a chord in a particular context but not uniformly.

[19] Lutfullah, *Seamless Boundaries*, p. xxxi.

An average Muslim preferred to fashion his life on the basis of local ties, traditions, and relationships. Richard Eaton's erudite study concludes with the remark: 'What made Islam in Bengal not only historically successful but a continuing vital social reality has been its capacity to adapt to the land and the culture of its people, even while transforming both.'[20] Religious syncretism, therefore, posed the greatest threat to pietism and stringent fulfilment of the Quranic injunctions in the veneration of numerous Sufi *sheikhs*, *syeds*, and *pirs*.[21]

In Arampur, a village in Bihar, the local narratives incorporated both Hindu and Muslim histories.[22] At Zeradei in Saran district, the story was no different. In this village lived Rajendra Prasad (1884–1963), first President of the Republic. He began schooling under a *maulvi*, who initiated him into the alphabet and taught him Persian. Of course, religion permeated village life but it did so without disturbing Hindu–Muslim harmony. Muslims participated in the boisterous festival of Holi. Often children would draw beautiful paintings on sheets of paper and the maulvi would inscribe on them his verses, an interesting hotchpotch of Persian and Hindustani. Likewise, Hindus participated in Muharram. The *tazias* of the well-to-do Hindus in Zeradei and Jamapur were bigger and brighter than those of the poor Muslims. They were eventually taken to Karbala. Prasad recalled the atmosphere being surcharged with enthusiasm.[23]

A long tradition of inter-community interaction and a great diversity of Sufi and other expressions of Islam existed in the Deccan. More generally, the Asaf Jah dynasty, heir to a unique regional culture, nurtured a distinctively Deccani approach to Islam and even at times transcended religious denominations altogether.[24] Jackie Assayag traces such a blend of narratives that fashions a group identity in south India, carefully scrutinizing Hindu–Muslim ties in the village and urban milieu

[20] Richard M. Eaton, *The Rise of Islam and the Bengal Frontier, 1204–1760* (Delhi, 1997), p. 31.

[21] Anna Suvorova, *Muslim Saints of South Asia: The Eleventh to the Fifteenth Centuries* (London, 2006), p. 5; Arthur Buehler, *Sufi Heirs of the Prophet: The Indian Naqshbandiyya and the Rise of the Mediating Sufi Shaykh* (Columbia, 1998).

[22] Peter Gottschalk, *Beyond Hindu and Muslim: Multiple Identity in Narratives from Village India* (New Delhi, 2000).

[23] Rajendra Prasad, *Autobiography* (Bombay, 1957).

[24] Nile Green, *Indian Sufism since the Seventeenth Century: Saints, Books, and Empires in the Muslim Deccan* (London, 2006), p. 108.

through saints, *fakirs*, hybrid cults, and even within the individual, community, everyday life and festivals. He also looks at communal conflict and demonstrates how new boundaries, even if secular, highlight a communitarian exclusivism which extends to the core of collective memories.[25] Thus the modes of thought and action of thousands of people in a part of South Asia suggest that Hindus and Muslims have been living together and not in separate compartments.[26] This, too, exposes the myth of the 'pre-history' of communalism.

In Gujarat's Imamshahi tradition, centred on Pirana in Ahmedabad, a sect called Satpanth (true path) admitted among its members Hindus as well as Muslims. Associated with Vishnu and his ten main incarnations was the figure of the Imam, so essential to the Shias, in particular in Ismaili philosophy.[27] Indeed, syncretism worked in Muharram rituals at multiple levels and was manifested differently. Malcolm Darling says about his experiences in Dewas (central India, now Madhya Pradesh) in the early twentieth century:

During my first month in Dewas there occurred two annual celebrations, one of importance to the Shia branch of Islam, the other to the Hindus. Muharram, as the former was called, came first. Its object was to mourn the martyrdom of Ali, the son-in-law of the Prophet, and his two sons, Hasan and Husain. The celebrations lasted several days, and they brought us one evening to Dewas' main bazaar. With its tiled houses, shadowing eaves and purely Indian atmosphere, Dewas by day was always a pleasant sight. But at night, and as now under a half moon, with scattered lamps throwing an uncertain light upon the houses and upon the turbaned heads passing to and fro, its charm was irresistible. We had come to see the customary procession. The sound of drums and the flare of torches announced its approach. At its head came one of the State's two 'serviceable' guns drawn by a pair of phlegmatic bullocks. The State infantry followed with glittering sabres and behind them came H.H. in brilliant yellow silk with the dashing Maratha puggaree on his head.[28]

Rafiuddin Ahmed appreciates, despite building a case for the existence of powerful Islamizing trends, that the objective Hindu–Muslim

[25] Jackie Assayag, *At the Confluence of Two Rivers: Muslims and Hindus in South India* (New Delhi, 2004).

[26] Ibid., pp. 250–1.

[27] Dominique-Sila Khan and Zawahir Moir, 'Co-existence and Communalism: The Shrine of Piranas in Gujarat', in Asim Roy (ed.), *Islam in History and Politics: Perspectives from South Asia* (New Delhi, 2006).

[28] Malcolm Darling, *Apprentice to Power: India 1904–8* (London, 1936), p. 146.

differences at mass level were themselves not strong enough to induce mutual conflict, and that it was only through skilful manipulation of certain religious symbols that the latent differences could be articulated and later used as a potent weapon in the conflict between elite groups.[29] We have irrefutable evidence on the common ties binding the Hindu and Muslim lower classes in north India. Works on Allahabad, Banaras, and Lucknow emphasize the importance of religious practice and belief on city life in particular.[30]

Situated on the banks of the holy Ganga, Banaras is the locus of both classical and modern, high and low, Hinduism as well as popular Islam. It is 'a city where communities remain different but live together, where there is not one but many different certainties'.[31] The intermixing of local culture and practices has given Banaras its vibrancy and compositeness. Apart from economic interdependence, Muslim weavers actively participate in public ceremonies that express a shared culture, including the day-to-day observances related to particular idols and shrines.[32] Another inspiring legitimation of the more mundane expressions of peaceful coexistence comes daily when Muslim *shehnai* players join in the *aarti* at Hindu temples, including that at the Vishwanath temple.[33]

In general, the hallmark of urban life has been the sharing of a similar lifestyle, the ideology of work, tenure, and public activity. Divisions among people, in order of importance, seem to be: men/women; lower class/upper class; educated/uneducated; and then on the basis of religion, mohalla, caste, language, community, and personal compatibility. Division at any of these levels did not necessarily mean antagonism but structural similarity, as with divisions along the lines of gender, religion, and mohalla.[34]

[29] Ahmed, *The Bengali Muslims*, p. 183.

[30] C.A. Bayly, *The Local Roots of Indian Politics: Allahabad 1880–1920* (Oxford, 1975); and also his *Rulers, Townsmen and Bazaars: North Indian Society in the Age of British Expansion 1770–1870* (New Delhi, 2002); Rosie Llewellyn-Jones, *A Fatal Friendship: The Nawabs, the British and the City of Lucknow* (New Delhi, 1992).

[31] Mark Tully, *India's Unending Journey: Finding Balance in a Time of Change* (London, 2007), p. 248.

[32] Sandria Frietag (ed.), *Culture and Power in Banaras: Community, Performance, and Environment, 1800–1980* (New Delhi, 1989), pp. 13–14, 168–9.

[33] Judith F. Pugh, 'Divination and Ideology in the Banaras Hindu Community', in Ewing, *Shariat and Ambiguity*, p. 289.

[34] Nita Kumar, *The Artisans of Banaras: Popular Culture and Identity, 1880–1986* (Delhi, 1995), p. 225, and her 'Work and Leisure in the Formation of Identity: Muslim

In Gujarat, now troubled by the legacy of the 1969 and 2002 violence, historical records provided no evidence of sustained Hindu–Muslim animus. From 1714 until 1969 Hindu–Muslim riots were recorded in Ahmedabad in 1941 and 1946. According to the Justice Reddy Commission of Inquiry into the Ahmedabad Communal Disturbances of 1969,

The people of Gujarat in general and those of Ahmedabad, in particular, were not prone to communal passions or excitement—both the Hindu and the Muslim community lived by and large in amity except in a few places here and there which had their own special reasons for communal disturbances.[35]

'Here and there in every *mohallah*,' wrote the novelist Ahmed Ali (1910–94), 'the mosques raise their white heads towards the sky, their domes spread out like the white breasts of a woman bared, as it were, to catch the starlight on their surfaces, and the minarets point to heaven, indicating, as it seems, that God is all-high and one.'[36] Even though mosques and *madaris* dotted Delhi's landscape, the capital of the patrimonial-bureaucratic Mughal empire offered spaces to diverse and multiple cultures and religions to prosper. Tension did occur, but not always along distinct religious lines. Mohamed Ali, editor of *Comrade*, wrote in 1912: 'Moslem Delhi is beyond the skill of the restorer .... The Hindus of Delhi can hardly be distinguished from their Moslem brethren.'[37] The Phoolwalon ki Sair and the Pankha festival attest to the assimilative character of Islam and Hinduism and to the Muslims living as a principal religious minority and in shared responsibility with people of other faiths and ideologies. C.F. Andrews sketches an idyllic picture:

One further fact deserves mentioning which is full of importance today. In Delhi city itself, the two communities, the Hindu and Musalman, had come to live peaceably side-by-side under the wise guidance of the Moghul emperors, who had learnt to

---

Weavers in a Hindu City', in Frietag, *Culture and Power*, p. 169.

[35] Ornit Shani, *Communalism, Caste and Hindu Nationalism: The Violence in Gujarat* (Cambridge, 2007), p. 91.

[36] Ahmed Ali, *Twilight in Delhi* (London, 1940), pp. 1–2.

[37] Stephen P. Blake, *Shahjahanabad: The Sovereign City in Mughal India 1639–1739* (New Delhi, 1993), p. 232; Sunil Kumar, *The Present in Delhi's Past* (New Delhi, 2002); Eckart Ehlers and Thomas Krafft (eds), *Shahjahanabad/Old Delhi: Tradition and Colonial Change* (New Delhi, 2003, 2nd edition).

trust the Hindus, and were trusted by them in return. Those of my informants who were Hindus among the old inhabitants of Delhi, told me without any reserve when I approached them for information, that their community was well treated under the last Moghuls and had no cause to complain. This general contentment of these later times had been a growth of centuries; and the Moghul emperors, in spite of much that can be said against them on other grounds, deserve credit for the manner in which they had overcome within themselves religious bigotry and prejudice, and on that account were able to treat their Hindu subjects with kindly consideration and a measure of impartial justice. They were also able to impress the same regard for the feelings of the Hindus upon the Musalman nobles of the royal court. Even if at times there were outbreaks of mob violence among the ignorant and illiterate masses over some insult to religion, these quarrels never reached beyond that substratum of society, and the animosity created was easily allayed. The Moghuls knew how to make peace.[38]

Again, Andrews wrote:

The intimate residence together side by side in the same city of Musalmans and Hindus had brought about a noticeable amalgamation of customs and usages among the common people. In Delhi—unlike further north in the central Punjab and on the Frontier—the Hindus had never been unequally matched in numbers with the Musalmans. The Hindu influence had told especially in commerce. The Musalmans had taken up the administration. Official posts were filled chiefly by them, with the exception of the revenue department. I have had more convincing and corroborative evidence about this especially friendly relationship between Hindus and Musalmans in Old Delhi than I have had concerning any other factor. The information has come to me from both sides, and has been practically the same. It was evidently a feature of the city of which the inhabitants themselves were proud. These older residents whom I approached, whether Hindu or Musalman, spoke of this fact with enthusiasm, and contrasted it with the bitterness of modern times. It was quite common, for instance, in those days, for the two communities to join together in different religious festivals. Hindus would go to a Muslim festival, and Musalmans would go to a Hindu festival. This had become a natural local custom, and none but the zealots and puritans on either side raised any objection to such friendly proceedings.[39]

Until the 1857 revolt, the Delhi College stood as the symbol of the Delhi Renaissance, a site of intellectual ferment that embraced Hindu,

[38] C.F. Andrews, *Zakaullah of Delhi*. With Introductions by Mushirul Hasan and Margrit Pernau (New Delhi, 2003), p. 27.
[39] Ibid., p. 129.

Muslim, and British teachers and administrators. The Archaeological Society, dedicated to preserving the city's great past, had a composite membership.[40] All this stimulates reflection on and reappraisal of theories on the 'pre-history' of communalism.

Bahadur Shah Zafar (1775–1862), the last Mughal Emperor bemoaned:

> Delhi was once a paradise,
> And great were the joys that used to be here;
> But they have ravished ths bride of peace,
> And now remains only ruins and care.

The post-1857 Delhi was not as bad as Bahadur Shah felt it to be; we have Ahmed Ali's testimony that 'the city stands still intact, as do many forts and tombs and monuments, remnants and reminders of old Delhi, holding on to life with a tenacity and purpose which is beyond comprehension and belief'.[41]

Turning to literary and historical figures living through Delhi's upheaval in 1857, we find them responding to the conditions of modern life with a strong and universalistic component in their thinking. They found wisdom in numerous religious traditions and, without advocating their cultural merging or the dissolution of boundaries, they were content to let a hundred flowers bloom. Even though Islam was a necessary cultural and spiritual ingredient of their personality, they viewed religion as a matter of personal choice and disposition. Again, while adhering to the personality paradigm of the Prophet, they also drew upon non-Muslim sacred figures in order to develop a conception of coexistence between religious institutions and the men of faith in different religions.

Consequently, one of the key themes in my historical explorations is the continuous relationship of the Indian civilization with other religions, cultures and civilizations, and the contact of Muslims with many religions, including Zoroastrianism and Manicheism, Hinduism and Buddhism, Sikhism, not to speak of Christianity and Judaism, inside and outside West Asia. Sure enough they discovered the congruence of the

---

[40] Ibid., p. 180; Narayani Gupta, *Delhi between Two Empires, 1803–1931: Society, Government and Urban Growth* (New Delhi, 1981), p. 6; and the essays in R. E. Frykenberg (ed.), *Delhi through the Ages: Essays in Urban History* (New Delhi, 1986).

[41] Ali, *Twilight in Delhi*, p. 8.

basic tenets of all religions. Mujeeb asserted that if the Muslim and the Sikh walk steadfastly on what is their true path they will discover their paths and the goal to be the same. That discovery will itself be a spiritual experience, 'an occurrence of the heart', a fulfilment of what God, in a story related to Maulana Jalaluddin Rumi (1207–73), the Balkh-born Persian poet, said to Moses, the Hebrew prophet: 'You have been sent to unite, not to divide.'[42]

Even though British travellers viewed Islam in a binary and essentialist manner and the likes of William Muir (1819–1905) felt sufficiently uneasy about Islam to denigrate it and indulge in a character assassination of Prophet Mohammad, Mir Taqi Mir had this to say in a couplet: 'It is the power of His beauty fills the world with light/Be it the Kaaba's candle or the light that that lights Somnath.' Let me use Ghalib, his successor in terms of greatness, to make a point about religious tolerance. The ideological element in his poetry and letters is not, of course, a new discovery, but a shift in perspective can sometimes help in uncovering new elements in the past.

According to Hali, 'It is clear that not only in poetry, but also in his manners, dress and address, food habits, life style and even in the art of living and dying, Ghalib disliked to follow the popular, conventional ways.' Ill at ease with religious dogmas and discarding outward religious observances, he announced virtually from the rooftops: 'Faith stops me, if impiety pulls me towards itself/Kaaba is behind me, the church is in front of me.' Ghalib makes his meaning clearer in another verse:

> What is the temple, what is the Kaaba?
> Baffled passion for union constructing
> Myths and illusions, asylums to shelter
> Its ardour, its hopes, its dreams and despair.

The true faith can be attained only if we go beyond religion.

> God is One, that is our faith,
> All rituals we abjure,
> 'Tis only when religions vanish
> That belief is pure.[43]

---

[42] Mohammad Mujeeb, 'Guru Nanak through Muslim Eyes', in *Islam and the Modern Age* (Delhi), August–October 2003, p. 168.

[43] Mohammed Mujeeb, *Ghalib* (Delhi, 1969), pp. 6–7.

He could thus demand from God treatment consistent with his self-respect and question why the angels' written testimony and not the witnesses' defence will be accepted on the Day of Judgement.[44] He could also question the very notion of Paradise that constitutes a vital part of the Muslim faith. One gets a glimpse of his irrepressible sense of humour in the following miscalleneous verses:

> *Hum ko maaloom hai jannat ki haqiqat lekin,*
> *Dil ko khush rakhne ko Ghalib ye khayal achchha hai.*

> I know the truth, but, be that what it will,
> The thought of Paradise beguiles me still.

> *Sunte hain jo behisht ki taarif sab durust*
> *Lekin, khuda kare wo tera jalwa-gaah ho*

> All that they say of paradise is true, and yet
> God grant it be illumined by your radiance.

And, on a lively note:

> *Wo cheez, jis ke liye hum ko ho behisht aziz*
> *Sewaye baada-i gulfaam-i mushkboo kya hai?*

> For what else should I value Paradise
> If not the rose-red wine, fragrant with musk?

Ghalib wore no sectarian badge, no sectarian colour. 'I hold mankind to be my kin,' he told Hargopal Tufta, a devotee of Persian poetry, 'and look upon all men—Muslim, Hindu and Christian—as my brothers, no matter what others may think.' 'Every son of Adam,' he says in another letter, 'be he Muslim, Hindu or Christian, I hold dear and regard as my brother. I do not care if others believe in this or not.' Once, while gazing at the sky, the apparent chaos in the distribution of the stars struck him and he proclaimed, 'There is no rhyme or reason in anything the self-willed do. Just look at the stars scattered in complete disorder. No proportion, no system, no sense, and no pattern. But their King has absolute power, and no one can breathe a word against Him.'

For the Muslim elites to whom Ghalib belonged by virtue of his family lineage and his ancestral social status, Islam was neither the only nor in

---

[44] The angels write, and we are seized. Where is the justice there?
We too had someone present when they wrote their record down.

all circumstances the most important identity.[45] Once during Ramazan, the month of fasting, his close friend, Mufti Sadruddin Azurda, visited him about midday. He was then in the cell, playing chess or *chausar* with a friend. The Mufti found his way to the cell, and seeing Ghalib playing games in the month of fasting, said, 'I have read in the *Hadith* (Tradition) that Satan is kept locked up during Ramazan, but now I have doubts about the genuineness of this *Hadith*.' 'No, my venerable friend,' Ghalib replied, 'the *Hadith* is perfectly genuine. Only, you must know that this cell is the place where Satan is kept locked up.'[46]

Ghalib admired Hindu rituals and Hindu sites. In October 1827, he set out for Calcutta. He travelled, part of the way by river, and did the final stage, from Banaras to Calcutta, on horseback. He reached Kolkata on 20 February 1828—almost a full year after he had set out from Delhi. Banaras enchanted him; hence the long lyrical Persian poem of 108 couplets in its praise. It is entitled 'Chiragh-e dair' (The Lamp of the Temple). According to him, the beauties of Banaras have 'their coquetry in a rose garden intoxicated and brimful of blandishment; their graceful walking embraces the hundred turmoils of judgment Day!' By contrast, Allahabad (Prayag) was a ghost, 'dull and uninspiring, its people unfriendly and inhospitable'. He decided not to touch Allahabad on his journey back home.

From its alleged founding in the sixth century BC, Kashi had grown to be one of northern India's largest cities in the early nineteenth century. With pilgrims seeking salvation or taking part in seasonal fairs and eclipses, Ghalib enjoyed the paradise-like environment of natural beauty, the temple bells ringing and the devotees walking hurriedly towards the Ganga. Invigorated by the salubrious climate, the forests along the river, and the streams and waterways all through the city, he makes a patriotic revaluation of the common cultural and religious inheritance.

Preservation of customs is Ghalib's theme in 'Chiragh-e dair'. In this he rejects infidelity (*rasm-e kufr*) but not the Divine Bounty. 'Negation without affirmation is nothing but error'; indeed, one cannot affirm God and deny His signs. Kashi was thus a 'sign' of God. Besides being a centre

---

[45] Margrit Pernau, 'Multiple Identities and Communities; Re-Contextualizing Religion', in Jamal Malik and Helmut Reifeld (eds), *Religious Pluralism in South Asia and Europe* (New Delhi, 2005), p. 156.

[46] Mujeeb, *Ghalib*, pp. 26–7.

for pilgrimage and worship, it was a microcosm of Indian life, customs, and popular belief. It was, so wrote Ghalib, the Kaaba of India.

More than thirty years later Ghalib remembered his stay in Banaras with pleasure: 'What praise is too high for it? Where else is there a city to equal it? The days of my youth were almost over when I went there. Had I been young in those days I would have settled down there and never come back this way.' Arguments for tolerance, when not purely pragmatic, took recourse to other values, some of which, including respect for cultural diversity, play a central role in the thinking of Urdu's greatest poet.

Without suggesting any causal relationship between Ghalib's interest in Hindu sites and symbols and his eclecticism, it is important to point out his interest in them in order to indicate something of the significance of these histories for composite traditions and even composite nationalism. It is not as if he did not pay sufficient attention to religiously defined cultures. The fact is that he tried to tease out the subtle ways in which conflicts could be avoided.

PLURALISM IN PRACTICE

If nineteenth-century Delhi was, for the most part, a place of cultural synthesis rather than a pure and simple cultural crusade of one kind or another, so were the qasbas in colonial Awadh. Here, one is able to knit the micro-narrative, as revealed in family histories and documented local tales, to the grander narrative of national movement and partition.[47] I have attempted in From Pluralism to Separatim: Qasbas in Colonial Awadh to unfold the story of the qasbas through the family history of the Kidwais of Masauli, and to scrutinize their private and public domains to generalize about the larger qasbati culture. The lives of the Kidwais reveal the existence of a vibrant political culture that was pluralistic and in which religion occupied an important place but did not conflict with the concern for the nation or relations with people of other religions. Indeed, qasba culture produced new styles of appearance, behaviour, language, expression, and communication which were pluralistic, distanced from communitarian politics, and yet not entirely isolated from religion.

[47] Review of Mushirul Hasan, From Pluralism to Separatism: Qasbas in Colonial Awadh (New Delhi, 2004) by Seema Alavi in The Indian Economic and Social History Review, vol. 44, no. 1, 2007, p. 105.

The qasbas predisposed *ashraf* or families comprising the gentry to the rational and ethical dimensions of Islam, to the virtues of charity,[48] tolerance, generosity, good-neighbourly conduct, and to those elements of piety that go into the making of the Perfect Man or *Insan-e kamil*. Without denying the existence of negative critiques or the wide gap between ideals and reality, it is worth drawing attention to one *Weltanschauung* of significance, the rationalist and humanist construction of Islam. To be educated in the second half of the nineteenth century meant to be steeped in those values, and promised dignity and advancement in life. Hence the comment that, presumably, alludes to such people, especially the aspiring intellectuals: 'The Mussalmans of Oudh cannot, as a body, be accused of bigotry or intolerance.'[49] This is corroborated by Meer Hasan Ali's experience in Lucknow, of being received without prejudice and being allowed to observe her European habits and Christian faith.[50] Some, if not all, of the men who figure in her narrative thus were typical carriers of moral and ethical piety or *akhuwat* in the qasbas. Hence the authors of nineteenth- and twentieth-century *tazkiras* prided themselves on being the elite gazing self-consciously into the mirror of history, or historical fantasy.

The gentry's patronage and the common man's veneration of Muslim shrines and holy men enhanced the qasba's solidarity as a unique entity. It is true that religious attributions were common, but more often than not they were banners under which different economic and social groups organized themselves. The point is that their motives had little to do with religion, and qasba society only rarely witnessed polarization along religious lines. Expressions of orthodoxies were minimal not because religious 'secularism' replaced religious stridency but because local ties and networks supplanted formal religious structures. One result of all this was the mutual interpenetrating of Sufi ethics and the Hindu way of life in the village and qasba-based *khanqas* rather than in urban centres where Hindus and Muslims led more self-centred, if not exclusive, lives. Hence coexistence became the rule in qasba society.

[48] Meer Hasan Ali, a British lady married to a Shia in Lucknow, stressed this point, that is 'the spirit of philanthropy'. Meer Hasan Ali, *Observations on the Mussulmans of India* in 2 vols (London, 1832), vol. 1, pp. 4–6.

[49] H.C. Irwin, The *Garden of India* (London, 1980), p. 38.

[50] Ali, *Observations on the Mussulmans of India*, vol. 2, p. 424.

Peasants and craftsmen forged bonds through festivals, *melas*, and shared religious traditions, such as Muharram, whereas gentry families interacted with one another in the high tradition of a specifically Indo-Persian culture. Even though some nursed sectarian prejudices, most consciously resisted attempts to create fissures in the broadly unified and consensual model of social and cultural living. Bonds of friendship and understanding remained intact among all classes who shared a language and literature and a cultural heritage. Indeed, while sharp social divisions and cultural fragmentation marked city people, the qasba people invoked their unity of experience. As the temple bells rang and the *muezzin's* cadences floated in the air, service families celebrated Basant and Diwali with much fanfare. A longer tradition of aiding the process of acculturation existed among such families.

Shrines in Rudauli, Dewa, and Bansa came to constitute nuclei of ascetic pietism. They offered shelter and refuge to the devotee, Hindu and Muslim alike. It is instructive to turn to the life of Shah Abdul Razzaq of Bansa, a site of piety and devotion in Barabanki district, and to observe the triumph with which he brought back, from his forays into the neighbouring districts, the 'Little Traditions' into his worldview. He visited Allahabad's Magh mela, interacted with *jogis* and *bairagis*, joined the theatrical performances featuring popular stories about Krishna and the *gopis*, and listened to the verses of Kabir. In this dimension, the Hindu gods were his friends and thereby the well-wishers of all the disciples and followers amongst the Muslims as well.

Hopefully the histories of qasbas and the erstwhile imperial capital will prove a source of knowledge of a cultural and intellectual heritage that belongs to the entirety of South Asia. Hopefully, when the history of ideas of the countries bordering India is better explored and therefore better known, the historian will take note of the currents of influence, which, from Pakistan to Bangladesh, constitute the very fabric of the history of Islam in the region.

Halide Edib quoted a simple story told by Nobel Prize winner Jane Adams (1860–1935) and reproduced by Gandhi in the March number of *Harijan* in 1937:

There was a woman down at the bottom of a pit where she felt so very hot and uncomfortable that she sent prayer after prayer to the throne above, begging that she might be taken out. Finally the word came down to her, that if she could think of one unselfish thing she had done it might be sufficient to save her. She thought and thought a long time, and because she had been a very selfish person she simply could not think of one really unselfish act. Finally she remembered that one day she was sitting in from of her house preparing some carrots for dinner; a blind beggar came along and asked for something to eat—and she gave him a bad carrot. She realized that it was not a remarkably fine deed, but as it was the only one she could think of, she sent that up as her one unselfish act. Very soon there came down into the pit a carrot on a string. She was told to take hold of it, Clinging to the carrot she went up and up into an atmosphere less lurid where she was getting quite comfortable. Then all of a sudden, as she looked down she saw that somebody was hanging on to her feet, and as she gazed further down she was horrified to see that somebody was hanging on to his feet, and someone on his, so that there was a long line of humanity suspended below her. Suddenly she realized that the carrot was bad—a rotten one, in fact, so that she grew frightened and thought that it would break. She called down, 'Let go of me; it is my carrot. It is my chance to get up!' And immediately the carrot did break—and they all went down together.

Jane Adams concluded: 'No one is going to get up by himself; we must all go up together if we go up at all.'[51]

[51] Halide Edib, *Inside India*. With an Introduction and Notes by Mushirul Hasan (New Delhi, 2002), p. 248.

6

Education and Faith
Exalting Orthodoxies

Khuda tujhe kisi toofan se ashna kar de
Ke tere behr ki maujon me iztirab nahin

Tujhe kitab se mumkin nahin faragh ke tu
Kitab-khwan hai mugar sahib-e kitab nahin.

God bring you acquainted with some storm!
No billows in your sea break in foam,

And never from books can you be weaned
Which you declaim, not comprehend.

—Mohammad Iqbal [Victor Kiernan (ed.),
Poems from Iqbal (p. 180)]

According to Christopher Hill, historians are interested in ideas not only because they influence societies, but also because they offer insights into the societies that gave rise to them. In this section, I cover some important writings on the history of ideas in Islam as they were formulated in and expressed through educational institutions in India.

In the late 1970s, two major conferences in the United States deliberated upon the relationship between codes of behaviour derived

from Islam and codes of behaviour derived from other sources.[1] Some of
the contributors debated the histories of certain educational centres in
India. They did so because India had been the home of traditional Islamic
learning since the advent of Turkish rule in 1206. Delhi alone had a
thousand *madaris* during the reign of Mohammad bin Tughlaq (1325–
51). Jaunpur had thirty. A sixteenth-century traveller visiting Thata—
near Karachi in Pakistan—found four hundred large and small madaris.
Working with an elaborate curriculum,[2] they made adjustments in
religious thought and organization. Ostensibly, their aim was not only
to sift the false from the true but also to assist the pregnant mind to bring
forth its own truths, but in reality the well-drilled array of 'historians'
hardly ever went beyond extolling the *Dars-e Nizamia* devised by Mulla
Nizamuddin (1679–1748).

It is different with *Islamic Revival in British India: Deoband 1860–1900*.
The scene of Barbara Daly Metcalf's book is laid, and truly laid, in a
qasba, a semi-rural area in Deoband in UP's Saharanpur district. The
evocation of the character of such towns in north India is very specifically
historical. Her sensitivity to its changing character appears in the whole
of her work. In the overall setting, one notices different moods and hears
different voices. As the story from 1857 onwards unfolds, one sees light
as well as shades of darkness. *Islamic Revival in British India* is the product
of meticulous research and testifies to remarkable erudition.[3]

Barbara Metcalf's thesis is that Islam in nineteenth-century India did
not stagnate and that significant cultural changes occurred only through
the adoption and incorporation of Western values. As evidence of this,
she turns to the *ulama* engaged in a self-conscious reformulation of their
religious thought—a reformulation involving new emphases and new
concerns from within the framework of their own received tradition. The
origins of the Dar al-ulum show that scholars had already prepared the
groundwork for the setting up of a seminary. Barbara Metcalf offers us
glimpses of their world and the ways in which they experienced colonial
rule, of a teacher's life, of the growing up of a student thrown into a

---

[1] Barbara Daly Metcalf (ed.), *Moral Conduct and Authority: The Place of Adab in
South Asian Islam* (London, 1984); Katherine P. Ewing (ed.), *Shariat and Ambiguity in
South Asian Islam* (New Delhi, 1988).

[2] H.S. Reid, *Report on Indigeneous Education and Vernacular Schools* (Agra, 1852); R.
Nathan, *Progress of Education in India 1896–97 to 1901–2*, vol. 1 (Calcutta, 1904).

[3] Review of Barbara Metcalf, 'Islamic Revival', in Francis Robinson, *Islam and Muslim
History in South Asia* (New Delhi, 2000), pp. 254–64.

particular social milieu, and of the evolution of religious ideas. She introduces the interpretation of religious/theological thought with finesse, though she discusses much less its impact on the construction of a society modelled on the *sharia*.

Deoband's history reveals the existence of long and deep traditions of Islamic apoliticism and a de facto embracing of democratic and liberal traditions. The goals and satisfactions that come from participation in Islamic movements may well have little to do with opposition or resistance to non-Muslims or the West. What institutions like the Dar al-ulum offer their participants may be the fulfilment of desires for individual empowerment, transcendental meaning, and moral socialization that do not engage directly with national or global political life at all.

That there was much that was admirable in the learning and public conduct of its scholars is readily granted; equally, the presence of godly, spirited, and self-sacrificing men. It is also true that their views carried weight; the ulama used tracts, treatises, and *fatawa* to draw the dispersed nodes of teaching and influence into a larger framework of common imaginings.[4] The Deobandi ulama issued 147,851 fatawa from 1911 to 1951. Rashid Ahmad Gangohi (1828–1905), for example, gave rulings that it was lawful to learn English if there was no danger to religion and that it was unlawful to take interest from a Christian and to use money-orders and bills of exchange in which the element of interest enters. He also ruled that the wearing of a cross or a *topi* was sinful. The ten volumes of fatawa from Deoband cover issues of marriage, divorce, inheritance, and forms of prayer.

However, contemporary accounts do not display undiluted enthusiasm for the institution. Idealizing the Deobandi ulama runs contrary to the widespread critique of their conduct and performance by their detractors. Maulana Abul Ala Maududi (1903–79), founder of the Jamaat-e Islami, launched a vituperative attack on the Deobandis; he derided secularism, nationalism, and democracy and dreamt of a theo-democracy where the entire Muslim community would administer the Kingdom of God—the only legislator.[5]

    [4] Francis Robinson, 'Technology and Religious Change: Islam and the Impact of Print', *Modern Asian Studies*, vol. 27, no. 1, February 1993, pp. 229–31; David Gilmartin, 'A Networked Civilization', in Miriam Cooke and Bruce B. Lawrence (eds), *Muslim Networks: From Medieval Scholars to Modern Feminists* (New Delhi, 2000).
    [5] Annemarie Schimmel, *Islam in the Indian Subcontinent* (Leiden, 1980), p. 238.

The story of the Barelwi–Deoband animus is fairly well known. The bitter legacy lives on as is apparent from a recent report about a Reserve Police commandant being turned away from a mosque in Gondal, 30 km from Rajkot, and of a police inspector and judge being turned away from prayers. This is because Barelwi mosques in the Saurashtra-Kutch region have put up boards asking non-Barelwis not to enter.[6]

Sections of the ulama themselves realized, soon after the establishment of the seminary at Deoband, that the curriculum they had worked out—*Dars-e Nizamia*—was woefully inadequate in many ways. Shibli was one of them. He criticized the traditional curriculum which clung to the texts and, in science, neglected everything that had been discovered after the Greeks. He therefore founded the Nadwat al-ulama in 1894.

Poets and writers have critiqued some of Deoband's scholars for being pretentious, stridently religious, and anti-modernist.[7] Syed Ahmad Khan, who was 'deadly poison' to the early Deobandis, had no patience with *taqlid* (conformity) and many had long been prepared to accept his view. Azad expressed fervent agreement with him. In the early twentieth century, he established the Dar al-Irshad and the Madarsa-e Islamia in Calcutta. These initiatives reveal the dissatisfaction with the form, method, and content of teaching in traditional schools. More generally, he was prepared to question accepted beliefs. In an eloquent passage from *Ghubar-e khatir*, he observes:

As a rule man receives his belief by tradition, and with me it was the same. Yet I could not be content with the traditional doctrines. The drink they gave could not quench my thirst. Abandoning the old paths I had to search on my own for new ways. Before my fifteenth year I already began to doubt. ... Firstly, I found diverse trends within Islam, and the mutually contradicting convictions and discrepant dogmas both alarmed and confounded me. Then, when I penetrated still further into the matter, I noticed that in the heart of religion itself there were points in dispute, and this brought me from uneasiness to doubt, from doubt to unbelief. ... Vital questions which I had seldom posed myself, arose one by one... questions, like: What is truth? Where is it? Does it actually exist? If it should exist, it ought to be one, for there cannot be more than one truth. Why, then, does one see such various ways to attain it?... Over against all those conflicting ways Science stands with the light of its unshakable and well-

---

[6] *Indian Express*, 7 August 2007, p. 1.

[7] For example, T.N. Madan, *Modern Myths, Locked Minds: Secularism and Fundamentalism in India* (New Delhi,1998), p. 139.

founded truths in hand, and in that pitiless light all those old obscure mysteries of
former times and tradition, at which mankind had got accustomed to look with awe,
are dimmed one by one. This path begins with doubt and mostly ends with atheism.
And if one runs down it to the end, one has finally nothing left but despair. ... I too
had to pass those stages, but I did not walk down the road to the end. My thirst refused
to be satisfied with despair. ... It became clear to me that amidst the conflicting ways
and the dense darkness of fallacies and delusive ideas a bright and safe course is still
open, leading to security and a firm ground for faith. ... The belief I lost by searching
for truth, I got back with the aid of this very searching. What had been the cause of
my illness turned out to be eventually the means for recovery.[8]

Azad's convictions here about the unity of faiths and pluralism are
his own—deeply felt and experienced—and addressed as much to himself
as to the reader.

The view that taqlid stopped the development of religious thought is
succinctly reasoned by a number of scholars.[9] The ulama, those from
Deoband included, studied not events and occurrences but the old texts
to discover the working of God's will.[10] Hence Rashid Ahmad Gangohi,
co-founder of Deoband, banished philosophy because it led the faithful
to get lost in the dark and fathomless world of *falsafa*.[11] With taqlid as
their favourite pastime, they abrogated the individual's right to hold an
independent opinion about right and wrong. Taqlid degenerated into a
farce, especially in the second half of the nineteenth century when the
Muslim elites lost every vestige of political power and the religious
minded practised the type of casuistry which the Urdu poet Akbar
Allahabadi ridiculed:

> You can wear these socks and shoes
> And make love to Miss D'Souze,
> If only you fast and pray
> You can live and love as you choose.[12]

One should not assume that the ulama alone lived a life of piety and
learning, or that they alone represented 'true' Islam and interpreted its

---

[8] J.M.S. Baljon, *Modern Muslim Interpretations, 1880–1960* (Brill, 1968), p. 9.
[9] Fazlur Rahman, *Islam* (London, 1966), p. 201.
[10] Mohammad Mujeeb, *Islamic Influence on Indian Society* (Meerut, 1972), p. 56.
[11] Schimmel, *Islam in the Indian Subcontinent*, p. 210.
[12] Ibid., p. 39.

doctrines authoritatively in a world torn by materialism, as Metcalf and Robinson have done. In other words, overemphasis on religious belief, practice, and institutions at the expense of other social factors can lead to mistaken conclusions about the role of religion among Muslims.[13]

To what extent does *madarsa* education in general and the *Dars-e Nizamia*, in particular, create a mindset? What is its impact on the modes of thinking on education, gender, justice, and other aspects of family life? Without denying the ulama's strong presence and influence, one is inclined to probe if their overbearing presence could not have been curbed. One is equally tempted to deliberate upon the proposition that although Deoband's seminary may have prepared its students for religious life, it did not do enough to equip them to cope with the modern world. Several scholars have argued that the Dar al-ulum has worked for a kind of stagnation of the spirit by reaffirming traditional beliefs even to the extent of denying such scientific facts as the movement of planets round the sun. They have described it as a stronghold of conservatism that brought the Muslims who were inclined to accept the existing conditions or saw no other alternative to acceptance into open conflict with the rest of society.[14]

Barbara Metcalf has written positively in some essays about the Tablighi Jamaat, an organization that has been in the limelight recently owing to its unproven links with terror outfits in Iran, Pakistan, and Afghanistan. She is favourably disposed to its cause, though I am not. The Tablighi Jamaat's organization and thought are well-nigh as conservative as those of its opponents. Glimmerings of its early missionary zeal are still visible, but it has, on the whole, settled down into well-worn dogmatic channels. It has purged itself of heresies and of orthodox zealots, but it persists with keeping women in *purdah*, resisting social reforms, and insulating its followers from the world around them. The same holds true of its attitude to politics. It is true that there is much that is wrong in politics and politicians can be short-sighted and greedy. But it does not follow that individuals and groups, being part and parcel of the existing order, can build a state system on this assumption. The Tablighi Jamaat has, perhaps involuntarily, surrendered its claim of

[13] Peter Gottschalk, *Beyond Hindu and Muslim: Multiple Identity in Narratives from Village India* (New Delhi, 2000).

[14] Mujeeb, *Islamic Influence on Indian Society*, p. 85.

citizenship. Instead of critically engaging with the multifarious challenges, it has enclosed Muslims in their own cultural world and insulated them from the rapid developments in the world around them.[15]

Nobody takes exception to piety or to religious obligations being fulfilled in private or public spaces, but it is disconcerting to see scores of not so well-to-do Muslims taking to *tabligh* when they should be concentrating on earning a decent livelihood. Ideally, the faithful should be allowed to seek his/her own salvation without a mediator.

The Mughal Emperor Aurangzeb granted the property of a European merchant to a learned family in Lucknow. This property was called Firangi Mahal, and this was the name by which the family came to be known. Any student of modern Indian history would know how some of its learned men made Firangi Mahal a centre for the study of medicine, religious jurisprudence, Islamic philosophy, logic, social and physical sciences, and theology. Any student would be equally familiar with its role during the Khilafat protest, the visit of Gandhi, and his parleys with the spiritual head, Maulana Abdul Bari (1876–1926). 'Those responsible for the introduction of (this) scholarship and erudition were the learned men of the Firangi Mahal', wrote Abdul Halim Sharar (1860–1926) the essayist-novelist and pupil of Maulvi Abdul Hai (d. 1886).[16]

Today the seminary, once the cloistered refuge of a few, exists only in name in a dark alley in Chowk, a bustling bazaar. But thanks to Francis Robinson, it has gained a fresh lease of life in the pages of history.[17] He introduces its scholars and teachers who, for nearly three centuries, drew students and disciples not only from all parts of India but also from Arabia and China. He writes about those family members who turned to other callings—government service, journalism, or the medical profession (*unani*)—but focuses on the teachers transmitting the word of God and the skills required to understand it. These teachers were the ones who exemplified the code of right conduct. 'Watch me,' stated Maulana

[15] Yoginder Sikand, 'The Reformist Sufism of the Tablighi Jamaat: The Case of the Meos of Mewat', in Mushirul Hasan (ed.), *Living with Secularism: The Destiny of India's Muslims* (New Delhi, 2007); see also his *The Origins and Development of the Tablighi Jamaat, 1920s–1990: A Cross-Country Comparative Study* (New Delhi, 2002), and *Reflections of the Believers: Madrasas and Islamic Education* in India (New Delhi, 2001).

[16] Abdul Halim Sharar, *Lucknow: The Last Phase of an Oriental Culture*. Translated and edited by E.S. Harcourt and Fakhir Hussain (London, 1975), p. 94.

[17] Francis Robinson, *The Ulama of Farangi Mahall and Islamic Culture in South Asia* (New Delhi, 2001).

Abdul Razzaq (d. 1889–90?), 'so long as I follow our pious predecessors, follow me; and if I do not follow our pious predecessors, do not follow me. Our predecessors were better than we are, because they lived closer to the time of the Holy Prophet.'[18]

Robinson's account, factually informative, clearly arranged, and well provided with footnotes, directs the reader to the relevant sources. What is more, he supplements the conventional outlines of the historians of South Asian Islam. The chapter on scholarship and mysticism in Awadh is instructive: it places Firangi Mahal in the context of an Islamic world system based on shared systems of formal and spiritual knowledge. The last two chapters offer a synthesis of the work of a generation and discuss the impact of colonialism on traditional societies. This is a central theme of nineteenth-century Islam in South Asia. Robinson provides a useful starting point for further study.

Robinson subscribes to a definition of culture as something that is carried out by a small elite and so is nobler and more beautiful. In this context, like most writers of a thesis, he sees Firangi Mahal's influence everywhere and is inclined to overstate his point. He writes with feeling, if sometimes repetitively, on how good and great were its ulama. But even if they possessed special attributes, and one has no reason to doubt that, so unceasingly and resolutely pious a family is difficult to believe in. One is inclined to wonder whether there were there no personal scandals, no disputes over property, marriages, divorce, and inheritances, no bickering, no squabbles; and whether the Firangi Mahalis never quarrelled amongst themselves and with the others over mundane affairs. In other words, were the Firangi Mahalis human or divine? What of the ideological disputes surfacing openly in the 1930s with some prominent family members joining the Congress and the socialist movements? Is it true that Firangi Mahal lost its influence with Abdul Bari's death and that his fame rested not so much on his scholarship but on his ability to gather around him publicists like the Ali brothers?

Some family members complain that Robinson idealizes only one branch of the family—the one led by Abdul Bari and inspired by pan-Islamism—and due to personal friendship with it refuses to give credit to or listen to the others who developed the system of education and served the Muslims of not only northern India but the entire subcontinent.

[18] Quoted in Francis Robinson, 'The Ulama of Farangi Mahall and their *Adab*', in Metcalf, *Moral Conduct and Authority*, p. 152.

There have been detailed studies of some other streams of modern Islamic thought in the subcontinent apart from the Deobandis and Firangi Mahalis. Usha Sanyal profiled Ahmad Rida Khan (1855–1919) Barelwi and his ideas.[19] Before her, C.W. Troll, a German Jesuit based at the Vidhya Jyoti in Old Delhi, had reflected on Islamic trends in South Asia. His essays on the *dargahs* were some of the early works on the subject. As is in the case of the scholar Louis Massignon (1883–1963), he and some of his fellow-contributors demonstrated how Sufism had grown, not by importation from Hinduism or eastern Christianity, but internally as some Muslims took the teachings of the Quran seriously, meditated on them, and tried to draw out their implications for the spiritual life.[20]

Three other competent and wide-ranging works on Islamic thought must be mentioned here. One is by Barbara Metcalf; the other two by Francis Robinson.[21] All three, while differing widely in interpretation, share a tendency to exclude from the argument all those who opposed the traditional modes of thinking. Hence the glorification of religious seminaries with fervent ardour. There is in all this an implicit desire to resurrect the old and overlook the liberal and secular trends among Muslims, attaching undue importance to theologians.

'The social dimensions of the Islamic project in South Asia have so far not been much explored in research,' asserts Dietrich Reetz.[22] The fact is that the 'Islamic project' alone appears to be a favourite project in the West. Even for educational, legal, and social welfare issues, Reetz himself turns to the 'religious Islamic groups'.[23] Mark Juergensmeyer expounds a typical version of this rather limited view by imagining 'the loss of faith in secular nationalism' and the consequent legitimacy acquired by the vision of religious nationalists.[24]

[19] Usha Sanyal, *Devotional Islam and Politics in British India: On Ahmad Riza Khan Barelwi and his Movement, 1870–1920* (New Delhi, 1996).

[20] Christian W. Troll (ed.), *Muslim Shrines in India* (New Delhi, 1992). For Massignon, see Albert Hourani, *Islam in European Thought* (Cambridge, 1991), pp. 43–4.

[21] Barbara Daly Metcalf, *Islamic Contestations: Essays on Muslims in India and Pakistan* (New Delhi, 2004); see also Robinson, *Islam and Muslim History in South Asia*, and his *Islam, South Asia and the West* (New Delhi, 2007).

[22] Dietrich Reetz, *Islam in the Public Sphere: Religious Groups in India, 1900–1947* (New Delhi, 2006), p. 298.

[23] Ibid., see Chapter 6.

[24] Mark Juergensmeyer, *Religious Nationalism Confronts the Secular State* (California, 1993), pp. 23, 24.

In an essay published in a Festschrift volume for Aziz Ahmad, Ralph Russell listed scholars from a modern Western tradition, Barbara Metcalf, Gail Minault, and Francis Robinson included, who were 'too timid in stating truths, and sometimes very important truths, that their knowledge of Urdu has taught them'. 'I sometimes have the impression that in the field of Islamic studies more than most, scholars feel a need to be "diplomatic" so that influential people will not be offended.'[25] For me the *truth* lies in studying and analysing, along with what Russell calls 'Islamic chauvinism', the liberal and secular currents in Indian Islam.

Sarah Ansari, Claudia Liebeskind, Mumtaz Currim, and George Michell are among those scholars who find traces of eclectic thought and religious tolerance in Indian Islam.[26] Liebeskind's book evocatively visualizes the qasba society in Awadh, with its powerful Sufi networks. The reader is taken on a journey to the shrines of Dewa Sharif and Bansa Sharif and can hear the *muezzin* calling the faithful to prayer or the *qawwal* reciting, in his loud but melodious voice, *Munkun to Maula* ... by Amir Khusrau. As night descends on the dargah, we hear those sentimental, tearful voices of joy and ecstasy, of the faithful uniting with the Almighty. In *'Namidanam che manzil bud shabgahi ki man budam'* Amir Khusrau describes a mysterious nightly festivity with wine and candles, which all of a sudden turns into praise of the Prophet: *'Mohammad shame mehfil bud shabgahi ki man budam.'*[27] Liebeskind makes us breathe in the atmosphere of the period.

Jamal Malik's big tome on the Nadwat al-ulama, an institution which appears to be frozen in time, is in German and therefore inaccessible to some of us. But his scholarly essays give us a good many historical particulars. *Colonialization of Islam: Dissolution of Traditional Institutions in Pakistan* (1996), and an edited volume, *Perspectives of Mutual Encounters in South Asian History 1760–1860* (2000) also offer evidence of his scholarship.

[25] Ralph Russell, 'Aziz Ahmad, South Asia, Islam and Urdu', in Milton Israel and N.K. Wagle (eds), *Islamic Society: Essays in Honour of Professor Aziz Ahmad* (New Delhi, 1983), p. 67.

[26] Sarah F. D. Ansari, *Sufi Saints and State Power: The Pirs of Sind, 1843–1947* (Cambridge, 1992); Claudia Liebeskind, *Piety on Its Knees, Three Sufi Traditions in South Asia in Modern Times* (New Delhi, 1998); M. Ishaq Khan, *Kashmir's Transition to Islam: The Role of Muslim Rishis* (New Delhi, 1994); Mumtaz Currim and George Michell, *Dargahs: Abodes of the Saints* (New Delhi, 2004).

[27] Annemarie Schimmel, *As through a Veil: Mystical Poetry in Islam* (New York, 1982), p. 171.

Avril Powell's favourite theme is India's encounter with the West.[28]
She clearly brings out the difference made by the 1857 Revolt to the
attitude of the missionaries. Aware of the charge that their activities
had had a big hand in provoking the uprisings, she shows the missionaries
following a cautious path in the aftermath of the risings.

C.W. Troll delineated the contours of Syed Ahmad Khan's religious
thought. He had a sense of the supreme importance of the Quran in the
inner life of Muslims. Fluent in Arabic and Urdu, he brought out Aligarh's
intellectual atmosphere and related it to the institution's cultural milieu.

Throughout the nineteenth and twentieth centuries, Indian Muslims
continued to show solicitous interest in Turkey's welfare. After the
Turko-Italian war, they founded the Anjuman-e Khuddam-e-Kaaba
(The Society of the Servants of the Kaaba) in May 1913. The Society
had its headquarters first in Delhi and later in Firangi Mahal; its chief
organizers were Maulana Abdul Bari, Mushir Hosain Kidwai (1878–
1937), and Shaukat Ali. Gail Minault has produced by far the best study
on these pan-Islamic trends from their inception until their collapse in
1924. She has examined various dimensions and shown that pan-Islamism
held together locally fragmented movements.[29] M. Naeem Qureshi's
intimidating study merits serious attention. A collection of essays
published some time ago, and the recently published provincial Khilafat
committee reports point to the part played by the Sufis in Sind and Punjab
in the Khilafat upsurge.

Scholarly interest in Sufism has gathered momentum, despite its
rejection by the Ahl-e Hadith, because it is still a deeply Islamic tradition
and still very much alive. Shrines dotting South Asia's landscape testify
to this fact. The mystical vocabulary is common stock for all, down to
the lowest strata. Sufi poetry and prose can be enjoyed only with

[28] Mujeeb Ashraf, *Muslim Attitudes towards British Rule and Western Culture in India*
(New Delhi, 1982); Avril A. Powell, *Muslims and Missionaries in Pre-Mutiny India* (London,
2003); Gulfishan Khan, *Indian Muslim Perceptions of the West during the Eighteenth
Century* (Karachi, 1998); Mushirul Hasan and Narayani Gupta (eds), *India's Colonial
Encounter: Essays in Memory of Eric Stokes* (New Delhi, 2004, second revised and enlarged
edition).

[29] Gail Minault, *The Khilafat Movement: Religious Symbolism and Mobilization in India*
(New Delhi, 1982); Mushirul Hasan (ed.), *Communal and Pan-Islamic Trends in Colonial
India* (New Delhi, 1985 revised edition); Mushirul Hasan and Margrit Pernau (eds),
Regionalizing Pan-Islamism: Documents on the Khilafat Movement (New Delhi, 2005);
Ayesha Jalal, *Self and Sovereignty: Individual and Community in South Asian Islam since
1850* (New Delhi, 2001), p. 197, n. 15; Ansari, *Sufi Saints and State Power*, p. 197.

knowledge of the mystical background.[30] In Delhi, almost every poet and nineteenth-century writer was connected in some way with the Chishti or Naqshbandi order. *Sair-ul Manazil* (1811) by Mirza Sangin Beg mentions centres of piety and devotion, and Syed Ahmad Khan lists eighteen *mashaikh* or Sufis in *Asar-us Sanadid* (The Remains of the Great Buildings), a study of Delhi's ruins and extant monuments. Ghalib's close relationship with the Chishti order rendered it appropriate that on his death, he was buried near the most famous of Delhi's Chishti saints, in the shrine of Hazrat Nizamuddin Auliya, the ancestor and namesake of his (Ghalib's) friend Nizamuddin Aurangabadi.[31]

AT THE SYED'S FEET

> We only talk and talk—while Syed (Ahmad Khan) used to work
> Remember that to talk is not the same thing as do.
> Men may say what they like of him; what Akbar says is this:
> God grant him peace now he is dead. His virtues were not few.
>   —Akbar Allahabadi

David Lelyveld joined the ranks of a growing number of scholars to explore what it meant to be an *Indian Muslim* in a colonial context and how that cultural/social identity changed meaning in British India.[32] He focuses on the formally organized, self-consciously created social establishment at the MAO College, which owed its birth to the defined goal of carrying out transitions of identity and loyalty suitable to the special circumstances of British India.

Not all Lelyveld's conclusions can be unquestioningly accepted; nor is his delineation of situations and predicaments free from the obscurities of sociological jargon. Yet he explains major aspects of his field of study better than anyone before. Many writers have, subsequently, followed his methodology and framework of analysis; many have studied much the same themes in other contexts; some have acknowledged their debt to him; some have not. But Lelyveld's contribution is widely recognized.

[30] Schimmel, *As through a Veil.*

[31] Nile Green, *Indian Sufism since the Seventeenth Century: Saints, Books, and Empires in the Muslim Deccan* (London, 2006), p. 110; See also P.M. Currie, *The Shrine and Cult of Muin-al-din Chishti of Ajmer* (New Delhi, 1989).

[32] David Lelyveld, *Aligarh's First Generation: Muslim Solidarity in British India* (Princeton, NJ, 1978).

It must be said, however, that Lelyveld tells us very little about the Aligarh ethos being fiercely contested internally and about the fact of the ideas of its leading figures being diverse and marked by internal rivalries.[33] We are indeed ignorant of the other groups, the 'Second Generation' for example, and the roads they had taken in a period of flux. One should therefore study the lives, mentalities, and activities of men like Mohammed Habib, whose books bear the imprint of a long experience of teaching and research, K.M. Ashraf (1903–62), a gifted historian, and Zakir Husain, an educationist. They looked out upon the world with confidence in the strength and survival of the intellectual tradition which they had received from their teachers and ancestors. What scores of poets and writers wrote expressed faith in the synthesis of Hindu and Muslim cultures which had taken place and would continue to exist. Their task was not simply the rejection and repudiation of colonial interpretations but the legitimization of a secular polity and society. They defended, for this reason, the composite tradition to prove the hollowness of the 'two-nation' theory as against the idea of a Hindu *rashtra*.

Lelyveld does not tell us about another Aligarh project for strengthening mutual knowledge and respect between Muslims and Christians. Certainly, Syed Ahmad Khan bought books on the Christian faith, read them systematically, and compared its tenets with those of the Quran. He wrote a commentary on the Bible to make it known to the Muslim public, and completed a commentary on Genesis I to II and on Mathew I to V. Having discovered close similarities between the two religions, he pleaded strongly for a closer understanding between Muslims and Christians. Traditions of tolerance, dissent, and camaraderie, he pointed out, served as the perfect antidote to a mode of thinking that accentuated difference, religious in this case. Mohamed Ali, a student, responded warmly to the idea. He perceived a need for Muslims to enter into conversation with Christian scholars so that the two groups might better understand their common history. The brief history of Islam that he outlines in his book shows us something of what he believed should be the attitude of India's Muslims to their historical relationship with Christianity.[34]

[33] Mushirul Hasan (ed.), *Knowledge, Power and Politics: Educational Institutions in India* (New Delhi, 1998).

[34] Mohamed Ali, *My Life A Fragment: An Autobiographical Sketch of Maulana Mohamed*

Today, there is talk of a new Islamic tradition for the postmodern age, a *fiqh* of our times, which treats the fundamental sources of Islam, the Quran and the *Sunnah*, as an integrated whole.[35] This would facilitate inter-religious dialogue at many levels and across many divides. But, for the dialogue to be successful, we need to expand tolerance in our approach to different religions, celebrate the variety in religious expressions, and encourage a readiness in believers of different faiths to 'fight the imperialism of their own traditions and move from servile conformity to a position where their worldviews are adoptive rather than ossified in a particular historic location'.[36] As Akbar Allahabadi put it:

> I say the same to Hindus and the Muslims.
> Be good, each, as your faith would have you be
> The world's a rod? Then you become as water.
> Clash like the waves, but still remain one sea.

During Non-Cooperation, Jamia Millia Islamia, a breakaway institution with serious intent, clung fast to a new system of education. It openly proclaimed that it was going to be the breeding ground of political leaders and educationists, segregating carefully the students who were best fitted for this responsibility from those who would be content with a teaching or research career. In the school, boys and girls were put together and the authorities made no distinction between them. The idea was to train their minds and bodies alike to accuracy and efficiency, and to the appreciation of an austere and simple lifestyle. Elements of science and mathematics and the study of language combined with the teaching of literature, drama, and music.

Progressive writers in Urdu, some having been nurtured on the Aligarh campus, broke the chain of custom, emancipated Urdu literature from its shackles, and freed it from its bondage to the past and from the enemies of its progress. Bold and innovative, they spoke for the poor and hungry and constructed pictures of a society that encouraged the young to envisage new possibilities and horizons. What is more, they were socialistically

---

Ali (New Delhi, 1999); Syed Ahmad, *The Mohamedan Commentary on the Holy Bible* (Ghazeepore, 1862).

[35] Sohail Inayatullah and Gail Boxwell (eds), *Islam, Postmodernism and Other Futures* (London, 1985), p. 175.

[36] Ibid.

inclined, echoing the sentiment expressed long ago by Ghalib in the line—*Rang laye gi humari faqamasti ek din* ('Some day our poverty will find its true colour'), and by Iqbal in the verse:

> *Jis khet se dehqan ko miyassar na ho roti*
> *Us khet ke har khosha-e gandum ko jala do.*

> If a field does not yield bread to a peasant;
> You should burn every grain of that field.

The desire for independence had two sources. On the one hand, the ideas of the enlightenment gave impetus to thoughts of freedom, reason, and social emancipation. Much more important, on the other hand, was the disenchantment with the capitalist order that engendered inequities as well as caste and communal distinctions. Young idealists therefore invoked socialism to get rid of communal rancour and to make independence a blessing to the poor as well as the elite.[37] Asrarul Haq Majaz (1911–55) sums up the achievements of the Progressive Writers' Movement:

> Human intellect, in the darkness of superstitions,
> The hard, stormy dark night,
> If nothing else, has at least dreamt of a dawn,
> Where none had looked hitherto,
> Has looked up to the morning.[38]

Syed Ahmad Khan became the centre of what may be called the first modern intelligentsia of north India: a socially mobile group dedicated to the discussion and spread of ideas. Therefore, Lelyveld's book should be read along with the researches on Ghalib, Hali (the poet's biographer),[39] Nazir Ahmad, Zakaullah, and Muhammad Husain Azad (1830–1910). Recent monographs offer glimpses of the Delhi Renaissance and, equally, the sense of loyalty and bonding between students, teachers, and colleagues of the Delhi College.[40] This loyalty was made stronger over

[37] Victor Kiernan (ed.), *Poems of Faiz* (London, 1971), Introduction, p. 23.

[38] Translated from the Urdu by Humyaun Zafar Zaidi, cited in Javed Akhtar, 'Progressive Writers' Movement in Urdu Literature', *Indian Literature*, vol. 142, 2007, p. 162.

[39] Christopher Shackle and Javed Majeed (trans.), *Hali's Musaddas: The Flow and Ebb of Islam*, (New Delhi, 1997).

[40] C.F. Andrews, *Zakaullah of Delhi*. With an Introduction by Mushirul Hasan and Margrit Pernau (New Delhi, 2004); Margrit Pernau (ed.), *The New Delhi College:*

time by the memory of certain events, such as the pan-Islamic ferment at the Aligarh College.[41]

Gail Minault has dealt with education for Muslim girls in colonial India in a book published in 1998.[42] Earlier, she edited Hali's *Majalis-un Nisa*, a text which stands, in tone and content, in sharp contrast to Maulana Ashraf Ali Thanawi's *Bihishti Zewar*. While the *Majalis-un Nisa* is unashamedly 'modern', taking tradition as the opposite of Western modernity, *Bihishti Zewar* represents the powerful voice of orthodoxy, conservative and authoritarian. Why should *Bihishti Zewar* be celebrated, as has been done by Barbara Metcalf, and not *Majalis-un Nisa*? Nobody questions the value of studying religious ideas or their interpretations and transmission, but this should not be done at the cost of downgrading the liberal and modernist stream in Indian Islam.

While Festschrifts and seminar proceedings have served as aids to constructing social and cultural histories of Indian Muslims,[43] music, religion, and science have remained generally neglected themes.[44] The few studies, especially those put together by the late M. Waseem, do not fill the gap.[45] Works on literature are of a high quality. I have recently written on wit and humour.[46] A recent study of Munshi Nawal Kishore

---

Traditional Elites, the Colonial State, and Education before 1857 (New Delhi, 2007); Nazir Ahmad, *The Bride's Mirror: Mirat ul-Arus, A Tale of Life in New Delhi a Hundred Years Ago*. Translated from the Urdu by G.E. Ward, with an Afterword by Frances W. Pritchett (New Delhi, 2001); *The Repentance of Nusooh (Taubat-Al-Nasuh)*. Translated from the Urdu by M. Kempson, edited by C.M. Naim (New Delhi, 2004); William Dalrymple, *The Last Mughal: The Fall of a Dynasty* (New Delhi, 2007).

[41] For example, Choudhry Khaliquzzaman, *Pathway to Pakistan* (Lahore, 1961), which discusses at length the pan-Islamic ferment even after reaching Karachi.

[42] Gail Minault, *Secluded Scholars: Women's Education and Muslim Social Reform in Colonial India* (New Delhi, 1998).

[43] Christopher Shackle (ed.), *Urdu and Muslim South Asia: Studies in Honour of Ralph Russell* (New Delhi, 1991); Kathryn Hansen and David Lelyveld (eds), *A Wilderness of Possibilities: Urdu Studies in Transnational Perspectives* (New Delhi, 2005).

[44] I have explained the reasons in Mushirul Hasan (ed.), *Islam and Indian Nationalism: Reflections on Maulana Abul Kalam Azad* (New Delhi, 2001 reprint).

[45] Garcin De Tassy, *Muslim Festivals in India and Other Essays*. Translated and edited by M. Waseem (New Delhi, 1997); M. Waseem (trans., and ed.), *On Becoming an Indian Muslim: French Essays on Aspects of Syncretism*. (New Delhi, 2003). See also, Muzaffar Alam, Francoise 'Nalini' Delvoye and Marc Gaborieau (eds), *The Making of Indo-Persian Culture: Indian and French Studies* (New Delhi, 2000).

[46] Mushirul Hasan, *Wit and Humour in Colonial North India* (New Delhi, 2007); Christina Oesterheld and Claus Peter Zoller (eds), *Of Clowns and Gods, Brahmans and Babus: Humour in South Asian Literatures* (New Delhi, 1999).

(1836–95) tells us much on the growth of print culture and on the literary and cultural trends in nineteenth-century Awadh.

Fortunately, the profiles of cities throw light on literary, social, and cultural life,[47] so that Delhi, the favourite hunting ground for Percival Spear (1901–82), the British historian, finds its due place in the historian's discourse not just as a site for Mughal architecture but as a dynamic, fluid, and ever-transforming city. Shamsur Rahman Faruqi's writings on Mir Taqi Mir (1733–1814), the famous Urdu poet, and his recent historical fiction Kai Chand the Sar-i Asmaan (2007) are impressive. Other researches cast light on Delhi's trauma under the British. They are sympathetic to the anti-British feelings during the 1857 Revolt, springing from the humiliation of the last Mughal emperor. They trace, moreover, what may now seem to be commonplaces, but were at that time radical ideas of social and cultural change.[48]

What is more, they give a sense of the 'secular' or the 'modern', a world far removed from that of the mujahidin wielding his sword or the theologian wielding his pen for the next fatwa. It is a relief to see creativity foregrounded, unencumbered by the stranglehold of religious dogma, and to see orthodoxies being relegated to the background. In another era, perhaps the orthodox Waliullahi tradition would have been assailed. This was much less possible in Ghalib's Delhi with its uninterrupted cultural fusion.

Delhi's poets and writers had an air of superiority, but Urdu progressed in other parts of the country as well. Sadly, though, there have been no rigorous studies of this progress; the history of its literature has been traced by writers like Ram Babu Saxena (1927), Mohammad Sadiq (1983), and

---

[47] Rosie Llewellyn-Jones, A Fatal Friendship: The Nawabs, the British and the City of Lucknow (New Delhi, 1985); Narayani Gupta, Delhi between Two Empires, 1803–1931: Society, Government and Urban Growth (New Delhi, 1981); Sharar, Lucknow; Veena Oldenburg, The Making of Colonial Lucknow, 1856–1877 (Princeton, NJ, 1984); Violette Graff (ed.), Lucknow: Memories of a City (New Delhi, 1997); C.A. Bayly, Rulers, Townsmen and Bazaars: North Indian Society in the Age of British Expansion 1770–1870 (New Delhi, 2002 edn); Avril A. Powell, Muslims and Missionaries in Pre-Mutiny India (London, 1993); Jamal Malik, (ed.), Perspectives of Mutual Encounters in South Asian History 1760–1860 (Brill, 2000). Recent writings on the 1857 Revolt are: Sabyasachi Bhattacharya (ed.), Rethinking 1857 (New Delhi, 2007); Pramod K. Nayar (ed.), The Trial of Bahadur Shah Zafar (New Delhi, 2007).

[48] See the works of Frances S. Pritchett, Christopher Shackle, C.M. Naim, Gail Minault, Margrit Pernau, and Christina Oesterheld.

Ali Jawaad Zaidi (1993), who draw largely upon their imagination, often conduct their disputes in the abstract, and make deductions from dogmatic propositions. While Russell and Pritchett are thorough in their presentation and provide a perspective on prose and poetry,[49] gaps exist in their writings. Russell's analysis of the Progressive Writers' Movement and his estimation of Faiz do not impress. His work on Iqbal is patchy and hardly a match for Annemarie Schimmel's.[50] Pritchett is conservative in her approach and interpretation and only dimly aware of the recent historical narratives.

Autobiographies and biographies of Indian Muslim religious and political leaders are plentiful, but none to compare with L. Massingnon's biography (1922) of al-Hallaj (d. 922), a mystic, poet, and theologian who is reported to have said: 'ana al-haqq', I am the Truth or I am God. Biographies on Jinnah are generally adulatory. Stanley Wolpert and Akbar S. Ahmed fail to impress with their accounts of Jinnah[51] but Ayesha Jalal tells her story dexterously.[52] The underlying ideas in her other major work—Self and Sovereignty—may be historic, albeit in the proper classicist manner, generalizing, and abstract. Instead of concentrating on the historical processes through which the relationship between the Muslim individual and the community of Islam configured, she makes exaggerated claims on behalf of poets, writers, and ideologues. These claims are not historically based but emerge out of the logic of the author's scheme. She advocates her case like a lawyer, proving a point not to students of Islam but to a law court based somewhere in India. Like Barbara Metcalf, she also either ignores or does not attach much importance to the secularized concerns of the Muslims and their cross-community networks.

Returning to biography, the life of M.A. Ansari, one of the architects of Jamia and Congress President in 1927, exemplifies two points: he offered an alternative to communitarian politics, but his alternative

[49] Ralph Russell, The Pursuit of Urdu Literature: A Select History (London, 1992); Frances W. Pritchett, Nets of Awareness: Urdu Poetry and its Critics (Berkeley, 1994).

[50] Gabriel's Wing: A Study into the Religious Ideas of Sir Muhammad Iqbal (Leiden, 1963).

[51] Stanley Wolpert, Jinnah of Pakistan (New York, 1984); Akbar S. Ahmed, Jinnah, Pakistan and Islamic Identity: The Search for Saladin (Karachi, 1997).

[52] Ayesha Jalal, The Sole Spokesman: Jinnah, the Muslim League and the Demand for Pakistan (Cambridge, 1985). See also Asim Roy 'The High Politics of India's Partition: The Revisionist Perspective', in Modern Asian Studies, vol. 24, no. 2, 1990.

failed. 'The question is,' Peter Robb asked, 'whether or not it could have succeeded.'[53] Francis Robinson, on the other hand, commented:

As the second half of the century has worn on, it has become noticeable how differently those who supported the movement for Pakistan have come to be remembered as compared with those who devoted themselves to Indian nationalism. Iqbal's tomb of sandstone, lapis lazuli and white marble ... is a place of pilgrimage. Jinnah's Mazar... is a symbol of Pakistan's identity and one of the first places to which the visitor to Karachi will be taken. Azad's mausoleum before Delhi's Juma Masjid, on the other hand, is not greatly frequented; not once on many visits to the city over twenty years has anyone taken me by the hand and said 'come, let us pay our respects to Abul Kalam.' Ansari, moreover, seems almost entirely forgotten; although I have visited the Jamia Millia Islamia a fair number of times, I had to read the biography [Mushirul Hasan, A Nationalist Conscience: M.A. Ansari, the Congress and the Raj] under review to learn that he is buried there. It may be said, of course, that regard for great men need not only be displayed at their tombs. But amongst Muslims, the Wahhabi sort apart, it is a natural instinct to respect the resting places of great souls and to frequent them in search of both solace and inspiration. The relative neglect of the tombs of Azad and Ansari suggests that many Indian Muslims may have lost interest in keeping their memories alive. It also suggests that Indian society as a whole may no longer value as before, and perhaps may not even know, the principles for which they stood.[54]

It is true that the sacrifices of the Congress Muslims were reduced to ashes: 'like the crumbling pillars of a mosque, they could neither be saved nor used', observed an author-journalist.[55] It is also true that many of them did not celebrate the joy of freedom, and yet individuals like Ansari, Ajmal Khan, Azad, and Khan Abdul Ghaffar Khan are important simply because of their strong secular, nationalist tradition which should not be forgotten or, to quote Robinson, 'submerged within the rationalization of the victors'. Bertrand Russell wrote of the intense and passionate nobility of Joseph Conrad (1857–1924) shining in his memory like a star seen

---

[53] Peter Robb, 'Muslim Identity and Separatism in India: The Significance of M.A. Ansari', in Peter Robb, Liberalism, Modernity, and the Nation (New Delhi, 2007), p. 198.

[54] Robinson, Islam and Muslim History in South Asia, p. 277; see also I.H. Douglas, Abul Kalam Azad: An Intellectual and Religious Biography. Edited by Gail Minault and Christian W. Troll (New Delhi, 1988); and Mushirul Hasan (ed.), A Nationalist Conscience: M.A. Ansari, the Congress and the Raj (New Delhi, 1987).

[55] Quoted in Mushirul Hasan (ed.), India Partitioned: The Other Face of Freedom (New Delhi, 1997), vol. 2, p. 146.

from the bottom of a well. I wish one could make the light of Azad and Ansari shine for others as it shone for me.

Syed Ahmad Khan's contemporaries have still not received their due and there are unanswered questions about the origins and nature of the intellectual effervescence which marked the first stirrings of the Delhi Renaissance and the Aligarh movement. Books in Urdu are mostly hagiographies: they do very little to enhance the understanding of the social scientist. Movements and ideologies falling outside the 'dominant' orthodoxies are neglected. A great deal more should have been written about the Progressive Writers' Movement,[56] the Jamiyat al-ulama, the Khudai Khidmatgars, the Ahrars, the Momins, and the National Conference in Kashmir. The late Papiya Ghosh is the only one to have researched the career of the All-Momin Conference and its leaders. Writings on the Ahrars, including memoirs of the activists, are considerable but they await analysis. The 1930s witnessed a new kind of Muslim activism—the Khaksar movement.[57] Led by Inaytullah Khan Mashraqi (1888–1963), it gave new shape and structure to Muslim politicization. He addressed primarily social and religious matters concerning the Muslims and contributed indirectly to the emergence of the Muslim League as a popular party.

Karl Marx has written in The Eighteenth Brumaire of Louis Bonaparte, 'They cannot represent themselves; they must be represented.' This is true of leaders like Ajmal Khan, Ansari, and Azad. As Francis Robinson puts it:

One of the problems of history is that it tends to be written by winners rather than losers, in this case by the historians of the Pakistan movement, of Congress-led Indian nationalism, and even those of British imperialism rather than those of nationalist Muslims. Through his work in general, and through this book in particular, [Mushirul] Hasan has made sure that the nationalist Muslim perspective, and the option which it offered the Congress, will not be submerged beneath the rationalizations of the victors. In the process he has added new understanding to the problem of how British India came to be divided in 1947.[58]

[56] Ali Husaini Mir and Raza Mir, A Celebration of Progressive Urdu Poetry: Anthems of Resistance (New Delhi, 2006), is one work dealing with the movement.

[57] Iftikhar H. Malik, 'Regionalism or Personality Cult? Allama Mashriqi and the Tehreek-i Khaksar in pre-1947 Punjab', in Ian Talbot and Gurharpal Singh (eds), Region and Partition: Bengal, Punjab and the Partition of the Subcontinent (New Delhi, 1999).

[58] Robinson, Islam and Muslim History in South Asia, p. 221.

However, the quality of work on the Ahmadis,[59] and the Shias must be recognized.[60] Of J.R.I. Cole's well-crafted book on the rationalist Usuli school of Shia Islamic law, one is inclined to exclaim: 'C'est magnifique, mais ce n'est pass l'histoires.'[61] Toby M. Howarth captures the ethos of *majalis*, a congregation to mourn Husain's martyrdom, in Hyderabad. What is new is that he takes Shiism's minority status into account to analyse how the community uses *majalis* to maintain and affirm its identity.[62] Vernon James Schubel defines Shiism on its own terms rather than by comparing it to the larger Sunni tradition. The focus is on Shiism 'lived in a particular context'.[63]

Not much has been written on the Bohras, the Khojas, and the Memons, all settled in western India. Most Bohras were of Hindu origin, their ancestors having been converted by Ismaili missionaries, the first of whom landed in Cambay in 1067. They had both a Sunni and a Shia branch; the former included most of the city traders, the latter the rural agriculturists. Most of them were, however, traders and merchants, and only a few sought careers in government or the professions.[64] Like the Bohras, the Khojas were mainly traders. Descendants of the Lohanas and of other trading castes, they embraced Islam in the fifteenth century. Over the centuries, they spread out of Sind, Kathiawar, and Punjab and then from the late nineteenth century, began to settle in Bombay. In 1921, they numbered just over 146,000. Among the leading Khojas in public life were: R.M. Sayani (1847–1902), Congress President in 1896;

[59] In 1974, the Pakistani parliament declared them non-Muslims, and a presidential order in 1984 transformed Ahmadi religious observance into a punishable offence. Yohanan Friedmann, Prophecy Continuous: Aspects of Religious Thought and Its Medieval Background (London, 1989); Spencer Lavan, The Ahmadiyah Movement: A History and Perspective (New Delhi, 1974).

[60] The list of the twelve Shia lmams begins with Ali and ends with the Imam Mahdi, who has for the present withdrawn from the world, but, it is believed, will appear again on the Day of Judgement. The religious life of the Shias centres round a body of traditions, beliefs, and observances which have their source in Ali, Fatima, and their sons Hasan and Husain, who with the Prophet, make up the Panjatan-i-Pak, the Five Holy Ones.

[61] J.R.I. Cole, Roots of North Indian Shi'ism in Iraq and Iran: Religion and State in Awadh 1772–1859 (Berkeley, 1968).

[62] Toby M. Howarth, The Twelver Shia as a Muslim Minority in India: Pulpit of Tears (London, 2005).

[63] Vernon James Schubel, Religious Performance in Contemporary Islam: Shia Devotional Rituals in South Asia (South Carolina, 1993), p. 157.

[64] On the Bohras, see Asghar Ali Engineer, The Bohras (New Delhi, 1980).

Ibrahim Rahimtullah (1862–1942), member of the Bombay Legislative
Council (1899–1911); and Jinnah, founder of Pakistan and its first
Governor-General.

PARTNERS IN FREEDOM[65]

> Chalo aao tum ko dikhaain hum jo bacha
> hai maqtal-i-shehr mein
> Yeh mazaar ahl-e safa ke hain yeh hain ahl-
> E sidq ki turbatein.

> Come along, I will show you what remains
> in the city's death row,
> These are the shrines of the pious, and here
> the graves of those with honesty and
> conviction.

'All action springs from faith,' Zakir Husain, the Vice-Chancellor of Jamia
Millia Islamia, would say.[66] Inner discipline, such as every free man must
achieve, was not possible without faith. Hence Jamia not only taught
Islamiat, but also the Quran (meaning and interpretation of eight suras
in the first year), 100 selected Hadis (Prophet's Traditions) from Siha-e
Sitta, Fiqh (Jurisprudence), and literature. At the same time Zakir Husain
and his colleagues preserved objective minds in regard to knowledge.
'They never go to the Quran for corroboration of the scientific discoveries
of the last centuries,' Edib remarked.[67] Students were meant to serve all
humanity and not a particular group or clan. They were the torchbearers
of knowledge that obliterated distinctions of race and lineage, and
rescued people from the perils of narrow sectarianism. Campus life was,
in essence, liberal if not cosmopolitan. Theological disputations between
the Barelwis and the Deobandis or the Shias and Sunnis did not exist.
Edib was struck by 'the mixture of freedom and discipline', Jamia's
strongest and happiest educational achievement.[68]

Jamia's post-Khilafat history experienced a paradigmatic shift

[65] This section is based on Mushirul Hasan and Rakhshanda Jalil, Partners in Freedom:
Jamia Millia Islamia (New Delhi, 2007), pp. 161–79.

[66] Halide Edib, Inside India. With an Introduction and Notes by Mushirul Hasan (New
Delhi, 2002), p. 64.

[67] Ibid.

[68] Ibid., p. 65.

embodied in intellectual trends and expressed in discourses by secular and religious intellectuals, who called for democracy, individual rights, tolerance, and gender equality as well as the separation of religion from state. They did not dismiss religious sensibilities, but talked of an inclusive religiosity that took cognizance of difference with harmony and composite living. Learning from the Khilafatists, many of whom had renounced their earlier ideas lamenting the danger of introducing religion into politics, they believed in a secular state maintaining religious ethics in society. They acknowledged universalism, inter-faith dialogue, and tolerance in theory and practice.

As the end of the Khilafat/Non-Cooperation movements triggered a qualitatively different discourse and politics, Jamia responded variously to the intellectual currents. In its political aspect, it seemed to stand for Islam's inalienable facet of democracy. Even before Jinnah expounded the two-nation theory, Mujeeb felt that Iqbal's plea for a Muslim state in north-western India did not conform to their cherished notion that Muslims must live and work with non-Muslims to realize common ideals of citizenship and culture. He discussed this view with the poet early in 1935. The conversation was free from the bitterness which later marred every exchange of views between nationalist and pro-League Muslims. Iqbal could find no reasonable ground for rejecting the principle being followed by Jamia; he only maintained his own point of view, and it became clear to Mujeeb that the Muslims he had in mind were Punjabi Muslims who, according to him, were still too weak to stand on their own feet and felt the need of political power to support them socially and economically.

The League's rhetoric in the 1940s created ripples on the campus. The partition proposal, called 'an untruth' by Gandhi, strained the faculty. Yet Mujeeb and others in Jamia wanted to be led by persons who would represent not communalism but faith, not numbers but values, not multitudes but effectiveness. The experience of living together had moulded the Hindus and Muslims into a common nationality, and they accepted the logic of fact and history and fashioned their destiny accordingly. Zakir Husain implored the participants of the Basic Education Conference, hosted at Jamia in 1940:

For heaven's sake, please pay attention to the prevailing political situation and build the foundation of a trustworthy society, in which the weak are not afraid of the strong, the poor are not kicked by the rich, in which our own culture can blossom, and we draw out the best from all human beings, where each person's latent capacities are nurtured and where everyone is ready to be of service to society.

By this time, the League had turned against Jamia. Basic education stood condemned not only as an attack on Muslim culture but on all ideas of decency. Such was Jamia's identification with the Gandhian project that primary and secondary schoolteachers wearing the Gandhi cap were abused and ridiculed. This forced Zakir Husain to change the cap. In 1945–6, Jinnah insisted on excluding the Congress Muslims, notably Maulana Azad, from the Simla Conference and the interim government. And when Zakir Husain's name figured in the Congress list, the future *Qaid* (leader) characterized him, as Wavell recorded in his journal of 19 June 1946, as a 'Quisling' and 'utterly and entirely unacceptable'. After meeting Wavell, Jinnah reiterated that he would not accept the nomination of any Muslim other than a Leaguer.[69]

After partition, Jamia became introverted, withdrawn from the centre of affairs, and cut off from the vital flow of young students. Its history in the 1950s and 1960s is uninspiring on the whole, even if some learned men made advances in scholarship. Its influence on society at large and its role as a nursery for future leaders of the nation diminished. There was talk of taking the college to Aligarh and of placing the school under the Delhi state government, but Jawaharlal resisted the move. While Aligarh progressed under Zakir Husain's leadership, Jamia survived uneasily on the margins of Delhi's academic life.

Jamia could have turned into a quasi-religious or quasi-communal institution, but this did not happen. 'I look on this as a secular school,' claimed Mujeeb.[70] As noted earlier, he drew upon the heritage of Gandhi, Tagore, and Nehru to affirm that secularism did not mean rejecting religion 'but a challenge to all of us to show through our actions the true social value of our beliefs', and that national integration, the principal motto of nationalism, derived from freedom, from service to the highest forms of the common interest, and from the most intense

[69] See references in Mushirul Hasan, 'Secular and Communitarian Representations of Indian Nationalism: Ideology and Praxis of Azad and Mohamed Ali' in Hasan, *Islam and Indian Nationalism*, p. 99. See also, Pyarelal, *Mahatma Gandhi: The Last Phase* (Ahmedabad, 1956), vol. 1, book One, p. 219.

[70] Greighton Lacy, *India Insights* (Delhi, 1972), p. 288.

realization that in cooperating with fellow citizens each person realized
his or her true self. Jamia inculcated in the youth ideas of their rights
and duties as citizens and ultimately helped to create a harmonious
nationhood. Mujeeb, who wanted the educator to draw upon his inner
resources, offered the following appraisal:

We agreed that Muslim or non-Muslim, our student should learn to represent the
values of his religion, of his moral and cultural tradition, that he should make himself
a useful citizen by being cultured, modest, thoughtful and competent. The forms in
which these qualities were to express themselves were those of the Indo-Muslim
culture of the nineteenth and twentieth century. This was the common culture of
the region.

To familiarize students with their own cultural heritage without
rejecting what was true and useful in other people's culture, Mujeeb
wanted them to be both good Muslims and good citizens. What is more,
he took pride in Jamia being co-educational. 'They [girls] leave their
homes with the *burqa* (veil) on, and somewhere along the way they take
it off,' he remarked.[71] The challenge of running such an institution had
to be met in order 'to strengthen the foundation of that culture which
must be created to enable us to realize the freedom and equality of a
democratic society'.

> I heard him out; then, smiling, said to him:
> 'It is not good to speak so ill of men.
> Who made you judge of others? You had best
> Thank God that one puts you to the test.'
>
> —Mirza Rafiuddin Sauda (1713–81)

---

[71] Ibid., p. 280.

7

Partition
A World Turned Upside Down

Kaise kaise khuda bana dale
Khel bande ka hai khuda kya hai

How many gods have been made!
What is God but the invention of man.

—Ghalib

Dina Nath belongs to a feudal Hindu household in a village near Lahore. When his *haveli* is burnt down and all the family members are put to death, he survives but flees to Amritsar. The scene remains the same even there—humanity is under fire. Haunted by barbarism, death, and destruction, Dina Nath ponders over the hollowness of the pride that man takes in civilization, which is like a veil torn apart by a freak event in history, laying bare the primeval forests of human instincts. Towards the end of the novel *Ghaddar* by the Urdu writer Krishan Chandar (1913–77), Dina Nath stands alone in a field where a group of Muslims had been massacred earlier in the day. Corpses lie all around. Dina Nath hears the cry of a child and detaches it from the dead mother. He embraces the child and says to himself 'Dina Nath, you are not following the logic of mutual hatred between the two nations. Where do you go from here?'[1] Where do we go from here was the uppermost question in everybody's mind as India made its tryst with destiny.

Anthony Smith observed that nation building and state building in post-colonial societies have often been very difficult.[2] As India celebrates its liberation from colonial bondage after six decades, the media focuses on success and triumph—the Incredible India.[3] Freedom has given India and its people national self respect: 'The gain in self-respect offset to a huge extent the debit items in our independent ledger.'[4] The greatest achivement has been this: Independence was worked for by people more or less at the top; the freedom it brought has worked its way down. 'People everywhere,' Naipaul reported, 'have ideas now of who they are and what they owe themselves.'[5]

Prophecies of doom and destruction have not come true. The stories of demolition, war, floods, cyclones, and disease are over, Rahi Masoom Reza the Hindi writer and author of *Adha-Gaon* (Half a Village) declared. Instead, the stories of life have begun, because the stories of life never end: the resilience of parliamentary democracy, success of a federal polity, the upward mobility of Dalits, backward classes and women, and informed citizens turning against religious nationalism and rallying behind the values of pluralism and equality.[6] India is a global poster country for dynamic growth and infinite investment opportunities: by contrast, in the 1950s and 1960s, it had been synonymous with misery and starvation, hunger and famine.[7]

[1] Javed Akhtar, 'Progressive Writers' Movement in Urdu Literature', *Indian Literature*, vol. 142, 2007, p. 154.

[2] Anthony D. Smith, 'State-Making and Nation-Building', in John A. Hall (ed.), *States in History* (Oxford, 1986).

[3] 'So long as the constitution is not amended beyond recognition, so long as elections are held regularly and fairly and the ethos of secularism broadly prevails, so long as citizens can speak and write in the language of their choosing, so long as there is an integrated market and a moderately efficient civil service and army, and ... so long as Hindi films are watched and their songs sung, India will survive.' Ramachandra Guha, *India after Gandhi: The History of the World's Largest Democracy* (New Delhi, 2007), p. 771. For a different perspective, see Patwant Singh, *The Second Partition: Fault-Lines in India's Democracy* (New Delhi, 2007).

[4] Frank Moraes, *Witness to an Era* (Delhi, 1973), p. 307.

[5] V.S. Naipaul, *India: A Million Mutinies* (New Delhi, 1990), p. 517.

[6] Martha C. Nussbaum, *The Clash Within: Democracy, Religious Violence, and India's Future* (Cambridge: Massachusets, 2007), p. 3; Alex von Tunzelmann, *Indian Summer: The Secret History of the End of an Empire* (London, 2007).

[7] Meghnad Desai, 'Our Economic Growth: 1947–2007', *India Sixty, IIC Quarterly*,

As in 1959 so also now, India is, in Jawaharlal Nehru's words, a very mixed picture of hope and anguish, of remarkable advances and at the same time of inertia, of a new spirit and also the dead hand of the past and of privilege, of an overall and growing unity and many disruptive tendencies.[8] All said and done, the 'India idea' is alive. As 'the most innovative national philosophy to have emerged in the postcolonial period', it deserves celebration, because 'it is an idea that has enemies, within India as well as outside her frontiers, and to celebrate it is also to defend it against its foes.'[9]

Mujeeb, the historian, had poignantly remarked:

There is no end to what we can discover of India once we have prepared ourselves for the adventure. We shall not all discover the same things or respond in the same way to the challenge to our understanding. But India will be all the richer for every sincere attempt made to discover her secrets and to become intellectually and spiritually aware of what she represents.[10]

This would apply to partition studies. This chapter deals with cities turning into flaming volcanoes, of village after village being set on fire, of men, women and children fleeing from the valleys to safety on high slopes, and of hate-blinded vengeful men committing violence, murder, rape, and mutilation. I cover the general, the political, and the human aspects of a grim and sordid story.

All through this work I have pointed to the bewildering diversity of Muslim communities,[11] the variety in their social and cultural traits, and the range and depth of their divisions. Hence no organization could authoritatively claim to represent a specifically Muslim constituency.[12] Even though tension brewed, inter-communal networks weakened, and the Muslims, having been politicized during and after the Khilafat movement, demanded their share of the benefits of office, my premise is that India

---

spring 2007, p. 35.

[8] Uma Iyengar (ed.), *The Oxford India Nehru* (New Delhi, 2007), p. 73.

[9] Salman Rushdie, quoted in *Time*, 11 August 1997.

[10] Mohammad Mujeeb, 'The Discovery of India', *Islam and the Modern Age*, August–October 2003, p. 173.

[11] Mushirul Hasan, *Nationalism and Communal Politics in India, 1916–1928* (New Delhi, 1979).

[12] In 1918, for example, India's Secretary of State received forty-four deputations from Muslim groups/organizations; each one of them played a different tune.

after the Non-Cooperation movement cannot be characterized as a communally polarized society. The political landscape underwent a change only in the late 1930s and early 1940s. Those were indeed terrible years, years in which the lives of millions were cast. One stroke of the pen endorsing partition falsified the composite culture: romanticism became a pose, religious beliefs turned into hypocrisy, and neighbourly friendship into deceit. *Mere bhi Sanam Khane*, the novel by Qurratulain Hyder (1927–2007), portrays the sparks of partition igniting the pathways of composite culture, leaving behind charred dust.

In effect, if one were to slice the 1940s as an era and view the cross-section of layers, one would, inevitably, find partition under the icing of Independence. No other country in the twentieth century offers two such contrary movements in simultaneous layering. If one is a nationalist struggle, unique in global history for ousting the colonizers through non-violent means, the other appears to be the countermovement that sprang from its belly, marked by violence, cruelty, bloodshed, displacement, and massacre. If one led to celebration, the other anguished and angered millions. If one symbolized independence and sovereignty, the other tore asunder the subcontinent along religious lines. Thus wrote Jigar Moradabadi (1890–1960), the Urdu poet, in December 1947:

> *Kahan ke lala-o-gul, kya bahar-e-tauba-shikan*
> *Khile hue hain dilon ki jarahaton ke chaman.*

> Do not talk of the tulips and roses; do not speak of the exciting spring,
> These are the wounds of the heart, open like flowers.

> *Rug-o-pai mein kabhi sahba raqs karti thi,*
> *Magar ab zindagi hi zindagi hai maujzan saqi.*

> It was wine and wine only that circulated in the veins before,
> Now it is only the waves of life in my body, O Saqi.

> *Fikr-e- jameel khwab-e-parishan hai aajkal,*
> *Shair nahin hai who jo ghazal-khwan hai aajkal.*

> These days a beautiful thought is like a dream shattered,
> The singer of simple lyrics cannot be considered a poet today.

While some exulted in freedom, most mourned the 'vivisection' and the accompanying violence. For an ideologically-driven poet like Faiz,

the dawn of freedom signified the non-fulfilment of a dream. Fear and
hope gripped Siraj Lakhnavi, a lesser-known poet. As the clock struck
the midnight hour, he began his walk into the alleys of uncertainties.

Khabar Rihaii ki mil chuki hai, charagh phoolon ke jal rahe hain,
Magar bahut tez roshni hai, qafas ka dar soojhta nahin hai.

We have received the news of our release from the prison; lamps of flowers
are burning bright
But there is so much light that the door of the cage is invisible.

Sharah-e naadari hain khali haath sookhi aastin,
Ab to maathe par mashaqqat ka paseena bhi nahin.

The empty hands and dry sleeve is a commentary on our poverty,
There is not even a drop of perspiration of labour on our forehead.

These and many such verses in other languages vividly capture the bizarre
and horrific simultaneity of the two layerings, of freedom and partition.

THE POLITICAL

Emotions have a way of upsetting logic, and we may not ignore them
simply because they seem so unreasonable. But this idea of a Muslim
nation is the figment of a few imaginations only, and, but for the
publicity given to it by the Press, few people would have heard of it.
And even if people believed in it, it would still vanish at the touch of
reality.

—Jawaharlal Nehru, *An Autobiography*, p. 469

One can go on debating whether partition or the more general
conflagration that preceded and followed it were inevitable or whether
they might have been averted by skilled negotiations, goodwill, and a
non-partisan role by the government. To explore the alternatives, it may
be worth the while, first of all, to recapitulate some of the important
milestones on the road to Pakistan, and to then recall the violent
communal upsurge that Gandhi and Nehru, the two topmost leaders,
had to face. As Badruddin Tyabji (1907–96), civil servant, recalled: 'It
was Panditji and the Mahatma who went about the country rallying the
broken-down spirit of the left-over minorities. They risked their lives to

inspire faith in the new India that would come into being, whatever happened across the border.'[13]

The Government of India Act of 1935 and the provincial election two years later ushered in a number of important political and constitutional changes. The Congress, having contested 1161 of the 1585 seats and winning 716, gained a majority in six of the eleven provinces. It emerged as the largest single party in three others. A sense of adventure filled the air, and this excitement crept into remote villages and intoxicated its inhabitants. 'There was relief,' Jawaharlal wrote 'from the burden of the old and a glad welcoming of the new.'[14] The League's performance, on the other hand, was lacklustre. The Muslim electorates, with principally 'provincial or 'local' concerns, hitched their fortunes with the Krishak Lok Party in Bengal and the Unionist Party in Punjab. It made greater sense to them to safeguard their interests at this level rather than wrestle with the intricacies of devolution of power in the national arena.

Meanwhile the war clouds gathered over Europe. Hitler invaded Poland on 1 September 1939, and two days later Britain and France declared war on Germany. Within a few hours of the declaration of war, the Viceroy announced India's participation on the side of the Allies. He did this without consulting the provincial governments or the people's representatives in the legislatures. In the dominions of Canada and Australia, on the other hand, prior consultations were held with the elected representatives. Nehru announced on 21 March 1939: 'India will not submit to any form of exploitation to further Britain's war effort. But how can India fight for democracy if she herself does not have it?'[15] Subsequently, he prepared the first draft of the Congress resolution on India and the War.

The War declaration was followed by an amendment to the Government of India Act of 1935 which granted Linlithgow (1887–1952), the Viceroy, the power to override its provisions for co-coordinating the activities of the central and provincial governments in prosecuting the War. He was also empowered to direct the provincial governments to exercise their executive authority, and, if required, enact laws to this end. The Congress asked its members not to attend the Central

[13] Badruddin Tyabji, *Memoirs of an Egoist*, vol. 1 (Delhi, n.d), p. 177.

[14] Editorial in the *National Herald*, 9 November 1939, Iyengar, *The Oxford India Nehru*, p. 144.

[15] Iyengar, *The Oxford India Nehru*, pp. 134–8.

Assembly's next session: the amendment struck at the very root of responsible government and rendered provincial autonomy ineffective.

The Viceroy and the Secretary of State realized the gravity of the situation arising out of Congress's intransigence. Both agreed to set up a consultative group of political parties in British India and Indian princes. The Viceroy also mentioned Dominion Status as the goal of British policy. But the Congress Working Committee, at its meeting on 22–3 October 1939, described the proposals as 'an unequivocal reiteration of the old imperialist policy'. Its resolution laid down that if the War was

to defend the status quo, imperialist possessions, colonies, vested interests and privileges then India can have nothing to do with it. If, however, the issue is democracy, then India is intensely interested in it. If Great Britain was fighting for the maintenance and extension of democracy, then she must necessarily end imperialism in her own possessions and establish full democracy in India.

The British government was called upon to declare its war aims 'in regard to democracy and imperialism' and also to announce whether those aims would apply to India. Importantly enough, the Congress demanded that India be freed from colonial bondage. The Congress could either resign or hold on to the reins of office at provincial level. After much debate and disagreement, the Congress High Command announced in November 1939 that 'in no event can the Congress accept the responsibility of the Government even in the transitional period without real power being given to popular representatives'. It insisted on convening a Constituent Assembly in order to determine the country's democratic constitution. The Viceroy turned to the Muslim League and 'Muslim India', as he termed it, to buttress his claims. Now, critically, Jinnah made his support to the War effort dependent on justice for Muslims and a guarantee of no constitutional advance without its approval. The League resolution of 18 September 1939 challenged the Congress's imperious claim to represent all India.

Already the row over the Communal Award, the messy coalition debate after the 1937 elections, and 'miscalculated moves' on the part of the Congress, including the Muslim Mass Contact Campaigns, Nehru's brainchild, had widened the Hindu–Muslim divide. Although the excesses during the reign of the Congress Ministries (1937–9) were exaggerated, the Urdu Press raised the spectre of 'Hindu Raj' by publicizing the dangers of the Wardha Scheme of education and the Vidya Mandir Scheme in the Central Provinces, the introduction of 'Vande Mataram' in schools, and the imposition of Hindi as the national language. To them, the pattern of the Ministry's cultural and educational policies seemed a substitution and suppression of the British by Hindu institutions—a situation in which they feared the annihilation of their religious-cultural identity.[16]

Jinnah had been more of an ally of the Congress than its adversary from the All Parties National Convention in December 1928 until the League's March 1940 resolution. But his attempts not to wreck secular democracy were frustrated by the inability of the Congress to overcome the influence of the Hindu Mahasabha or a sizable section of its own communalized membership. An intransigent Congress rejected not only Jinnah's overtures but settled for a soft option—treating the Muslims as a homogeneous political entity and, on that basis, forging unprincipled alliances for short-term gains. Now, in the changed political scenario, Jinnah virtually held the trump card.

Jinnah declared 22 December 1939 as the 'Day of Deliverance'. Although this act of unspeakable folly embittered Hindu–Muslim relations, the gamble paid off. The Quit India Movement raised fresh hopes in the minds of the League leadership; it stimulated the awakening of the Muslim masses. Though it would be no more than a parlour-game to decide on the exact date when the *Qaid* managed to weld the disparate elements into a unified 'community', the post-1942 period yielded success to Jinnah; and, though he may not yet have known this, he now stood at the pinnacle of his fame and success. Years of negotiations with the British and the Congress had given him a sense of invincibility and an arrogant contempt for opponents. He appears to have predicted the outcome of his finely-tuned efforts and carefully orchestrated demands— that is partition. So, for one reason or another, the partition bandwagon rolled on.

On 29 July 1946, Jinnah embarked on a policy of direct confrontation —the Direct Action Day resolution. The result was the spread of violence in Calcutta, followed by the tragedies of Noakhali and Tippera. Jinnah

---

[16] Aziz Ahmad, 'India and Pakistan', in P.M. Holt, Ann K.S. Lambton, and Bernard Lewis (eds), *The Cambridge History of Islam*, vol. 2A (Cambridge, 1970), p. 106.

had, after a series of manoeuvres, achieved the impossible—the polarization of Hindus and Muslims into opposite camps. E.J. Benthall, vice-president of the Bengal Chamber of Commerce, provided the big picture on the growing Hindu–Muslim animus, the heavy constraints on the leaders by the escalation of civil strife, and their inability to rein in the communal monster.[17]

In the autumn of 1947 Gandhi arrived in Calcutta and stayed in a tumbledown house on the outskirts of Calcutta, near the scene of one of the worst Hindu–Muslim riots. He soon realized that one of the principal causes of the rioting was people's poverty. Millions lived in slums of the worst description. Indeed creative writers, then and now, dwell on the suffering of the ordinary people, not those protected by wealth and power. After having hidden in a Hindu's house during the riots, a Muslim worker in Manik Bandopadhyay's *Khatian* (The Ledger) returns home. On the way he passes through the localities of the rich that stand undisturbed. 'We belong to the poor community,' he says to his friend, discerningly. Poverty is a greater identity marker than any religion. In other stories, class consciousness binds the poor together, making them disregard religious differences.[18]

To return to Benthall, he set off for a rendezvous with Gandhi, but encountered a riot on his way. 'Bombs were exploding and guns were being fired, and the streets were littered with glass and stones,' he wrote. When he reached the place Gandhi was staying, he found him sitting on a low wooden platform and spinning, wearing only a loincloth. A small girl sat on the platform near him, apparently learning to spin, or perhaps ministering to his needs.

Twenty minutes after the Gandhi–Benthall meeting, a mob broke into the house. They were furious because the Mahatma's influence had prevented them from organizing a general massacre of Muslims in Calcutta. They demanded that he should immediately withdraw his opposition and if he did not, they would kill him. The Mahatma did not stop spinning. One of the young men then aimed a blow at his head with a *lathi*. The little girl sitting beside him caught the blow on her arm. Gandhi continued spinning.

[17] Benthall Papers, Centre for South Asian Studies, Cambridge.
[18] Such as Achintya Kumar Sengupta's *Swakkhar* (Treaty) and Nabendu Ghosh's *Ulukhar* (Insignificance).

Nobody else in the crowd had the courage to strike the Mahatma again. They vented their fury on the building, pulling the window frames out of the walls, smashing the doors, and reducing the scanty furniture to matchwood. And yet, from the moment when the little girl saved the Mahatma's life, the rioting ceased and nothing of the sort occurred in Calcutta for a good many months.

From 1947 to 1950, Benthall, as representative of the Bengal Chamber of Commerce and the Associated Chambers of Commerce, had numerous meetings with Nehru, sometimes in company with others, and sometimes alone. He recalled being in Calcutta, soon after Independence, to end the rioting and massacres in Bengal. The Prime Minister sat at a desk which had on it a large inkpot, some pens and pencils, and the weighty volume of *Thacker's Indian Directory*.

A discussion took place about how best to combat the communal ill-feeling. It proceeded on sensible lines for some time, but after a bit some discussants made an impassioned plea for the Indian Army to go into East Pakistan to rescue the Hindus. Nehru listened for a short time, but then suddenly appeared to lose his temper. He picked up the *Directory*, raised it to the full length of his arms above his head, and brought it smashing down on the desk. He repeated this action three or four times, with greater and greater force. The ink-pot, pens, etc., scattered on to the floor. He accused them of deliberately planning a war and a massacre of Muslims. He continued with extraordinary eloquence until those demanding the Indian Army's entry into East Pakistan slunk out of the room, leaving the others to listen to the Prime Minister. Shortly after that the discussion returned to a minor key, and the meeting dispersed.

No Hindus were massacred in East Bengal at that time, though hundreds of thousands were driven out and had to take refuge in West Bengal. Nehru was of course right in refusing to send the army across the new frontier, and his violent reaction to such a suggestion was typical of the man.

The message from the pre- and post-1947 negotiations was simple enough for Uncle Hamid in Attia Hosain's *Sunlight on a Broken Column*:

Through the years he passively allowed himself to be battered by the speeches and statements that poured from the legion of leaders and propagandists of every party as they bargained with the British and each other, incited emotions and pleaded for peace, spoke for and to the people, unscathed while blood flowed and hatred spawned.[19]

THE HUMAN

Bam-o-dar khamushi ke bojh se chur,
Asmanon se ju-e-dard rawan,
Chand ka dukh-bhara fasana-e-nur
Shahrahon ki khak men ghaltan,
Khwabgahon men nim tariki,
Muzmahil lai rabab-e-hasti ki
Halke halke suron men nauha-kunan!

On gate and roof a crushing load of silence—
From heaven a flowing tide of desolation—
The moon's pale beams, whispered regrets, lying
In pools ebbing away on dusty highroads—
In the abodes of sleep a half formed darkness—
From Nature's harp a dying strain of music
On muted strings faintly, faintly lamenting.

The World Wars, the rise of fascism, concentration camps, and Hiroshima and Nagasaki found critical and emotional representation in art forms almost immediately. Likewise, cinema, painting, and theatre unravel the depth and scale of the human tragedy in August 1947. While historians nowadays lend meaning to the survivors of the 1947 holocaust by covering the enormity of violence, its shifting meanings and contours, and the continuous entanglement of 'event and interpretation',[20] creative writers and poets enhance their vividness by expressing moral outrage, revulsion towards violence, the fear of its recurrence, and the hope of its prevention.[21] Biographies, too, enhance the vividness of partition violence.

[19] Attia Hosain, *Sunlight on a Broken Column* (New Delhi, 1992), p. 283.

[20] Gyanendra Pandey, *Remembering Partition* (Cambridge, 2001); and *Routine Violence, Nations, Fragments, Histories* (New Delhi, 2006); see also Ian Talbot, *Freedom's Cry: The Popular Dimension in the Pakistan Movement and Partition Experiences in North-West India* (Karachi, 1996); Ahmad Salim (ed.), *Lahore 1947* (New Delhi, 2001).

[21] For Amrita Pritam, see Nonica Datta, 'Transcending Religious Identities: Amrita Pritam and Partition', in Satish Saberwal and Mushirul Hasan (eds), *Assertive Religious*

Ismat Chughtai drew themes from the lives of Urdu-speaking women for her short stories, sketches, essays, plays, novellas, and novels. She wrote on these themes with an authenticity that no male writer could have matched. By bringing into the ambit of Urdu fiction the hitherto forbidden terrain of female sexuality, she led her female contemporaries on a remarkable journey of self-awareness and undaunted self-expression. She made use of vapid or clichéd characters from the *zenana* or from the popular tales and fables to give them her own twist of meaning, wit, and penetration. In more ways than one, she changed the complexion of Urdu fiction.

Ismat Chughtai mirrors the joy and expectancy of an era and captures the mood of transition from the colonial era to freedom and partition. Although some of her stories often give an impression of deliberate indulgence and comic relaxation, she is poised, controlled, and almost magisterial in voicing anger and dismay at the spread of Hindu–Muslim violence. Violence and freedom is so muddled that she finds it difficult to distinguish between the two. Anyone who secured a measure of freedom discovered that violence came alongside. She proceeds to elaborate:

Most of the Progressive writers in Hindustan and Pakistan turned their attention to this issue and, helped by other progressive elements, began their work in earnest. The force of the pen thwarted the attacks of the knife and dagger. Although the reactionaries sided with the dagger and the knife, it was the progressive elements that finally won. This was a time when the value of life was equivalent to a fistful of sand. The helpless victims had been unleashed in the field; every demand was met by adding fuel to the blaze of communal violence. The organizers were standing with their back turned; the reformers of the nation were dozing somewhere out of sight. This was the moment when writers provided the ammunition in the form of plays, sketches, stories and poems, scattering them everywhere. [22]

This is the impression of a writer of the effect partition writing had on her generation.

'Here lies Saadat Hasan Manto. With him lie buried all the arts and mysteries of story writing. Under tons of earth he lies, wondering if he is

---

Identities: India and Europe (New Delhi, 2006), pp. 439–67; K.S. Duggal, *Abducted Not and Other Stories of Partition Holocaust* (New Delhi, 2007).

[22] Ismat Chughtai, in Ritu Menon (ed.), *No Woman's Land* (New Delhi, 2004), p. 44; Tahira Naqvi (ed.), *My Friend, My Enemy: Essays, Reminiscences, Portraits* (New Delhi, 2000).

a greater short story writer than God.'[23] This is not frivolity; this is what Manto, the enfant terrible of Urdu literature, wrote as his own epitaph on 18 August 1954, a year before his death at the age of forty-four. When party workers and their blind followers in the National Guards and the RSS, with savage and barbaric instincts, did their worst, Manto referred to 'the single minded dedication with which men had killed men, about the remorse felt by some of them, about the tears shed by murderers who could not understand why they still had some human feelings left'.[24]

Nobody can deny that his works have won a permanent place, and a significant one, in Urdu literature. As a writer his stock has risen remarkably in our own times. Villified in his own day as obscene and suspected of moral corruption, for which he was prosecuted in the early 1940s and for a second time in 1948, Manto was attacked by his detractors, of whom he has always had many, for sensationalizing a tragedy, desecrating the dead, and robbing them of their possession to build a collection.[25] The truth is that Manto's stories generate a measure of antagonism between him and his reader: a relation that might be likened to certain kinds of confrontations in the art world. The fact is that he asks questions that trouble every thoughtful reader, and are too often felt to have been either swept under the carpet or evasively answered. As he put it: 'I am not seditious. I do not want to stir up people's ideas and feelings. If I take off the blouse of culture and society, then it is naked. I do not try to put clothes back on, because that is not my job.'[26]

Manto managed to build out of all that—the moans and the cries of anguish—a powerful discourse which has filled even his severest critics with awe. That is because he touched hearts and minds. His worldview was not fundamentally different from that of his detractors, notably the progressives. Like them, his ideals sprang from his hopes and dreams of an equitable and just society. He too believed in a realistic depiction of social issues in literature: indeed, he insisted that the literati must 'present life as it is, not as it was, not as it will be, nor as it ought to be'.

[23] Saadat Hasan Manto, *Kingdom's End and Other Stories*. Translated from the Urdu by Khalid Hasan (New Delhi, 1989), p. 10.
[24] Alok Bhalla (ed.), *Stories about the Partition of India*, 3 vols. (New Delhi, 1994); see also Muhammad Umar Memon (ed.), *An Epic Unwritten: The Penguin Book of Partition Stories in Urdu* (New Delhi, 1998).
[25] Leslie Flemming, *Another Lonely Voice: The Life and Works of Saadat Hasan Manto*. Translated by Tahira Naqvi (Lahore, 1985), pp. 27–30.
[26] Ibid., p. 33.

Answering the various charges levelled against him, he argued that 'literature is not a sickness, but rather a response to sickness. It is also not a medicine. ... Literature is a measure of temperature, of its country, of its nation. It informs of its health and sickness'.[27]

Generally speaking, short stories focus on the individual protagonist from the ranks of the ordinary and portray the 'small' destinies of those cleft asunder by history's 'big' events. Their authors command sublime realms because they reconstitute life in its wholeness. Stories like 'Cold Meat' and 'Open it' and the aphoristic sketches in *Black Marginilia* (Black Margins) are intense representations of violence characterized by sheer vividness of observation. Manto as novelist, Manto as moral prophet, Manto as an atheist: these are the moving forces which impelled him towards the creation of the new prose style in *Black Marginilia*. This was the prose with which he satisfied his artistic conscience by speaking with his innermost voice and with the voices of all his known selves.

Tremors of his iconoclastic impatience can be felt in Manto's stories. They articulate the 'little' narratives against the grand; the unofficial histories against the official. What is peripheral to recorded history— the actual impact of official decisions on the everyday life of the people— is central to Manto's description. Mostly of a realist dispensation, he brings out the comic and earthy side of human beings as well as their aspirations. At the same time neither the essays nor the stories are simple transcripts of his personal experience. They are all creative artefacts, and, as one might expect, they mirror the perception of an age, its contradictions, travails, anxieties, and cares.

Acquitting Manto, the judge told him, 'If I had rejected your appeal, you would have gone around saying that you had been done in by a bearded Maulvi.'[28]

Other languages too engaged with the horror and deeply felt sorrow of partition. The circumstances are in each of the many cases related not only vividly, but with a subtle sense of distinctions. The train of thought is continued; in the final reckoning, the short story, the oldest genre in the world, holds a pre-eminent position by encapsulating individual fates. It holds its own against the unfolding of multiple histories in the novel; the short duration carries as much punch as the epic sweep of novelistic time.

[27] Ibid., p. 32.
[28] Manto, *Kingdom's End and Other Stories*, p. 8.

A recent collection of Bangla stories, translated into English, covers a wide time span, from pre-partition days to the present. It includes stories by eminent Bengali authors of the older generation as well as younger writers from both sides of the border.[29]

One of the stories in the collection tackles the theme of the ambiguity of notions of border/boundary and nation/homeland extremely well. Unlike standard textbooks that show coldly and irrevocably drawn borders and nations, the protagonists in Amar Mitra's 'Bana Hangshir Deshe' (Wild-Goose Country) see only fuzzy frontiers and emotional homelands. To the trader involved in selling and buying, legally or illegally, the border is, at best, a porous entity. Thus the shortage of Vicks balm on one side is met from the other side. If Vicks cannot be procured, perhaps Jhandu Balm will do.

The Urdu writer, Fikr Tausvi (1918–87), tackles the same theme dexterously in *Wagah ki Nehar* (Wagah Canal), 'the canal which watered the fields, both on the east and west (of the new border between India and Pakistan), would now be used to divide east and west.'[30] His naturally flowing humour knits together fun and frolic with sarcasm and exposure.

Inventing borders and boundaries did not always achieve the desirable result. Without being able to ascertain the numbers, it is fair to assume that a good many people would have found themselves, thanks to the Radcliffe Award and just after 'Sikka Badal Gaya', on a side of the border they had least expected to be. Bibhutibhushan Bandyopadhyay's 'Acharya Kripalani Colony' is, in fact, a humorous take on the politics of the dividing line. Land colonizers who promise ideal location on the banks of the river exploit the fear of relocation and displacement. The fact is that the actual location was different from the alluring advertisements for a plot of land.

The border that is 'just across' for the traders is the distance of the 'near abroad' for Mazarul in 'Bana Hangshir Deshe' who cannot understand why his uncles and aunts did not acknowledge letters from East Pakistan. Although on the threshold, he is unable to take the short step

[29] Bashabi Fraser (ed.), *Bengal Partition Stories, An Unclosed Chapter* (London, 2006). See also Basudeb Chakrabarty, *India Partition Fiction in English and in English Translation: A Text on Hindu–Muslim Relations* (Calcutta, 2007).

[30] Mushirul Hasan (ed.) *India Partitioned: The Other Face of Freedom* (New Delhi, 1997), vol. 1, pp. 248–9.

to crossing over to check out the reason. Those who see undefined frontiers take the white objects flying in the skies to be wild geese; those who see borders assume they are warplanes. While the border on land can be fenced off with barbed wire, how to enforce the border running through water? Again, let us turn to Manto's Toba Tek Singh:

As to where Pakistan was located, the inmates knew nothing. That was why both the mad and the partially mad were unable to decide whether they were now in India or in Pakistan. If they were in India where on earth was Pakistan? And if they were in Pakistan, then how come that until only the other day it was India ....

Those who had tried to solve this mystery had become utterly confused when told that Sialkot, which used to be in India, was now in Pakistan. It was anybody's guess what was going to happen to Lahore, which was currently in Pakistan, but could slide into India any moment. It was still possible that the entire subcontinent of India might become Pakistan. And who could say if both India and Pakistan might not entirely vanish from the map of the world one day? ...

Just before sunrise, Bisham Singh, the man who had stood on his legs for fifteen years, screamed and as officials from the two sides rushed towards him, he collapsed on the ground.

There, behind barbed wire, on one side, lay India and behind more barbed wire, on the other hand, lay Pakistan. In between, on a bit of earth, which had no name, lay Toba Tek Singh.[31]

So many other complexities in interpersonal relationships come to the fore through the medium of the short story. 'Oh, God, who can tell how many more Pakistans were created with the creation of that one Pakistan? It's such a mix up. Things have become more complicated,' writes Kamleshwar (1932–2007), one of the famed 'Nai Kahani' trio. *Kitne Pakistan* (How many Pakistans?), from which these lines are drawn, is typical of Kamleshwar's simple, yet incisive prose and his insight into the hidden layers of reality, which are then constructed in a disturbing manner. This is where literature scores over archival materials, in deciphering the unwritten codes and unfolding the unstated assumptions. Literature reveals the obvious and the hidden and, for this reason, takes us into the world of realism and imaginings.

As an example of the diversity of themes, some of which may not even figure in the imagination of the historian, consider the navy launch

[31] Manto, *Kingdom's End and Other Stories*, pp. 14, 18.

Pomfret getting parked in the middle of the river on sandy land and causing the protagonist to fret: What if it floats off when there is water into the 'other' territory, or gets lost in the Bay of Bengal? Luckily, Muslims who take advantage of the floods upstream, board it. Ready to start the engine as soon as it moved, they bring the launch back. 'One should not distrust a man just for his religious belief. Whatever you preserve today comes to your rescue later on,'[32] says the magistrate in the border district in the post-partition years. He had built up a relationship of trust with the Muslims of the area.

Consider, too, the internal stratification of communities during turbulent times, a theme that is the sociologist's delight. In Nabendu Ghosh's 'Traankarta' (The Saviour), the Bengali Hindu elite use the low-caste *doms* to protect them from Muslim assault. At the end of the story the narrator ironically states that Jhogru, the leader, died because people like him were born to save the likes of Mr Bose. The Pandavas would not have lived if the five Nishads (alluding to the Mahabharata where the five Pandavas saved themselves and their mother from the fire in a house built of lacquer in the forests) had not died in their place.[33]

Stories also remind us that it was not all milk and honey for individuals immigrating to Pakistan. Manto himself fared poorly, failing to secure a job for seven years in Lahore. Josh Malihabadi (1898–1982), the great Urdu poet, felt let down and, like Manto, died with his soul restless. His autobiography, *Yadon ki Baraat*, is a tale of woes. Recalling his experiences in Pakistan, he wrote: 'I looked like a pauper sitting on the stairs of Delhi's Juma Masjid flashing his teeth and begging for alms.'[34] Similarly, the divided families had a mixed experience. In *Sunlight on a Broken Column*, an incisive novel by the Lucknow-born Attia Hosain (1913–98), Waliuddin tries to straddle one fence too many and falls into obscurity as a lawyer in a small town in Pakistan.[35]

Others, however, negotiated the border profitably. In Imdadul Haq Milan's 'Sonadas Bauler Kathakata' (The Story of Sonadas Baul), Gaganbabu stayed back in East Pakistan and continued to trade in grain, while he sent his money to West Bengal and even built a three-storied

[32] Annada Shankar Ray's *'Angina Bidesh'* ('Alien Land'), in Fraser, *Bengal Partition Stories*, p. 283.

[33] Ibid., p. 145.

[34] Hasan, *India Partitioned*, vol. 2, p. 206.

[35] Hosain, *Sunlight on a Broken Column*, p. 294.

house for his wife and children. When the trader migrated to Kolkata in his old age, so that his son might light his pyre, the old homeless baul Sonadas, lost his place of shelter, for he had slept in Gaganbabu's ware-house for years. The rich cross over; the poor become homeless within their own nation.[36]

Sonadas was struck dumb for a few minutes. Quickly glancing at the storehouse he felt it had turned black like new moon night, yet it was full moon, the night was intoxicatingly drenched in moonlight. Sonadas forgot everything.

Gaganbabu said, 'Feel sorry for you, Sonadas. 'Ave spent m' life 'ere, do I want to go? But what to do? Am old. Can die any moment. If I die here, who'll light my funeral pyre? It's better to die near Golapan.'

After this neither Gaganbabu nor Sonadas uttered a word. The dimly lit lantern sat between the two.

Sonadas got up after some time.

'Where are you going?' said Gaganbabu.

'Coming ,' said Sonadas in a sad voice.

As he came out, Sonadas had a funny feeling deep within him. In this old age, should he weep? Shout and thump his forehead?

People would laugh to see him cry.

He lit a *bidi* and went towards the back of the bazaar.

There was a huge field. Beyond the field were wetlands for paddy extending across many miles. In the far distance were more fields and villages. The moon blossomed atop the village. The place was heady with the moonlight.

With weary steps, the miserable Sonadas walked on through the fields. Who knows where he went! In this whole wide world, there was no place for Sonadas.[37]

'A Man's Country' by Hasan Manzar is set against the background of the break-up of Pakistan in 1971, violence, and the cyclone in Bangladesh. These added to the misfortunes of Mobinurrohman's family. One day he was asked:

'What brings you to Karachi?'

'Coming to signing of a seep,' he finally responded.

'But you have your Bangladesh now, don't you?' I sputtered, as crudely and inappropriately as the Hindus and Sikhs in India, I hear, used to say to Muslims, 'You have your Pakistan now. Why don't you go there?'

[36] Fraser, *Bengal Partition Stories*, pp. 372–3.
[37] Ibid., pp. 371–3.

Almost vengefully I asked him, 'You didn't go to Bangladesh?'
He ignored the mercilessness of my tone and said, 'My Bangladesh right here.'
'What?' I asked.
He repeated his answer, as if explaining something to an ignoramus:
'My contree—this office, this work, right here.'[38]

TYRANNY OF LABELS

Ghizalaan tum to waqif ho, kaho Majnu ke marne ki
Deewana mar gaya, aakhir ko veerane pe kya guzri.[39]

O gazelle, you know, tell me how did Majnu die
What happened to the forest after the crazy man's death.

While blood flowed and hatred spawned, nobody kept count of the dead; G.D. Khosla (1901–96) estimates a death toll of half a million.[40] Nobody knows the size of the displaced and dispossessed population, except that, by early September, 1.25 million people had crossed from West Punjab into East Punjab and vice versa, while perhaps a million more were 'on the move'. Between 1946 and 1951, nearly nine million Hindus and Sikhs came to India, and about six million Muslims went to Pakistan. Of the nine million, five million came from what became West Pakistan, and four million from East Pakistan.[41] Between August and October 1947, civil war engulfed Punjab, the land of the five great rivers. In her heart-rending poem 'Aj Akhan Waris Sah Nun' (I say unto Waris Shah), addressed to the celebrated eighteenth-century poet Waris Shah, Amrita Pritam (1919–2006) implored the author of the immortal *Heer*:

Today a million daughters weep
But where is Waris Shah
To give voice to their woes?
Arise, O friend of the distressed!

[38] Hasan Manzar, *A Requiem for the Earth: Selected Stories* (Karachi, 1998), p. 69
[39] This is Ram Narain Mouzoon's one-couplet elegy to the defeat of Siraj-ud-daulah at the hands of the British.
[40] Gopal Das Khosla, *Stern Reckoning: A Survey of Events Leading up to and Following the Partition of India* (New Delhi, 1989).
[41] Iqbal A. Ansari, *Life after Partition: Migration, Community and Strife in Sind 1947–1962* (Karachi, 2002).

Corpses lie strewn in the pastures
And the Chenab has turned crimson.

By 1951 nearly 3,29,000 Muslims from Delhi had headed off to
Karachi. Hence the Muslim population dropped from 33.22 per cent in
1941 to 5.71 per cent a decade later. In Sind, on the other hand, Muslims
comprised around 90 per cent of the population, compared with only 2.9
per cent Hindus and 6.9 per cent Scheduled Castes. The Muslims in
effect rose by around 38 per cent while the strength of the non-Muslims
fell by close to 84 per cent of what it had been before 1947.[42]

Nearly 4.75 million refugees from the North West Frontier Province
and West Punjab came to Delhi. Ravinder Kaur narrates their story of
displacement, loss, resettlement, and restoration. Beside memories of
personal and inherited experiences,[43] she deals with the social background of the migration, government policies on resettlement, the
migrants' claiming a new place as their own, and the making of a Punjabi
Hindu identity. Step by step, she questions existing theories and
assumptions. Step by step, she takes her inquiry into uncharted territory.
Step by step, she opens up new vistas of research.

Most existing works limit themselves to, say, a decade after partition;
her book critically investigates the period between 1947 and 1965, the
year the Ministry of Relief and Rehabilitation merged into the Ministry
of Home Affairs as a department. Kaur covers the twin processes of
transformation that turn (a) ordinary people into refugees and (b)
refugees into citizens and then into locals. Earlier studies focused on
resettlement; her book goes a step further and brings alive the hardships
of the migrants, their everyday life, and their strategy to cope with a
harsh and unfriendly new world. Again, earlier works based their
conclusions on the experiences of upper caste/middle class narrators and
left out the lower class/untouchable migrants. Since 1947 draws on the
latter's experiences as a supplementary narrative to the mainstream story
of the Punjabi middle classes.

With the experience of migration and resettlement at multiple levels,
it is impossible to conceive of a single narrative that would represent

[42] Ibid., p. 75.
[43] Ravinder Kaur, Since 1947: Partition Narratives among Punjabi Migrants of Delhi
(New Delhi, 2007). On Bengal, see Joya Chatterji, 'Right or Charity? The Debate over
Relief and Rehabilitation in West Bengal', in Suvir Kaul (ed.), The Partition of Memory:
The Afterlife of the Division of India (New Delhi, 2001).

the partition reality. Thus the experience of those travelling by air (across the borders) was different from that of the foot travellers. And yet 'air travel has never been part of the national narrative of partition, in which the birth of the nation is linked with traumatic territorial dismemberment and loss, followed later by rejuvenation attained through clear political vision'. It is Khushwant Singh's *Train to Pakistan* (1954) or Krishan Chandar's *Peshawar Express* that fits the national narrative on the struggle, sacrifice, and the indomitable spirit of the refugees.

Of Kaur's many insights, one is that the master narrative is told by the Punjabi elites, though their own experiences differ from the general experiences they narrate; second, women and poor refugee men do not author their own history, because 'they exist only as a mass of refugees' whose individual plight are condensed as collective experiences that are essential to the larger narration of the epic partition drama; third, 'untouchables' are excluded, because of the assiduously cultivated myth of the upper caste, middle class Punjabis emerging as heroic survivors battling all odds to successfully reconstruct their lives. 'The purity of this myth cannot be polluted by opening it to the experiences of untouchables,' Kaur concludes.

Even though there is sufficient evidence of the autonomy of literary representation in articulating the range of imaginative experiences,[44] memories of violence and uprooting colour the 'remembered' (and re-remembered) trauma. Even without a commemorative memorial for the survivors, they live in everyday forms among the migrants. As Karl K. Duetsch points out, memories are essential, although they are not directly observable. Some can be observed by analysing literature, mass-media transmissions, and other sources.[45]

This brings us to violence against women. Sentimentality about the bloody maniacs of 1947–8 apart, there is nothing incomplete, arbitrary, or untenable in the poignant descriptions of the women survivors. They bore the brunt of violence, uprooting, and relocation in more ways than one. Of the many stories in Bangla that bring out the trauma of gendered suffering, two are remarkable for the representation of their triumph.

Mahashweta Devi's 'Ram Rahimer Katha' (Of Ram and Rahim) has two mothers who have lost their sons to the rioting. They realize that

[44] Sukrita Paul Kumar, *Narrating Partition: Texts, Interpretations, Ideas* (Delhi, 2004).
[45] 'Communication Theory and Political Integration', in P.E. Jacob and J.V. Toscano, *The Integration of Political Communities* (Philadelphia, 1964), p. 64.

they are together in grief and find a way of looking ahead, bridging the Hindu–Muslim divide.[46] In 'Bharatatbarsha' (India), Sayyed Mustafa Siraj tells the tale of an old, irreverent woman, who is quick to reply to the fun the men in a tea stall make of her. She walks up to a banyan tree and settles comfortably into a hole in its roots. When she is discovered later, she appears to be dead. Men of both communities fight over her last rites, claiming that she belonged to 'them'. But then she is suddenly 'resurrected' and walks away, telling the people they did not recognize her for what she is. She could be a ghost; she could be the subcontinent.

Whatever she is, the image of the old, withered woman is a haunting one, for she transgresses all the spaces, boundaries, and identities that could be imposed on her. She rises again, not to destroy, or wreak revenge, but to go her way. She is an indomitable spirit beyond all violation and can, on the contrary, instil fear in the hearts of men who have not learnt their lessons from violence and hatred.

'Buri, are you Hindu or Muslim,' she is asked by people from both the groups.

'Have you had your eyes plucked out, you rascals?' she says to them. 'Can't you see? You devils of hell, you vulture-eyes! Can't you see for yourself what I am? Run! Get out of my sight or I'll have your eyes plucked out!'

Having said this she began to hobble away unsteadily along the road. The mob made way for her. She moved further away and gradually faded into the soft glow of the golden sunset.[47]

In Imdadul Haq Milan's 'Meyertir Kono Dosh Chhilona Na' (The Girl Was Innocent), love is constrained in the ethics of the feudal village community and does not enjoy the sanctity of privacy. It is Kusum, the daughter of a poor artisan, who bears the double burden of being a woman and a poor Muslim. The boy, a Hindu, is better off and can buy his release from the Imam when caught meeting the girl. Kusum, unable to pay the fine, suffers a hundred lashes in front of her people. She commits suicide, even as the Hindu boy waits for her by the river.

God's earth looks strangely romantic at that moment. The moon is exactly in the centre of the sky. Silver moonlight is flooding all sides. The leaves and their shadows dangle in the desolate night wind. Somewhere far away, the cry of a lone night bird

---

[46] Fraser, *Bengal Partition Stories*, pp. 375–88.
[47] Ibid., p. 296.

can be heard. The bird's cry is wafted close by the wind, then swept far away. The music of nocturnal insects was soothing the warm earth. This generous beauty of nature is marred somewhat by Kusum's tears. Tears flood Kusum's cheeks, they flood her heart. Standing in the courtyard, she was looking at the heavens; she is looking at the moon. Then she has upturned the bottle of insecticide over her mouth. That liquid fire flows down burning Kusum's breast. In a split second it makes her vision hazy. Slowly, gently, Kusum collapses on the courtyard floor. Her nose-stud shines brilliantly in the moonlight. In her dazed, hazy vision, Kusum can still see, a strangely beautiful river flowing on. Almost darkening the river shore stands a lone tree. Under the tree, with the pain of waiting in his breast, sits a daring lover. He does not follow any laws, he does not believe in any religion.[48]

In the recent gendered narratives, women are sometimes represented as 'theatrical', both as victimized yet empowered. Aunt Saira in *Sunlight on a Broken Column* 'refused to see dust and decay; they created a twilight that did not pick out cobwebs'.[49] Although examples of women gaining independence, identity, and control over their lives are not scarce, they and the poor refugee men, in general, seldom tell their story.

The women appear in Partition accounts chiefly as victims of violence, abductions, and forcible conversions, while the poor men appear in the vast background of the Partition drama as part of the crowd, fleeing on train tops or in foot columns. They never appear as individuals in their own right. Their individual experiences are condensed as collective experiences that are essential to the larger narration of the Partition drama. Thus, poor men and women exist only as a mass of refugees who on the one hand constitute integral ingredients of the Partition migration, and on the other, serve as a background against which individual experiences of middle class migrants are narrated.[50]

Let me, however, conclude this section by a discussion of a novel written by a woman, this time in English and from across the border. In this quasi-autobiographical first and only novel, Mumtaz Shah Nawaz (1912–48), or 'Tazi', traces her own 'conversion' to the idea of a separate homeland for the Muslims through the lives of two sisters, Zohra and Sughra Jamaluddin—one an ardent Congress supporter and the other an equally enthusiastic League worker in Punjab. By the end of the novel

[48] Ibid., p. 517.
[49] Hosain, *Sunlight on a Broken Column*, p. 275.
[50] Kaur, *Since 1947*, p. 254.

a change is wrought in Zohra's heart through a process of slow churning that started sometime in the 1930s.

There were many speeches, poems and songs, and it was almost dusk before they (the people) began their journey back to Amritsar. She was very silent, for her mind had been to the full that day.
'A new land—Pakistan!' said the Leaguers.
'A new world!' cried the workers ....
And she thought of Iqbal's words:
'Change alone hath stability.'
Her eyes were thoughtful and he smiled and let her think.[51]

The Heart Divided focuses on the years 1930 to 1942, 'weaving the many dimensions of those turbulent years and the painful ambivalence of those who live through them.' While the first draft had been completed in March 1948, the novel appeared several years after the author's death in a plane crash. 'Those who know Mumtaz', recounted her brother, 'have often wondered how she would have reacted to the "iron curtain" which had grown up by then between India and Pakistan. It was not what she had envisaged in the closing chapters of *The Heart Divided*.'[52] Unlike the family's loyalist, Mumtaz Shah Nawaz corresponded with Nehru, wrote socialist poetry during the years 1939–42, attended Congress sessions, and linked up with socialist groups. But her disillusionment began with the Quit India movement and she took to organizing Muslim women in Delhi and Punjab under the League's aegis.

What happened to the heady days of 1919 when the Hindus and the Muslims had united to fight the British? What caused Mumtaz Shah Nawaz's disenchantment with the Congress? What of the Muslim renaissance spelt out in Iqbal's soul-stirring verses? In turn, why did the Congress baulk at separate electorates, calling them anti-national and narrow-minded? Why did it do nothing to allay the Muslim fear that the freedom the Congress promised meant freedom for Hindus alone, not freedom for all? Seen from the *Muslim* point of view, 'nationalism' increasingly began to mean thinking and living in the 'Hindu Congress' way and none other. Those living or thinking another way became anti-Indian. Mumtaz Shah Nawaz traces the gradual shift from the early

[51] Hasan, *India Partitioned*, vol. 2, p. 26.
[52] Ibid., pp. 13–26.

Muslim demands for safeguards, for checks and balances, then reserved seats and separate electorates, to finally the intractable demand: a separate homeland, the land of the pure, Pakistan.

What would have been the state of the subcontinent today had the League and the Congress reached a compromise? Was the cleavage of hearts and land inevitable or could it have been averted? In the end, there is the poignancy of what might have been: 'Had they tried to keep us with love perhaps we would not want to break away.' Both sides allowed the rift to become a chasm and the chasm a sea of blood and tears. Both sides are 'guilty'.[53]

Yes indeed. This makes partition 'a complex and convoluted human tragedy which raised many questions and doubts'.[54] One of them is, of course, 'a deeply ambiguous, transitional position between empire and nationhood'; the other is the protracted, unruly end of empire that destabilized life for millions; and the third and last theme is the collusion of leading political parties with the killers and their actions.[55] However much one may try to come to terms with the 'reality', these questions will continue to haunt the people in the subcontinent.

THE HEARTBROKEN GENERATION

Ahmed Ali and Attia Hosain portray change, decay, and the uncertainties of their age with great effect. They reveal a rare sensitivity to the changes in Awadh, to the imminent decline of the feudal order therein, and the confusion and insecurities of those trying to cope with the transition around them.

Hundreds of thousands of families were faced with the necessity of changing habits of mind and living conditioned by centuries, hundreds and thousands of landowners and the hangers-on who had lived on the largesse, their weaknesses and their follies. Faced by prospects of poverty, by the actual loss of privilege, there were many that lost their balance of mind when their world cracked apart. Others retired to anonymity in their villages.... This was the end my uncle had prophesied. This was the end our

---

[53] Personal Communication to Rakhshanda Jalil.

[54] Intizar Husain, *The Seventh Door and Other Stories*. Edited and with an Introduction by Muhammad Umar Memon (London, 1998), p.14.

[55] Yasmin Khan, *The Great Partition: The Making of India and Pakistan* (New Delhi, 2007), pp. 206–7.

theories and enthusiasm had supported. Like death and all dissolution it was an end easier to accept with the mind than as a fact.[56]

The concluding lines from Ahmed Ali's novel *Twilight in Delhi* picture a world undergoing a change, nay fast disappearing: 'And night came striding fast, bringing silence in its train, and covered up the empires of the world in its blanket of darkness and gloom'.[57] Ali delicately and sensitively summarizes the moods of a city wherein, wrote Mir Taqi Mir, 'dwelt the chosen spirits of the age'. He depicts 'the decay of a whole culture, a particular mode of thought and living, now dead and, gone already right before our eyes'. Yet he would have preferred living and dying in Delhi. But his Indian identity was snatched away from him and he languished in Karachi,[58] alien, remote, and distant for a *Dehalvi*.

Attia Hosain, a consummate stylist, sums up a range of human emotions in a sentence or two. Her prose is exquisite, delicate, and charming. It is, in the words of Anita Desai, the literary equivalent of the miniature school of painting in India, introduced by the Mughals. Her novel and collection of stories 'are delicate and tender, like new grass, and they stir with life and the play of sunlight and rain. To read them is as if one had parted a curtain, or opened a door, and strayed into the past'.[59] *Sunlight on a Broken Column* is mostly about a feudal society trying to come to terms with the uncertainties and insecurities ushered in by the World War. There is tension in the air as Uncle Hamid tells his son Saleem:

No one seemed to talk anymore, everyone argued, and not in the graceful tradition of our city where conversation was treated as a fine art, words were loved as mediums of expression, and verbal battles were enjoyed as much as any delicate, scintillating, sparkling display of pyrotechnic skill. It was as if someone had sneaked in live ammunition among the fireworks. In the thrust and parry there was a desire to inflict wounds. Even visitors argued. A new type of person now frequented the house. Fanatic, bearded men and young zealots.[60]

Attia Hosain was deeply familiar with the social and cultural milieu her novel is set in. She came from a *taluqdari* family of Awadh and was

---

[56] Hosain, *Sunlight on a Broken Column*, p. 277.
[57] Ahmed Ali, *Twilight in Delhi* (London, 1940), p. 318.
[58] William Dalrymple, *City of Djinns: A Year in Delhi* (Delhi, 1993), p. 65.
[59] Anita Desai, 'Introduction', in Hosain, *Sunlight on a Broken Column*, p. vi.
[60] Hosain, *Sunlight on a Broken Column*, p. 230.

privileged to study at La Martiniere School for Girls and the Isabela Thoburn College in Lucknow. She was the first woman graduate from any *taluqdari* family. And yet her feudal background did not deter her from taking part in left-wing activities and attending the first Progressive Writers' Conference and the All-India Women's Conference in Calcutta in 1933. She moved to London in 1947.

Events during and after Partition are to this day very painful to me. And now, in my old age, the strength of my roots is very strong; it also causes pain, because it makes one a 'stranger' everywhere in the deeper areas of one's mind and spirit *except where one was born and brought up.*[61]

Ahmed Ali and Attia Hosain were brought up differently and in completely different environments, and yet they had much in common. Both were attached to liberal and composite values, the hallmark of Delhi's and Lucknow's social and cultural ambience. Both were wedded to a humanistic world-view, free of bigotry, intolerance, and sectarianism. Both were uneasy with and anguished by partition; indeed, they belonged to a generation that had lived with its heart shattered. And both ended living and dying in countries that were not theirs. If they had exchanged letters, they would probably have written the following to each other:

> *Rahi nagufta mere dil me daastan meri*
> *na is dayar me samjha koi zabaan meri*
> —Mir Taqi Mir

> How could I tell my tale in this strange land?
> I speak a tongue they do not understand.

THE HEALING TOUCH

Jamia had no role in the production of narratives on partition, but its response to the accompanying tragedy was an unequivocal call for Hindu–Muslim cooperation to combat what Zakir Husain blasted as the enemies of life, of joy, and of the light of day. The opportunity came on an auspicious occasion—the belated celebration of Jamia's Silver Jubilee from 15 to 18 November 1946. Zakir Husain himself was increasingly busy

[61] Desai, 'Introduction', in ibid., p. ix.

with the preparations, for the inaugural ceremony was going to be the greatest symbolic production ever mounted by Jamia's public relations. A large tent of huge dimensions, known as Dal Badal, was borrowed from the princely state of Rampur, and Qudsia Zaidi (1912–60), a lady of immense charm and wife of B.H. Zaidi (1898–1992), the future Vice-Chancellor of the Aligarh Muslim University, took charge of the arrangements.

With his usual vision, imagination, breadth of mind, and high courage bordering on audacity, Zakir Husain used the occassion to bring together the Congress and League leaders on a common platform. Sitting beneath it were some of the country's prominent leaders from both sides of the Great Divide. Prominent amongst them were Jinnah and his devoted sister Fatima, Nehru, Azad, Liaquat Ali Khan (1895–1951), who became Pakistan's first Prime Minister, the nawabs of Bhopal and Rampur, K.A. Hamied (1898–1972), then a prosperous businessman, (Sir) Abdul Qadir (1874–1950) from Punjab, Abdul Haq, Urdu's linguist-scholar, and Syed Sulaiman Nadwi (1884–1953), the theologian of Nadwat-al ulama. Gandhi, who was engaged in Noakhali's riot-torn areas, sent a message: 'The goodness of a good man is itself his true jubilee. Dr. Zakir Husain's great work itself is his true greatness.' He had, however, paid a surprise visit to Jamia in the midst of his crowded time in March 1946, and had a quiet meeting with students and teachers. Pyarelal describes the visit:

One of the students asked what they could do to bring about Hindu–Muslim unity. The way was, Gandhiji replied, that even if all the Hindus turned rowdies and abused them, they should not cease to regard them as their blood-brothers and vice versa. 'If one return decency for decency, it is a bargain. Even thieves and dacoits do that. … Humanity disdains the calculation of profit and loss. … If all the Hindus listened to my advice, or in the alternative the Muslims listened to me, there would be peace in India which nothing would be able to shatter. The mischief-maker will weary of the sorry business of stabbing, when there is no retaliation or counter provocation. An Unseen Power will arrest his uplifted arm and it will refuse to obey his wicked will. … God is good and does not allow wickedness to proceed beyond a certain length.[62]

Before leaving the campus, Gandhi stood by the tomb of Ansari, Jamia's founder-benefactor. Pyarelal describes the pilgrimage:

[62] Pyarelal, *Mahatma Gandhi: The Last Phase* (Ahmdedabad, 1956), vol. 1, Book One, pp. 175–6.

The doctor had been like a brother to Gandhiji. During his twenty-one days' self-purification fast at Poona in 1933 when Gandhiji's condition suddenly became critical, Gandhiji sent him a message at Delhi that he would love nothing better than to die in his lap. Back came the good doctor's reply; he would not let him die either in his or anyone else's lap! And interrupting his visit to Europe, he hastened to the bedside of his friend to see him safely through the fast. A platform thrown up into a series of terraces marked the burial place. A plain marble tablet at the foot bore the doctor's name and the dates of his birth and death. The austere simplicity of the monument added to the poignancy of the visit. The visit symbolized Gandhiji's undying faith in the ultimate inevitability of Hindu–Muslim unity.[63]

Gandhi acknowledged Zakir Husain as 'the spiritual successor' to Ansari, and, in 1938, sought his views and advice on the Hindu–Muslim riots in Bombay, and the Hindi–Urdu controversy in Bihar and Madras. He wrote to him on 24 May:

The question I wanted to ask was and I still want to ask is, will you be to me what the Doctor was on the Hindu–Muslim question? What distracts me is not the absence of the warmth of a gentleman-friend, of a God-believing and God-fearing doctor. It is the absence of an unfailing guide in the matter of Hindu–Muslim unity. My silence at the present time of this question is not a sign of my apathy, it is a sign of an ever-deepening conviction that the unity has got to come. Then I ask, will you take Dr. A [nsari]'s place? In answer, do not think of your status in society. If you have self-confidence, you must say 'yes.' If you have not, you must say 'No.' I shall not misunderstand you. I know and love you too well to misunderstand you.

Zakir Husain responded with his usual warmth. To his response, Gandhi wrote the following on 8/9 July.

Your frank, generous and full acceptance of my proposal relieves me of tremendous anxiety. It is like fire buckets which you always give [keep?] full up to the brim though you may never have to use them. They provide the assurance that if there is a fire, those buckets will enable you to put it out promptly. Dr. Ansari eminently served that purpose. You have now become that for me. I did not need to utilize that special function of his very often. I may not have to trouble you so frequently as to take a lot of your time. But the fact that you are always available for reference at critical moments is a great consolation.

[63] Ibid., p. 175.

Returning to the 1946 celebrations, Zakir Husain's immense task was to be a peacemaker, a role he played with remarkable dexterity. He made an earnest request to those present in the following words:

You are all stars of the political firmament; there is love and respect for you not only in thousands but in millions of hearts. I wish to take advantage of your presence here to convey to you with the deepest sorrow the sentiments of those engaged in educational work. The fire of mutual hatred which is ablaze in this country makes our work of laying out and tending gardens appear as sheer madness. This fire is scorching the earth, in which nobility and humanity are bred, how can the flowers of virtuous and balanced personalities be made to grow on it? How can we provide adornment for the moral nature of man when the level of conduct is lower than that of beasts? How shall we save culture when barbarism holds sway everywhere, how shall we train man for its service? How shall we safeguard human values in a world of wild beasts? These words might appear harsh to you, but the harshest words would be too mild to describe the conditions that prevail around us. We are obliged by the demands of our own vocation to cultivate reverence for children; how shall I tell you of the anguish we suffer when we hear that in this upsurge of bestiality even innocent children are not spared? For God's sake, put your heads together and extinguish this fire. ... For God's sake do not allow the very foundations of civilized life in this country to be destroyed as they are being destroyed now.

Zakir Husain brought together the most eminent Congress and League leaders on the same platform, and obtained from both, Mujeeb recalled proudly, an 'acknowledgement of the value of religious, cultural and political aims to which it was committed'. At the same time, he conceded that Jinnah's presence was 'due more to the tact and persuasive power of Dr. Zakir Husain than to any change in the attitude of the League'. Zakir Husain was, as Mujeeb recalled on the occasion of Jamia's Fifty Years of Celebrations on 30 October 1970, 'an example of the organic assimilation of spiritual, cultural and political values'.

Years before, writing of the Great War, Iqbal had said: 'That is not the rosy dawn of a new age on the horizon of the West, but a torrent of blood.' The same might have been written in 1947. In Jamia itself, the sound of the mob was indistinct and seemed to come from far away as the buzz of a swarm of bees. Mobs had gathered close to Jamia, but Mujeeb quickly got the authorities on the phone and demanded that they take control of them. On 8 September 1947, Gandhi came to the campus to inspire confidence: General Cariappa, the Commander-in-Chief, the

Prime Minister, and the Health Minister followed his visit. The Madras Regiment was posted around the campus. 'We could see the city burning,' recalled Abdul Sattar, then a Jamia student.

Our ration depleted gradually, and from two chappatis we were reduced to one! The villagers around Jamia helped as much as they could, and we got some wheat from the stores of Masih Garh Church, thanks to Mr. Kellat. Conditions deteriorated day by day. There was a rumour that an organized group could come to attack us any time. The government was powerless, and the administration on the point of collapse. Zakir Sahib, even at that time, took the whole Okhla village under his wings. The people from the village would come to Jamia at night, and we, the students would stand guard throughout the night, till they went back in the morning.

Alighting on a Punjab Railway platform in Jalandhar on 21 August 1947, Zakir Husain would almost certainly have been killed by the mob if a railway official had not recognized him and locked him up in a room. 'From then,' he used to say, 'I have been living on borrowed time.' Jamia's property in Karol Bagh was either looted or destroyed. The Maktaba Jamia was set ablaze. Shafiqur Rahman Kidwai (1901–53), Head of Idara-e Taleem-o-Taraqqi, ran for his life and escaped miraculously. The police were, for all intents and purposes, helpless. Religious leaders did not calm people down; they seemed to have precisely the opposite effect.

Jamia's *biradari*, retaining the impress of the ideal, the old inspiration and enthusiasm, did its best to restore peace. Akhtar Hameed Khan, who had joined Jamia only recently looked after the Jamia Nagar camp. A.J. Kellat, a teacher, procured some licensed guns. He commanded the volunteers and supervised night patrolling. Chowdhary Mohammad Ali took charge of the information control room. He dispelled rumours and gathered correct and authentic information. For this, he and his comrades would leave for the camp at Humayun's Tomb in the morning and return just before sunset. Begum Anis Kidwai (1906–82) found such volunteers to be the most efficient. Zakir Husain, who organized a public meeting at Bara Hindu Rao on 10 January 1948 to promote fraternal feelings amongst the old town residents, told the volunteers:

Those among you who are working at the Humayun's Tomb are doing very valuable work. If you are able to save Humayun's Tomb, you will be able to save Delhi and if you have saved Delhi, you will be able to save India. Keep this thought with you always, and you shall be able to increase your ability to work ten fold.

Likewise, he exhorted Jamia's women in the following rousing words:

This is not the time for tears; this is the time for action. You must share the burden with the men. Winter is about to set in. Think of those who are living out under the open skies. You must try to reduce your own needs. Try to give as many of your quilts, pillows and blankets as you can to those living in the camps. Darn and mend your old clothes, make them fit for use and give to those at the Humayun's Tomb camp. Strengthen your hearts. Do the best you possibly can in these circumstances and leave the rest to God.

Others talk of those days spent in volunteer work in the camps, of performing the grim task of counting the dead when smallpox and typhoid broke out among the inmates. Going deep into the innards of the tomb, into the many passages and hidden chambers, they had to look for the dead and dying among the huddled refugees. Some took to educating wandering children: 'We adopted them as our own and conveyed the message of friendship and affection through them to their homes,' recalled Mujeeb, years later, on the occasion of Jamia's Golden Jubilee Celebrations in 1970. For this, Shafiqur Rahman Kidwai and Zakir Husain started five centres in the old city. Nehru, the Prime Minister, desired refugee education to be handed over lock, stock, and barrel to the Nai Talim Association in Wardha and Jamia. From March 1948, fifty refugees in groups, men and women, were trained as teachers. Mujeeb claimed that 'we were able to heal their wounds and to give them enough of solace and encouragement to change their perspective on life'.

THE HISTORIAN'S AGENDA

Historians have, in recent years, expressed their dissatisfaction with the old ways of scholarship.[64] At the same time, very little 'new' has emerged so far so as to make us cast all our textbooks onto the death heap and learn anew the partition history. As for Pakistan, most writers continue to cling to the two-nation theory despite the creation of Bangladesh and the ethnic strife that has acquired such violent proportions in recent years. Do these facts reveal that the Pakistan movement itself, a multifaceted process, was riven with contradictions, or do they reflect on the inherent flaws in Pakistan's nationbuilding process? Or is there

[64] In the works of Gyanendra Pandey; Kaul, *The Partition of Memory*, pp. 2–3.

merit in Maulana Azad's assertion that religious affinity could not unite areas which were different from each other?[65]

The campaign for a Muslim homeland itself has been interpreted in a variety of ways: as the struggle for *azadi* for democratic rights, of Muslim awakening against resurgent Hindu revivalism, of Muslim nationalism against Hinduism, of minority rights against the tyranny of the majority. To some it was a noble battle over political and religious ideals; to others, it was an ugly scramble after material gains. The fact is that during most of the twentieth century, the Congress and the League, the two parties cast in adversarial role, had been classless; for the struggle between classes, as in rural Bengal, Punjab, and Sind, was only one of the many polarities criss-crossing the political scene. It is therefore more realistic to talk in terms of 'interests' than classes, some vertical, some horizontal: the clash of landowner/moneylender and tenant, land and business, small manufacturer and large manufacturer, and town and country. Party politics, factional goals, and personal ambitions were very much in evidence in the list of issues that influenced the Boundary Commission in shaping the border.[66] By dint of skilful organization and intense moral indignation, some of these 'interests' managed to make their cause seem like the nation's or the community's.

Social scientists have begun to question some of the certitudes about post-independence states and societies in South Asia.[67] Aziz Ahmad had talked of the 'conservative religious lower middle class' and the anxieties of the Western-educated intelligentsia regarding 'the dangerous growth of religious fanaticism'.[68] Hamza Alavi, by contrast, describes the all-powerful military-bureaucratic oligarchy mediating between the competing demands of the three propertied classes—the indigenous bourgeoisie, the neocolonial metropolitan bourgeoisie, and the landowning classes. In playing this role the military-bureaucratic oligarchy represented the relative autonomy of the post-colonial state of Pakistan.[69]

[65] Kaul, *The Partition of Memory*.

[66] Joya Chatterji, 'The Making of a Borderline: The Radcliffe Award for Bengal', in Ian Talbot and Gurharpal Singh (eds), *Region and Partition: Bengal, Punjab and the Partition of the Subcontinent* (New Delhi, 1999), p. 191.

[67] Tariq Rahman, *Denizens of Alien Worlds: A Study of Education, Inequality and Polarization in Pakistan* (Karachi, 2004); Pervez Hoodbhoy, 'Jinnah and the Islamic State: Setting the Record Straight', *Economic and Political Weekly*, 11 August 2007, p. 3300.

[68] Ahmad, 'India and Pakistan', p. 112.

[69] Hamza Alavi, 'The State in Postcolonial Societies: Pakistan and Bangladesh', in

Ayesha Jalal reminds us about the structural and ideational features of colonialism in the post-colonial era, though her attempt to discover the common strands of authoritarianism in the political experiences of India and Pakistan is, to say the least, off the mark.[70] As India probably gets ready to give its million voters yet another chance to elect a government, Pakistan appears to be in total disarray under a military dictatorship. More and more we see weak institutions debilitated further by stresses arising out of political exigencies, the incompatibility of Islam and democracy, and what Farzana Shaikh calls the contradictions between the Islamic notions of community and the recently instituted idea of electoral competition.

Ayesha Jalal states that her countrymen have the 'state' if not quite the 'nation' of their collective imaginings. She exposes the hollowness of civil society, the weakness of state institutions, and the ideological contradictions. Having accomplished Pakistan on such a basis, the newly created state denied democratic rights and basic rights of citizenship to the Bengalis in its eastern wing (now Bangladesh), the *muhajirs* in Sindh, and the Baluchis and Pathans in the North-West Frontier Province.[71] Ironically, language as marker of national identity became one of the main issues of contention between East and West Pakistan soon after Pakistan was constituted. 'Phire Dekha' (Looking Back), a Bangla story by Selina Hossain, shows the ruthlessness of Pakistan's rulers in dealing with the Bengali Language Movement in 1952.

She looked to her right. Last night a *poster* had been pasted on the trunk of a big mango tree. 'We want a nation for the Bengali language.' She felt that there was no other scene around her, only the abstract artwork of the *poster* on the wider *canvas* of time. It was not possible to write it in any other colour apart from that of blood.[72]

Ayesha Jalal rightly argues that exclusive nationalism cannot be a substitute for nationalism based on equal citizenship rights, the nation

---

Kathleen Gough and Hari P. Sharma (eds), *Imperialism and Revolution in South Asia* (New York, 1973), pp. 159-61.

[70] Ayesha Jalal, *Democracy and Authoritarianism in South Asia: A Comparative and Historical Perspective* (Cambridge, 1995), pp. 249-50.

[71] Ayesha Jalal, 'Ideology and the Struggle for Democratic Institutions', in Victoria Schofeld (ed.), *Old Roads New Highways* (Karachi, 1997), pp. 135, 136.

[72] Fraser, *Bengal Partition Stories*, pp. 398-9.

state's main claim to legitimacy. She points to the inherited colonial structures that were not realigned with the dominant conceptions that had fired the Muslim struggle for equality, solidarity and freedom, and bemoans Iqbal's lofty equation of Islam and civil society being lost sight of in the confusion surrounding conceptions of national identity and state sovereignty. One should add that Iqbal's identification of Islam with civil society was itself riddled with contradictions; equally, his philosophical legacy was ignored, partly because his politics-mongering followers misunderstood and misused his ideas.[73] Lately, Mohammad Waseem, the political scientist, has talked of 'the Islamic idiom' as 'a function of the perennial crisis of civil-military relations'.[74]

Existing secondary literature points to the possibilities of charting new territories and breaking free of the boundaries defined hitherto by partition historiography. In this context, it is worth our while to reintroduce some of questions which were raised a while ago by Kenneth Cragg, a scholar of Comparative Religions. Was separate nationhood mandatory in those areas where population majorities made it feasible? Or could, and should, Islam see its authentic destiny as participating with Hindus and others in a free and united subcontinent? And ought the issue to be decided in terms only of social equity and justice? Should Muslims follow the logic for independent statehood which divided them by a political frontier and rescued some only by excluding others, in exclusion highly prejudicial to their future?[75]

These issues are still not settled. In the concluding chapter, I will discuss how Azad and Husain Ahmad Madani and their followers addressed them.[76] Meanwhile, the search for more answers and explanations has gone on. Some have given up midway; others are more persistent. But most may end up echoing the views of George Abell (1904–89), private secretary to the last two Viceroys, who told David

---

[73] Fazlur Rahman, *Islam* (London, 1966), p. 226.

[74] Mohammad Waseem, 'Functioning of Democracy in Pakistan', in Zoya Hasan (ed.), *Democracy in Muslim Societies: The Asian Experience* (New Delhi, 2007), p. 214.

[75] Kenneth Cragg, *The Pen and the Faith: Eight Modern Muslim Writers and the Quran* (New Delhi, 1988).

[76] For Madani, see Barbara Daly Metcalf, 'Observant Muslims, Secular Indians: The Political Vision of Maulana Husain Ahmad Madani, 1938–57', in Dipesh Chakrabarty, Rochona Majumdar, and Andrew Sartori (eds), *From the Colonial to the Postcolonial* (New Delhi, 2007).

Page: 'I was in India for twenty years and I didn't manage to get to the bottom of it (the communal problem) and you certainly won't in three.'[77]

The foregoing discussion suggests that partition cannot be attributed to a consistent and inevitable conflict between irreconcilable forces. Page after page, there is testimony that the communal conflagration did not indicate a complete and irreversible divide. Page after page stands witness to hate artificially created, suspicion artificially fuelled. In 'The New Regime' (originally 'Sikka Badal Gaya') by Krishna Sobti (b. 1925), one of the earlier stories on the transformation that partition wrought, the peasant Shera half decided to kill the wife of the Hindu zamindar, who had always been like a mother to him, because of the temptation to please a political conspirator named Firoz. In other stories, the killers came from outside, although the village joined them later.[78] Who then was responsible? 'From what I understand,' said Amrik Singh of Doberan village, after suffering unspeakable horrors, 'partition is all politics'.[79]

The Pakistan movement has to be analysed in terms of group interests, and the swiftness with which the idea concretized and the intensity of emotions involved had more to do with material interests than with a profound urge to create an Islamic/Muslim state. Hence so few could divide so many in so short a time. Hasan Manzar, the Urdu writer from Hapur in UP, canvassed for the League among burqa-clad women. But, like many others,[80] he had no idea of Pakistan becoming his destination. He recalls his arrival well:

There, under the shade of peepal trees in the school yard, we chanted Hindi hain ham vatan hai sara jahan hamara. (We are Indians; the entire world is ours.) Later, after I'd migrated to Pakistan, I asked my schoolmates, 'what did you chant on 14 August?' I'd guessed right: they had chanted 'Muslim hain ham vatan hai sara jahan hamara' ('We are Muslims; the entire world is ours'). He served two warring powers equally well. Anyway, we'd become Pakistanis overnight, but somehow it was hard to get rid of the feeling of being strangers in this new country of ours.[81]

[77] David Page, quoted in Introduction to the paperback edition, The Partition Omnibus (New Delhi, 2002), p. vi.

[78] Hasan, India Partitioned, vol. 2, p. 32.

[79] Ibid., p. 133.

[80] See Mushirul Hasan, 'Memories of a Fragmented Nation: Rewriting the Histories of Partition', in Mushirul Hasan (ed.), Inventing Boundaries: Gender, Politics and the Partition of India (New Delhi, 2000).

[81] Manzar, A Requiem for the Earth, p. xxxiii.

The 'Partition Plan' of 2 June 1947 was devised with haste and with utmost cynicism. It ignored, among other things, the feelings and interests of the millions who had not even heard of a Hindu *rashtra* or a *dar al-Islam*.[82] Moreover, nobody tried to stop the bandwagon from rolling on. Even the left groups did not put up a people's front in their areas of influence to counter the votaries of a divided India. The socialists, though in theory opposed to partition, decided to swim with the current.[83] Leaders of other large and small political formations fixed their sights on the transfer of power and bought their way through a policy of conciliation and concession. Kamaladevi Chattopadhyaya (1903–90), founder member of the All-India Women's Conference, remarked: 'Secularism was one of the concepts we wanted to wear more as a jewel on our chest … rather than practise as an article of faith. We flaunted it rather than practise it.'[84]

A distressed Prime Minister told the Parliament on 10 April 1950:

All the ideals I had stood for since fate and circmstance pushed me into public affairs appeared to fade away and a sense of utter nakesness came to me. Was it for this that we had laboured through the years? Was it for this that we had the high privelege of discipleship of the Father of the Nation? [85]

In describing the horror stories and the countless tales of woes, to which Nehru alluded, there is always danger of repetition, more trains to India or Pakistan full of bodies, more hacked limbs. At the same time, there is, in these tales of despair, a redeeming repetition of hope and optimism. According to Amrik Singh, the Muslims from Doberan village in Rawalpindi district neither wanted to send the non-Muslims away nor kill them. Murder was brought to the village by outsiders.[86] In the North West Frontier Province, the Red Shirts saved the lives of thousands of Hindus. Major Khushdeva Singh, a medical doctor, loved Muslims as much as he loved his own kith and kin.[87] Many like him rose above the

[82] Ibid., p. 48.

[83] Hari Dev Sharma (ed.), *Selected Works of Acharya Narendra Deva* (New Delhi, 1998), vol. 2, p. 181.

[84] Kamaladevi Chattopadhyay, *Inner Recesses Outer Spaces: Memoirs* (New Delhi, 1986), p. 306.

[85] Iyengar, *The Oxford India Nehru*, pp. 359–60.

[86] Hasan, *India Partitioned*, vol. 2, p. 124.

[87] Ibid., p. 87.

macabre and sinister politics to espouse principles of humaneness and compassion and help others at the risk of their own lives. Shorish Kashmiri (b. 1917), a prominent Ahrari and a journalist of repute, saved a Hindu girl: 'As I handed her over, the sadness in her ... eyes deepened. She looked at me from their depths. It seemed she doubted my being a Muslim and thought that, had I been a real Muslim, I too would have had a taste of her.'[88]

By the summer of 1947, ten million people were in flight. By the time the monsoon broke, almost a million were dead: 'Death spared (them) the putrescent culmination, the violent orgasm of love that followed the independence.'[89] Almost all of northern India was in arms, in terror, or in hiding; the only remaining oases of peace were a few scattered little villages in the remote reaches of the frontier. Mani Majra was one such village. Here the Sikhs and Muslims lived amicably.[90] Here and elsewhere people found the strength to move beyond the diktats of the times and their own groups to help each other and to create small enclaves of humanity and sanity in the surrounding bloodshed. Encouraged by such examples, Khosla, who saw Punjab aflame, ends his story on a reconciliatory note:

Perhaps, there are some who will take warning from this sad chapter in our history and endeavour to guard against a repetition of these events. So long as sectarianism and narrow provincialism are allowed to poison the minds of the people, so long as there are ambitious men with corruption inside them, seeking power and position, so long will the people continue to be deluded and misled, as the Muslim masses were deluded and misled by the League leaders and so long will discord and disruption continue to threaten our peace and integrity.[91]

Many other stories conjure up sparks of humaneness in dark times. Whether it is the boatman Yasin, who responded to a woman passenger's cry for help and gave up his own chance of happiness to take her safely across ('Boatman', Prafulla Roy), a woman finding refuge with a Muslim shopkeeper during a riot, both equally nervous about the other's presence ('Loss', Gour Kishore Ghosh), or a Muslim, redefining the meaning of 'infidel' ('Infidel', Atin Bandyopadhyay). Other tales are sombre in tone.

[88] Ibid., p. 147.
[89] Hosain, *Sunlight on a Broken Column*, p. 283.
[90] Khushwant Singh, *Train to Pakistan* (New Delhi, 2007 reprint),
[91] Khosla, *Stern Reckoning*, p. 299.

In Dibyendu Palit's 'Hindu', Mathuranath wants to secure medical aid for a dying person on the road. His humanitarian impulse withers away when he discovers the dying man to be a Muslim. Everyone is, in fact, eager to wash his hands off the corpse.

Lastly, two histories of nationalism might be written. One is the history of its beginning, development, and culmination in freedom. The other is the history of trial and error resulting in partition. Initially the Congress invoked national unity and secularism to contest the two-nation theory. Soon, however, it conceded the ground to Jinnah. Even though V.N. Datta, Azad's biographer, details some 'pivotal situations' which had the possibility of resolving the communal impasse, nobody knows why the change occurred. Not even Gandhi. Not even Azad. If so, historians should discuss more closely than they have done so far whether these opportunities were missed by the Congress in dealing with the communal imbroglio.[92]

Whatever might be the outcome of the discussion, one agrees with Azad that 'the new State of Pakistan is a fact', and that India and Pakistan should be on friendly terms with each other. It is therefore time to build anew and stop, in the words of poet-filmmaker Gulzar, 'this constant scratching of the wounds'.[93] We cannot say today which reading is correct. Let history decide whether our leaders acted wisely and correctly in accepting partition.[94] Meanwhile, we must inculcate a respect for the past and the curiosity to make sense of it in countries like India and Pakistan where denial of the past and the urge to change it have enjoyed validity.[95]

[92] V.N. Datta, *Maulana Azad* (Delhi, 1990), p. 220.

[93] *Hindu* (Friday Review), 7 September 2007, p. 1.

[94] Abul Kalam Azad, *India Wins Freedom: An Autobiographical Narrative* (Bombay, 1959) p. 227.

[95] Krishna Kumar, *Prejudice and Pride: School Histories of the Freedom Struggle in India and Pakistan* (New Delhi, 2004).

8

The Choices and the Roads Taken

A Muslim meant someone with a beard. The word also conjured up
an unclean appearance, uncouth behaviour, lack of education and
culture .... In their routine existence, most Hindus had very little to
do in Muslim localities ... except passing through them in a tram or a
bus. For them, it was an alien part of the city, segregated in their psyche
like the prostitute's area.

— Vijay Tendulkar, quoted in Rowena Robinson,
Tremors of Violence, p. 233

There's a despair emanating from Muslim pockets. I feel no matter
which government came into power and whatever the colour of its
ideology, the mindset of the majority remained unchanged. I feel the
communal biases have been institutionalized. Even if you are a leader
who's an embodiment of secularism the instruments you see to bring
about your goals have become contaminated by communal biases.

— Mahesh Bhatt, in *The Times of India*, 29 August 2007, p. 22

The 1990s saw the rise of a new force in Indian politics—the Bharatiya
Janata Party (BJP), the successor of the Jana Sangh. Even though Girilal
Jain exonerated the BJP from the charge of being communal on the
ostensible grounds that 'Hindus have never been, and are not, a
community in the accepted sense of the term',[1] its followers have shown

[1] Girilal Jain, *The Hindu Phenomenon* (Delhi, 1994), p. 149.

great belligerence towards religious minorities. They have not only fouled politics but also undermined the legitimacy of the police, the bureaucracy, and the judiciary.[2]

The notion of the aggressive and alien anti-national Muslim is deeply embedded in RSS (Rashtriya Swyamsevak Sangh) ideological doctrine through Savarkar's evocation of the Muslim as the 'threatening Other', and also by orientalist stereotyping of a threatening Islam.[3] Thus, on the eve of the Assembly elections in Uttar Pradesh (UP) in April 2007, the BJP's officially-released CDs graphically detailed the slaughter of a cow at the hands of Muslim butchers, and warned of Muslims 'breeding like dogs' and of Muslim youth duping Hindu girls. One CD shows scenes of a woman grieving for her abducted daughter.[4] At other places, the video montage of invasion and battles shows an effort to create a new history for India by using fragments of the past and arranging them into the 'mocked order' of the new audiovisual media.

'After all,' observed a newspaper editorial, 'the BJP has got away, time and again, with inciting communal passions. ... The time has come to close the gap between precept and practice by enforcing the electoral and criminal law against the nth time offenders in UP.'[5] The BJP stood a poor third in the elections, but this brings no comfort to the beleaguered Muslims living in India's most populous state. They wait anxiously, as they have done from the time of the Ayodhya episode and the anti-Muslim pogroms in Gujarat, for the bridging of the yawning gap between theory and practice.

The *Tehelka* report in November 2007 is, in fact, a pointer to this danger faced by Muslims, for it showed how violence against them was planned by influential men in politics, police, and the bureaucracy. 'After this,' writes a social activist, 'middle class, upper-caste Gujarat can no longer the refuge in the long-cherished myth of its own non-violence. Because we planned, killed, raped, slit open wounds and celebrated own masculinity'.

The long course of misfortunes, of cruel vicissitudes, and of the ignominy of being suspected of extra-territorial loyalties is well

---

[2] Iqbal A. Ansari, 'Course of the Law on Riots and Terror', *Economic and Political Weekly*, 1 September 2007, pp. 3527–31.

[3] Christiane Brosius, *Empowering Visions: The Politics of Representation of Hindu Nationalism* (London, 2005), p. 127.

[4] *Indian Express*, 5 April 2007, p. 1; *Hindu*, 6 April 2007, p. 12.

[5] *Hindu*, 7 April 2007, p. 10.

documented. With 'many a Congressman [being] a communalist under his national cloak',[6] a remark Jawaharlal Nehru made in 1936 in his autobiography but which applied to free India as well, efforts to draw the Muslims generally into the nation-building schemes yielded few results. 'We have also,' he wrote to his chief ministers, 'communalism not only in the minority but very much so in the majority. The chief difference is that in the majority it puts on the garb of nationalism and democracy.'[7] Except for some well-established Muslim families in UP and Bihar, the Muslim 'middle classes' declined in mega cities like Bombay and Calcutta, in trading and business centres, and in Lucknow, Bhopal, and Hyderabad, once centres of Muslim power. In Lucknow, Naipaul found 'the cramped, shut-in, stultifying life of the Muslim ghetto of the old town.'[8] Palaces and great houses wore signs of neglect. Shops and surgeries, brothels, and law courts lost their best customers.[9] Lawyers lost their briefs owing to the virtual ban on Urdu. The UP government eliminated most Muslims from the police force, reducing their numbers from approximately half to less than 5 per cent.[10] Their share in other branches of government fell gradually, a fear anticipated in the legislative council on 29 May 1947, months before independence, but denied by the Congress Chief Minister.[11] This was the end some people had prophesied. This was the end their theories had supported: 'Death and all dissolution it was an end easier to accept with the mind than as a fact.'[12] There was rubble and dust in Lucknow and Bhopal, as in Delhi and Hyderabad.

The displacement of an estimated 12.5 million people (about 3 per cent of undivided India) meant that educational institutions were depleted of students and teachers, and traditional Muslim centres lost a major segment of their professional classes.[13] The ambivalence towards

---

[6] Jawaharlal Nehru, *An Autobiography* (London, 1936), p. 136.

[7] Uma Iyengar (ed.), *The Oxford India Nehru* (New Delhi, 2007), p. 440.

[8] V.S. Naipaul, *India: A Million Mutinies* (New Delhi, 1990), p. 354.

[9] Attia Hosain, *Sunlight on a Broken Column* (New Delhi, 1992), p. 277.

[10] Paul R. Brass, *Theft of an Idol: Text and Context in the Representation of Collective Violence* (Princeton, NJ, 1997), p. 288.

[11] B.R. Nanda (ed.), *Selected Works of Govind Ballabh Pant*, vol. 11 (New Delhi, 1998).

[12] Hosain, *Sunlight on a Broken Column*, p. 277.

[13] Mushirul Hasan, *Legacy of a Divided Nation: India's Muslims since Independence*

'secular' education and its implied possibilities and dangers persisted in certain sections that stayed on in India.

The Muslim position in south India centred round Hyderabad for nearly 700 years. But 'Police Action' on 17 September 1948 brought to an end the life of the Asaf Jahi dynasty, as that of all the other 561 princes. The new Muslim elite, having been created by Osmania University, mostly went to Pakistan. The reshuffling of the state administration resulted in Muslims losing their near monopoly of government jobs.[14] When Hyderabad got trifurcated, Muslims of the Marathwada region joined the Bombay state, where they counted for little compared to Bombay's elite Muslims. The Muslims of the Karnataka region had to compete with the Muslim elite in Bangalore. The strength of the Muslim population diminished in Hyderabad; elsewhere in Andhra Pradesh, they became marginal.[15]

An era came to an end for the princely states in 1947: 'It was the end of old wealth, old customs and a glittering and protected way of life,' writes Princess Mehrunissa of Rampur, a princely state almost 1000 square miles in area and surrounded by the British-ruled territories of UP.[16] Its demise was inevitable despite the charge that the Congress violated the terms of power agreement with the British. Bhopal, founded in the nineteenth century and ruled by four remarkable women for over a century—Qudsiya Begum (1819–37), Sikander Begum (1843–68), Shah Jahan Begum (1868–1901), and Sultan Jahan Begum (1901–26)—merged into the Indian Union; its ruler died in forlorn obscurity.

The Congress government saw it all happen—the exclusion of Muslims from public services and the blatant discrimination against them in

---

(New Delhi, 1997), p. 289; Imtiaz Ahmad, 'Muslim Educational Backwardness—An Inferential Analysis', *Economic and Political Weekly*, vol. 16, 1981, p. 1461; N.C. Saxena, 'Public Employment and Educational Backwardness among Muslims in India', *Political Science Review*, vol. 22, no. 2, pp. 119–61; Abusaleh Shariff, 'Socio-Economic and Demographic Differentials between Hindus and Muslims in India', *Economic and Political Weekly*, 18 November 1995, pp. 2947–53, And, more recently, Sagarika Ghose, 'Minority Report', *Indian Express*, 13 July 2003, for the portrayal of a 'tense, anxious and depressed Muslim community'.

[14] John Zubrzycki, *The Last Nizam* (London, 2006), pp. 197–8; Margrit Pernau, *The Passing of Patrimonialism: Politics and Political Culture in Hyderabad 1911–1948* (New Delhi, 2000), pp. 336–7.

[15] B.P.R. Vitthal, 'Muslims of Hyderabad', *Economic and Political Weekly*, 13 July 2002.

[16] Mehrunissa, Princess of Rampur, *An Extraordinary Life* (Delhi, 2000), p. 76.

virtually every walk of life. Nehru, the first Prime Minister, made hesitant
conciliatory gestures. 'It is all very well to say that we shall not pay any
attention to communal like considerations in appointments,' he wrote
to his chief ministers, 'but ... we have to realize that in a vast and mixed
country like India we must produce a sense of balance and of assurance
of a square deal and future prospects in all parts of the country and in
all communities of India.'[17] But nobody listened to his admonitions. His
daughter responded to the mounting pressure on her to improve the
economic and educational condition of Muslims by appointing the Gopal
Singh Committee. At that time, Indira Gandhi had said: 'From my earliest
childhood I have been committed to the secular ideal. The India of our
dreams can survive only if Muslims and other minorities can live in
absolute safety and confidence.'[18] The fact is that, in June 1983, the
Gopal Singh Committee found that the Muslims were 'the hewers of
wood and drawers of water'.[19] Whether because of historical circumstance
or official neglect and discrimination, they were disproportionately
located towards the lower end of the socio-economic hierarchy.[20]

Since 1983, stories of poverty and deprivation have been confirmed.[21]
Recently, in November 2007, the Sachar Committee found 'deficits and
deprivation in practically all dimensions of development'. It pronounced
that 'the relevant facts are that Muslims are among the most deprived
of India's social groups and communities and their social, occupational
and economic profile is appalling. Marginalization, discrimination,

[17] 2 September 1953, Iyengar, *The Oxford India Nehru*, p. 398.

[18] *Muslim India*, June 1983, p. 249.

[19] In order to empower the minorities and to accelerate socio-economic change and
development, the Congress government in New Delhi constituted a panel on 10 May
1980. It submitted its interim report on 31 January 1981. The second report, drafted by
Gopal Singh, appeared on 14 June 1983. He found that a large majority of Muslims lived
in rural areas mostly as landless labourers, small and marginal farmers, artisans, craftsmen,
and shopkeepers. He found that more than half of the urban Muslim population—
approximately 35 million out of nearly 76 million—lived below the poverty line. The rest
was self-employed. He also discovered that fewer urban Muslims worked for a regular
wage or salary than did the members of other religious groups. He underlined, furthermore,
the limited access of Muslims to government-sponsored welfare projects and their small
share in private/ public employment.

[20] See 'Symposium on Sachar Committee Report', *Economic and Political Weekly*, 10–
16 March 2007.

[21] Rowena Robinson, *Tremors of Violence: Muslim Survivors of Ethnic Strife in Western
India* (New Delhi, 2005), pp. 83–105.

violence and social exclusion have further depressed Muslim aspirations and pushed down levels of achievement'.[22] Existing trends do not augur well for the future. Schooling and educational patterns suggest that Muslim children, especially in UP, India's most populous state, are unlikely to overcome the established processes of social and economic exclusion that perpetuate inequalities through generations. In the face of consumerism and with problematic access to employment, they are likely to be increasingly disaffected as they see the prizes of modernity and money eluding them.[23] Matters have come to a virtual standstill because the UP government has failed to provide minimally adequate schooling for them. As a result, in Bijnor district, to the east of the River Ganga, *madarsa* is a cheap alternative to school education.[24] This pattern in replicated in Bihar, Madhya Pradesh, and Rajasthan.

In Lucknow, poor and lower middle class Muslim parents resist sending children to schools, and various bold initiatives, such as the founding of the Unity College, have not been able to overcome the resistance. Even well-to-do Muslims who have prospered in the Gulf countries prefer traditional education to government and private schools. The picture is particularly grim in the Shia localities. Even though poverty and illiteracy are rampant, there is no evidence to suggest that the Shia organizations are grappling with these issues.

In the country as a whole, the proportion of illiterate Muslim women is high, 85 per cent in rural north India. Fewer than 17 per cent ever complete eight years of schooling and fewer than 10 per cent complete studies up to higher secondary level. This is far below the national average. Up the 'education ladder', there is a significant drop in the presence of Muslim women—3.56 per cent actually make it to the higher education tier. This is even below the figure for the Scheduled Castes.[25]

[22] Quoted in Rowena Robinson, 'Indian Muslims: The Varied Dimensions of Marginality', *Economic and Political Weekly*, 10–16 March 2007, p. 842. See also Tahir Mahmood (ed.), *Politics of Minority Educational Institutions* (New Delhi, 2007).

[23] Patricia Jeffery, Roger Jeffery, and Craig Jeffrey, 'Investing in the Future: Education in the Social and Cultural Reproduction of Muslims in UP', in Mushirul Hasan (ed.), *Living with Secularism: The Destiny of India's Muslims* (New Delhi, 2007), p. 84. See also, Omar Khalidi, *Muslims in Indian Economy* (New Delhi, 2006).

[24] Patricia Jeffery, Roger Jeffery, and Craig Jeffrey, 'The Mother's Lap and the Civlizing Mission: Madrasa Education and Rural Muslim Girls in Western Uttar Pradesh', in Zoya Hasan and Ritu Menon (eds), *In a Minority: Essays on Muslim Women in India* (New Delhi, 2005), pp. 108–48.

[25] *Frontline* (Chennai), 17 January 2003, p. 88.

Urbanization, which has a generally positive association with education, has not greatly impacted educational attainments of Muslim women.[26]

Poor and lower middle class parents still prefer the nearby madarsa, especially for the girl child. The bold among them withdraw their ward by the time she turns 15 or 16.[27] Their constraints are: first, attending a *mohalla* school means leaving the house daily; lower middle class parents resent this form of 'exposure' for a girl having reached marriageable age. Second, although it is possible to send girls to single-sex schools up to university level, there are not many single-sex universities or classes, which will not mix the sexes after puberty. Third, girl education is scarcely encouraged at the expense of household tasks. Lastly, girls are educated (if at all) not for employment but for marriage, and even the minimum schooling for them can lead to, so parents fear, the desired marriage not being contracted.[28] Invariably, brides, as among the Sheikhs in Qaziwala (in Bijnor district), have less schooling than their husbands, or at most an equal amount.

The picture from other areas is equally disturbing. In Delhi, the educational programme itself discourages Muslims from taking advantage of the opportunity in equal measure with non-Muslims. Muslims complain that books are in short supply, Urdu-medium schools are ill-equipped, and religious education poorly imparted.[29] The picture is the same in UP. Urdu having been downgraded to an optional language available only in select secondary schools, Muslim leaders, publicists, and theologians, though subscribing to a variety of ideological perspectives, have been criticizing the government for making it harder for them to learn Urdu, Arabic, and theology. Urdu-medium schools are either too few—one of the reasons why parents send their children to a madarsa—or not efficiently run. Whether empirically true or not, there are fewer schools in areas with a large population of relatively underprivileged Muslims and most Urdu-speakers do not have the choice of learning their mother

---

[26] *Indian Express*, 19 December 2002.

[27] E.S. Mann, *Boundaries and Identities: Muslims, Work and Status in Aligarh* (Delhi, 1992), and Chandralekha Lehri, *Socio-Demographic Profile of Muslims: Study of Bhopal City* (Jaipur, 1977).

[28] Jeffrey, Jeffrey, and Jeffrey, 'The Mother's Lap', pp. 183, 186.

[29] Ibid.; and David Lelyveld, 'The Fate of Hindustani: Colonial Language and the Project of a National Language', in Carol A. Breckenridge and Peter van der Veer (eds), *Orientalism and the Postcolonial Predicament: Perspectives on South Asia* (Philadelphia, 1993).

tongue or being educated through their mother tongue even at primary level. It is hard to tell whether this is by design or the result of the government's apathy; perhaps both factors act in tandem.

Urdu's eclipse has dried up a major source of livelihood in the police, judiciary, and the professions. But a greater source of worry is not just making both ends meet but the very survival of 'Muslim identity'. To recall some of the bare facts, Zakir Husain, Vice-Chancellor of Jamia Millia Islamia until 1948, had stated that 'Indian Muslims ... would not accept the complete loss of their cultural identity. They would like to be good Muslims as well as good Indians'.[30] Begum Anis Kidwai heard the alarm bells ringing during the first official Independence Day celebrations:

At that moment India was going back to the past, with people donning *tilaks* on their foreheads. And I wondered why they had sent for Brahmins. Why were they looking for a *Qazi* (reciter of the Qur'an)? What will *bhikshus* do in Government House? I felt suffocated. Lost in these thoughts I reached Government House. Momentarily I experienced a sense of pride. The national flag flew on the stately entrance which provided free passage to the common folk. Now, everything here was ours and our comrades in the national struggle lived in it. But soon my heart sank again. A language was being spoken there which was stranger to us than English, a language in the words of Josh Malihabadi:

> Jis ko dewom ke siva koi samajh na sake
> Zayr mashq hai woh andaze bayan ay saqi.

> What cannot be understood except by giants,
> Saqi, that is the current style of expression.

The *chowkis* on the right side of the dais were adorned with Buddhist priests. Many languages were spoken. English, Sanskrit, Arabic, chaste Hindi. But not a word in our precious language [Urdu], each expression of which 'sends a hundred flowers in bloom'.[31]

Mujeeb expressed similar anxieties:

I remember my own reaction when I visited Uttar Pradesh Assemby. It was, I believe the inaugural session. There were crowds of people in the visitors' galleries and the

[30] Quoted in Annemarie Schimmel, *Islam in the Indian Subcontinent* (Leiden, 1980), p. 223.

[31] Mushirul Hasan (ed.), *India Partitioned: The Other Face of Freedom* (New Delhi, 1997), vol. 2, p. 162.

hall, but hardly a face that was known to me. I was simple-minded enough to ask a
man standing next to me where the chief minister was, and I got in reply a reproachful
look and the remark, 'Can't you see he is sitting there?' I felt extremely uncomfortable.
I could not spot anyone dressed like me, the language spoken around was not the
Urdu which I thought was the language of Lucknow, the cultural metropolis of Uttar
Pradesh, and there seemed to be no one within sight worth talking to. I left the
assembly building with a feeling of mingled panic and disgust.[32]

Controversies deepened, chiefly in north India, between the votaries
of Hindi and those asserting their right to read and write in Urdu. The
contest had, in fact, begun in the 1860s: it gathered momentum under
the aegis of the Hindu revitalization movements.[33] In the Constituent
Assembly which came into existence in December 1946—a few months
before partition—the Hindi protagonists, also the torchbearers of Hindu
revivalism, depicted Urdu as a Muslim language, identified it with the
Pakistan demand, and insisted that there should be no legitimate
occasion to concede anything to a language that had functioned as a
symbol of secession. After Independence too a brute majority usurped
the right of Muslims to read and write in Urdu by stigmatizing the
language for its 'foreign' origin.

The UP Official Language Act 1951, and the wrangling in the Assembly
indicated which way the wind was blowing. Under Zakir Husain's leadership,
over ten thousand signatures were collected from Lucknow alone, but
nothing much happened either in Delhi or Lucknow to promote the
teaching of Urdu or accord it official status.[34] 'It is strange,' the poet Sardar
Jafri stated on 5 June 1998 in the presence of Atal Bihari Vajpayee, then
Prime Minister, 'that even after 50 years of independence both Ghalib
and Urdu are homeless. Urdu became a victim of communal politics.'[35]
Today, Urdu's fate is probably sealed forever. It survives lazily either in
government-sponsored institutes and academies or amongst the Punjabi
migrants from Punjab who congregate at Delhi's India International

[32] Mohammad Mujeeb, *The Indian Muslims* (London, 1967), pp. 410–11.
[33] Francis Robinson, *Separatism among Indian Muslims: The Politics of the United
Provinces' Muslims 1860–1923* (Cambridge, 1974), pp. 69–78.
[34] Jyotirindra Das Gupta, *Language Conflict and National Development: Group Politics
and National Language Policy in India* (Berkeley, 1970), pp. 127–50; Paul Brass, *Religion,
Language, and Politics in Northern India* (Cambridge, 1974), Chapter 4.
[35] Squadron Leader Anil Sehgal (ed.), *Ali Sardar Jafri: The Youth Boatman of Joy* (New
Delhi, 2001), p. 209.

Centre where they are regaled by *ghazals* or the resounding voice of Nusrat Fateh Ali Khan singing *Ali da pehla number*.

While Urdu's future is inextricably linked with employment—government and private—one must still ask why the Muslims lag behind, why the powers-that-be do not act on the principle of inclusion, and how one can mitigate the effects of those factors that make so many of them poorer and more backward than other Indians. Perhaps one can move state and society to devise a redress mechanism based on the minority rights the Constitution guarantees. The principle is simple enough: all citizens deserve to enter public spaces on equal terms and conditions. Democracy, Nehru reminded his chief ministers, meant rule by the majority, but it meant something more, that is full play and opportunity for the minorities.[36] Malini Parthasarathy, former editor of *Hindu*, echoed the same view a few years ago:

It is time that those Indians who pride themselves on being part of the global community yet have bought unquestioningly the notion that the minorities are responsible for some imagined economic deprivation, ask some hard questions. By driving the minorities to the margins of a civil society of which they are equal inheritors and thereby polarizing Indian society, rendering it more vulnerable to bitter internal conflicts, how can the dream of a modernizing India becoming part of a wider global community sharing a vision of faster economic growth and greater prosperity really materialize?[37]

To Nehru, secularism conveyed the idea of social and political equality.[38] Inclusive democracy means acknowledging social differentiations and divisions and encouraging differently situated groups to voice their needs, interests, and aspirations. This protection ensures equal respect for each and every citizen, a value at risk in any organization that is run by majority votes. Hence, even after partition and its terrible consequences, the founding fathers of the Constitution recognized the intrinsic connections between democracy, multiculturalism, and the obligation to protect minority rights. Articles 28, 29, and 30 protect and provide safeguards to *religious* minorities. Article 29 states: 'Protection of interests of minorities—(1) Any section of the citizens residing in the

[36] Iyengar, *The Oxford India Nehru*, p. 440.

[37] *Hindu*, 17 February 2003.

[38] Circular to the Pradesh Congress Committee, 5 August 1954, in Iyengar, *The Oxford India Nehru*, p. 66.

territory of India or any part thereof having a distinct language, script or culture of its own shall have the right to conserve the same.'[39] Consequently, the Constitution tried to ensure that no community is excluded or disadvantaged and, for this reason, provided autonomy to each religious community to pursue its own life.[40] Articles 14 [4] and 16 [4] too call for special treatment of historically disadvantaged groups in order to integrate them into the 'mainstream'.

The man in the street doubts the sincerity of those who constantly assure him that he is already in the Kingdom of Heaven. Religious minorities, in particular, do not expect miracles to transform their lives. But they do expect democratic institutions to be manageable for their interests so that they would find democracy worth defending. Regardless of whether the RSS–BJP decides that the Indian boat is full or overloaded, they expect the government to address their needs and interests, and ensure that the merchants of death are not let loose on them. 'Commissions and reports, sad to say, can never be a substitute for political will; political will that often refuses to rise above electoral calculations, and is guided by coalition calculations.'[41]

At the end of the day, a majoritarian democracy is no democracy at all, maintained Justice M.N. Venkatachaliah. It is only a participatory, representative, and inclusive democracy that can take a pluralistic society further and make it conflict-free.[42] Whether or not this goal is realizable will ultimately depend on how the minority citizens can share power and privilege and, at the same time, safeguard the religious and cultural interests enshrined in the Constitution. Nehru had exhorted in September 1950:

People should learn the great lesson that the inscriptions on Asoka's pillars teach that a man respecting the religion and culture of others increases the value of one's own. If the religion or culture of others is run down, to that extent the value of one's religion and culture is lowered.[43]

[39] For details see Arun Kumar, *Cultural and Educational Rights of the Minorities under Indian Constitution* (New Delhi, 1985).

[40] Gurpreet Mahajan, *Identities and Rights: Aspects of Liberal Democracy in India* (Delhi, 1988), p. 4.

[41] M.A. Kalam, 'Conditioned Lives', *Economic and Political Weekly*, 10 March 2007, p. 843.

[42] *Hindu*, 10 November 2001.

[43] Speech delivered on 22 September 1950, S. Gopal (ed.), *Selected Works of Jawaharlal Nehru*, second series, vol. 15, part 1, p. 81.

After Independence, Maulana Azad questioned the standard definition of a minority, as applied to Muslims, arguing that 'their heads are held so high' that it made no sense to look upon them as a minority deserving special concessions. Despite his short-term projections and the promise of long-term economic benefits accruing to the minorities in their new home in India, Azad's argument is too abstract to carry much persuasive force. Today, Muslims regard themselves, for right or wrong reasons, as a religious minority and, accordingly, demand rights and safeguards. This self-perception is unlikely to change. In other words, an executive fiat or a judicial judgement cannot take away the recognition, as a religious minority, by the colonial government and the Indian Constitution. Existing governments will, in turn, have to attend to the arduous and frustrating task of integrating their less fortunate citizens fully and not half-heartedly into the nation-building project. Despite the faith some repose in coalition governments and their compulsions to seek minority support,[44] heavy material investment and a change of heart will be required to bridge the gulf between 'Us' and 'Them'.

Social stratification and economic differentiation notwithstanding, Muslims are entitled to an equitable share of basic public resources. Entitlements include access to education even if it means departing from such norms of equity as merit and indifference to ascriptive religious characteristics. Today it is an open-ended question whether one takes the route of affirmative action or 'reservation', a practice prevalent in Kerala, Karnataka, and Andhra Pradesh. The debate goes on as more and more groups, including Dalit Muslims, distance themselves from *ashraf* Muslims and clamour for reservations.

Let me conclude on a cautionary note: 'majority' and 'minority' are not unified, exclusive, or antagonistic categories. A religious majority, that is the Hindus—and that is the sense in which the term is mostly employed in public discourses—is as fragmented as the minority, that is the Muslims. Added to this is the fact that they neither constitute a separate political 'majority' or 'minority' nor do they act as one. Indeed, the working of the electoral process itself proves that religious and political solidarities are fluid and changeable. Moreover, they are often

---

[44] Steven I. Wilkinson, *Votes and Violence: Electoral Competition and Communal Riots in India* (Cambridge, 2004), p. 237.

mediated by factors that bear no relationship to the presumed existence of 'majority' or minority' consciousness. Religious solidarities may coalesce with political processes in certain situations, but they may well dissipate rapidly. Thus the BJP, riding on the crest of a popular Hindutva wave, was spurned by its own following in UP after the demolition of the Babri Masjid. The same process is at work in Gujarat. Narendra Modi's appeal has diminished, though this has little to do with the success or the realignment of the secular forces. Modi is a victim of his politics, authoritarian, and blatantly partisan.

The predictions made on the base of the sudden rise of Hindutva have not borne fruit. The success of the Congress-led alliance in trouncing the BJP-led National Democratic Alliance (NDA) in the parliamentary election of May 2004 signals, among other things, the rejection of majoritarian politics.[45] Three years down the line, the Manmohan Singh government is on course while right-wing parties are in retreat, at least for the time being. The consolidation of the backward classes in UP and Bihar, the erosion of the BJP's electoral base, and the extraordinary displays of public outrage against right-wing violence and xenophobic intolerance have diminished the electoral appeal of the Sangh Parivar. Indeed, if the existing political trends are not reversed by some unforeseen factors, they may well lead us towards a new future, a future in which Muslim claims and issues may well be integrated and accommodated in India's multicultural agendas. If not, we may well replace the tune of 'Incredible India' with another one.

<hr/>

[45] Zoya Hasan, 'Bridging a Growing Divide? The Indian National Congress and Indian Democracy', *Contemporary South Asia*, vol. 15, no. 4, December 2006.

9

Miles to Go, Promises to Keep

Life has come full circle. My daughters go to the same school I did. The clamorous unruly Jana Sangh of my childhood has been replaced by the BJP.... My daughters, eight and ten, meet their share of Muslim baiters. I told them what my father said to me ('Wear you identity, if you must, as a badge of courage, not shame'). As I watch them grow ... I know that they shall cope, as I did. That they shall enjoy the dual yet in no way conflicting identities—of being Muslim and being Indian in no particular order. Despite Ayodhya and Gujarat, despite the many bad jokes about *katua*s (circumcised Muslims), despite the discrimination that is sometimes overt and often covert, I do feel, it is a good thing that families like mine chose not to hitch their star to the wagon of the League.
　　　　　　　　—Rakhshanda Jalil, *Hindustan Times*, 16 January 2007

Ziya Ahmed, well-known in Sringeri as a member of a community that constitutes a little less than 10 per cent of the population, opined: 'It is only in India's recent history that politicians have begun to see people only as Hindus or as Muslims. If they [politicians] sit down and talk, can't differences be sorted out?'.[1] At a time when the very vocabulary of discussion in certain quarters is structured to impede inter-faith dialogue and understanding, this is a pertinent comment. At this juncture in the

[1] Leela Prasad, *Ethics in Everyday Hindu Life: Narration and Tradition in a South Indian Town* (New Delhi, 2007), p. 44.

history of ethnic division and anti-Islamic prejudice, four points deserve to be underlined by way of concluding observations.

First, Islam in South Asia is a living tradition, howsoever defined, and a dynamic force whose traditions have been moulded by the region's unique cultures. Even though the social and cultural profile of its followers has undergone a fair degree of change, especially owing to the Tablighi Jamaat's influence, these traditions are inseparable from what Aziz Ahmad called the 'Indian envirnoment'. Even though Muslims have specific problems, they share them with the rest of society. Again, even though they have their own role to play, their role must be integrated within a larger complex of diversity, constituted in part by other men, more numerous and perhaps more powerful, with other values and with other roles. W.C. Smith pointed out that the future of Indian Muslims depended upon their own inner resources and creativity and their outward relations with their fellow men.[2]

Second, Islam persists not through rigid negation of but through adaptation to the forces of change. This has enabled its adherents to survive the endless vicissitudes of history. Mujeeb described Islam as a dynamic faith demanding continuous involvement of mind and energy in worldly affairs for fulfilling the purpose for which man was created. Instead of complacency and self-satisfaction, he desired the Muslim conscience to repeat to itself and to others, 'Nigh unto men has drawn their reckoning, while they in heedlessness are yet turning away (Quran, XLVII, 9)'.[3]

A.A.A. Fyzee (b. 1899), scholar of Islamic jurisprudence, positioned himself against the traditional belief that law and religion are coterminous in Islam, arguing that law, a product of social evolution, must change with time and circumstances.[4] The Deoband-educated Maulana Said Akbarabadi argued in the 1960s that a distinction had to be made between those Quranic injunctions that were specific to the Arab customary law and those applicable to Muslim societies in other

---

[2] W.C. Smith, *Islam in Modern History* (Princeton, NJ, 1957), p. 291.

[3] Mohammad Mujeeb, *Islamic Influence on Indian Society* (Meerut, 1972), p. 57.

[4] His best writings were on Muhammadan Law. A classical exposition of a modernist perspective is *A Modern Approach to Islam* (1963). See excerpts from this book in Aziz Ahmad and G.E. von Gruebaum (eds), *Muslim Self-Statement in India and Pakistan, 1857–1968* (Weisbaden, 1970), pp. 195–205; Mushirul Hasan, *Legacy of a Divided Nation: India's Muslims since Independence* (New Delhi, 1997), p. 249.

times. This distinction had been made, and that alone enabled Islam to pass through many stages of reorientation and readjustment. He also distinguished between various types of injunctions—ones that were explicit in the Quran and ones that were not so explicit. Where the Quranic injunctions were explicit, they could not be changed; others were changeable. He gave the example of polygamy which could be checked, controlled, or abolished if it was felt to be in the common interest.[5]

Others scholars, too, interpreted Islam liberally and reformulated some of the main premises of Islamic theology and jurisprudence. Ziya-ul Hasan Faruqi, Deoband educated, endorsed Akbarabadi's thesis of drawing a distinction between *din* (religion), immutable, and *sharia* which has been constantly changing.[6] Scholars like him found favourable response because great numbers of people saw in them an expression of their own identities or as related to their social and economic situations. If their voices were stifled, it is not because of cold or hostile reception to a secular ideology but because of the nexus between the ruling elites and Muslim orthodoxies of a wide variety. Added to this is the fact that the orthodoxies have not been able to solve the riddle at critical junctures in history as to what elements in their history they should emphasize and recombine for their effective self-statement in the present challenge; what they may modify and what they may reject.[7] The task is further complicated in the hands of those who interpret Islam as a closed system,[8] without taking adequate notice of the Prophet's statement: 'Do not put to me too many unnecessary questions, whoever does it is an enemy of the Muslims because the answers given will become binding on them and thereby the liberty of action would be curtailed.'

In South Asia, this admonition inspired Iqbal to justify the reinterpretation of the legal principles in the light of his own generation's experience and the altered conditions of modern life. The logical credentials of Iqbal's philosophy apart, a good number of Muslim intellectuals have demanded that the eclectic spirit of the Prophet's message is not throttled, its theology not gagged by history, and its vitality not sapped

[5] Aziz Ahmad, *Islamic Modernism in India and Pakistan 1857–1964* (New Delhi, 1967), pp. 254–5; and his 'Indian Muslims and the Ideology of the Secular State in India', in D.E. Smith (ed.), *South Asian Politics and Religion* (Princeton, NJ, 1966), p. 148.

[6] Ahmad, 'Indian Muslims and the Ideology of the Secular State in India', p. 148.

[7] Fazlur Rahman, *Islam* (London, 1966), p. 235.

[8] Smith, *Islam in Modern History*, p. 290.

by totalitarianism. The future history of reforms will, however, depend on the ability to fortify and carry forward this tradition.

Third, public intellectuals invariably found in their tradition the ideological resources to bridge their sense of 'difference' and participate fully and actively in the anti-colonial movement. This is exemplified in the writings of Azad and Madani, who championed composite nationalism and rejected the idea of Hindus and Muslims being two different nations.[9] Lesser men found conflict in the rich variety of Indian life. Mawdudi, for example, taught that Islam is different from, incompatible with, and superior to any other religion and criticized Western colonization, the corollary of political and military conquest.[10] His stern warning—one that alerted secular republics of the time—was: 'Whoever really wants to root out mischief and chaos from God's earth ... should stand up to finish the government run on wrong principles, snatch power from wrongdoers, and establish a government based on correct principles and following a proper system.'

Azad, on the other hand, saw the essential unity behind all that diversity, and realized that only in unity was there hope for India as a whole. He envisaged an Islam not of sectarian belligerence but of confident partnership in a cultural and spiritual diversity where a strident divisiveness would be its betrayal.[11] He talked of two aspects of religion. One separates and creates hatred; the other, the true spirit of religion, brings people together. It lies in the spirit of service, in sacrificing self for others. It implies belief in the essential unity of things.[12] He therefore asks mankind

to forge a nexus for human society so that believing in one God of all humanity, the several nations of the Earth might enter into fraternal or federal relations with one another and enjoy the good things of the Earth righteously as members of a single family, the 'Family of God' as described by the Prophet, or 'Fold every member of which shall be a shepherd unto every other and be accountable for the welfare of the entire world.[13]

[9] See Maulana Hussain Ahmad Madani, *Composite Nationalism and Islam*. Translated by Mohammad Anwer Hussain and Hasan Imam (Delhi, 2005).

[10] Peter R. Demant, *Islam vs. Islamism* (London, 2006), p. 99.

[11] Kenneth Cragg, *The Pen and the Faith: Eight Modern Muslim Writers and the Quran* (Delhi reprint, 1988), p. 29.

[12] Quoted in I.H. Douglas, *Abul Kalam Azad: An Intellectual and Religious Biography*. Edited by Gail Minault and Christian W. Troll (New Delhi, 1988), p. 276.

[13] Abul Kalam Azad, *Basic Concepts of the Quran*. Prepared by Syed Abdul Latif (Hyderabad, 1958), p. 113.

The *Tarjuman-al Quran* is one of the most profound statements on multiculturalism and inter-faith understanding. It is the finest example of constructive thinking enjoined on the Muslim in his discovery of 'a new world of religious thought to redress the balance of the old'.[14] Azad, the bridge between Deoband's *ulama* and the liberal modernists, shared in the effort to give the lie to the steady charge, or implication, that living without benefit of statehood would inevitably entail a slow assimilation of Muslims into the dominant ethos of Hinduism.[15]

Madani concluded that those trying to paint a hateful picture of composite nationalism were aiding the British, 'which their own army and arsenals have failed to achieve'.[16] He maintained that if individuals are to retain that measure of initiative and flexibility, which they ought to have, they must not be all drilled into one army. In the words of Faiz, 'Let colour fill the flowers, let breeze of early spring blow.' Literature mirrored such trends, as Victor Kiernan, the translator of Faiz, suggests:

Formerly the old dream-pictures of Persia and Turkestan could serve to express for Indo-Muslims their sense of being a community in, but not of, India. Now most of these Muslims have their own sub-Himalayan homeland, they may well want to hear from their poets about their own skies, flowers, lives, instead of those of the half-mythical native land of their half-mythical ancestors. To go on harping on too many old strings will be as fatal to Urdu poetry as to plunge into unintelligible modernism, and leave it to linger as a mere ghost of the past, haunting the hall of Faiz's poem where no-one will ever come any more.[17]

Saiyyid Fazlul Hasan 'Hasrat' (1878–1951) commended the crusade against exploitation and oppression that socialism expounded. Socialism alone meant an organized and harmonious cooperation of individuals with a view to securing universal well-being. Each year, the poet, once a committed *swadeshi*, took part in the Janamashtami celebrations in Mathura, the birthplace of Lord Krishna. In so doing, he followed the well-established Sufi tradition of revering Hindu gods and participating in Diwali. Love, as the Sufis proclaimed, becomes the reason for every motion:

[14] Mohammad Mujeeb, *Indian Muslims* (London, 1967); ibid., pp. 460, 463.

[15] Cragg, *The Pen and the Faith*, p. 29.

[16] Madani, *Composite Nationalism*, p. 152.

[17] Faiz Ahmad Faiz, *Poems by Faiz*. Translated and with an Introduction and Notes by V.G. Kiernan (New Delhi, 1971), p. 43; and V.G. Kiernan, *Across Time and Continents: A Tribute*. Edited by Prakash Karat (New Delhi, 2003).

If the earth and the mountains were not lovers,
Grass would not grow out of their breasts ....[18]

Large and small movements sympathized with or actively supported
the anti-colonial struggle. Throughout her analysis, Halide Edib is
favourably disposed towards the the Congress Muslims. Ansari, the bridge
between Hindus and Muslims, is her symbol of a new political
conception. Khan Abdul Ghaffar Khan (1890–1988), then 47 years old,
is the quintessential advocate of 'single nationhood' in the North West
Frontier Province. Ansari and Ghaffar Khan represented for her the two
fundamental principles in Islam towards which the world was moving.
For Ansari, 'it was democracy; or rather, the kind of democracy he believed
in. He had nothing to do with the facile democracy which backs a rabid
capitalism.... Abdul Ghaffar Khan is a socialist, a moderate and liberal
one. He also deems Socialism the only political creed compatible with
Islam'.[19]

Edib admires the 'Jamia men' for creating a harmonious Indian
nationhood while at the same time preserving their Islamic identity.
Painting an idyllic picture, she regards Jamia, founded in October 1920,
as the 'best' Muslim institution in India, for 'it leads to a simple life of
ideal and work'. Furthermore, 'it has no limitation in its intellectual
outlook'.[20] Zakir Husain, Mujeeb, and Abid Husain were the purest
minded of young men to invigorate campus life.

The All-India Momin Conference backed the Congress and stoutly
opposed the League. The Ahrars, having led an important movement
against the Maharaja of Kashmir, hitched their fortunes with the
Congress. Later, of course, they joined the Pakistan bandwagon. The
Jamiyat al-ulama did not waver in its commitment to the freedom
struggle. When a split occurred in 1947, most of the ulama connected
with it stayed in India. Individual leaders in Punjab, Sind, Bombay, and
UP were, by common definition, 'nationalist Muslims'. Although partition

[18] Annemarie Schimmel, As Through a Veil: Mystical Poetry in Islam (New York,
1982), p. 104.

[19] Halide Edib, Inside India. With an Introduction and Notes by Mushirul Hasan (New
Delhi, 2002), pp. 227–8.

[20] Bombay Chronicle, 16 March 1935. A.G. Noorani, the noted author-journalist, is
perhaps the only writer to have used her references to Jamia in President Zakir Husain: A
Quest for Excellence (Bombay, 1967).

left them sullen and demoralized, they determinedly carved out their future in Jawaharlal Nehru's India.

Rabindranath Tagore had warned in August 1911: 'A suppressed separateness is a terrible explosive force. Some time or other it would create a mighty upset by blowing up suddenly under pressure.' The Muslim engagement with composite nationalism continues to this day, sixty years after Independence and partition. Unlike Muslim societies of modern times in other parts of the world where the secular idea exists only in certain critical intellectual circles and where parliament and parliamentary processes are dismissed as Western heresies,[21] Indian Muslims, or Muslim Indians, as Syed Shahabuddin prefers to describe them in his magazine, accept secularism and hold firmly to the idea of an ecumenical society committed to social justice and freedom.[22] Maulana Abul Hasan Ali Nadwi or Ali Miyan (1914–99), Nadwat al-ulama's *alim*, stated in 1960 that the Muslims were not only citizens of equal status but also second to none for their selfless service to the motherland.[23] Mushirul Haq, educated at the same institution before joining Jamia, contended in 1972: 'The secular state in India is not only acceptable but, in the present circumstances, most welcome,' and 'that it is in accord with Islamic traditions.... This concept of secularism is not alien to a Muslim and therefore he sees no conflict between his religion, Islam and secularism.'[24]

Ziya-ul-Hasan Faruqi, Jamia professor, wanted fellow Muslims to maintain their Islamic individuality as well as prove themselves proud citizens. Urging them to realize that only the Indian brand of secularism, based on democratic traditions and liberal thought, could safeguard cultural and religious freedom and give them strength, he wrote with conviction that secularism was neither atheistic not antithetical to religion.[25] He probably took his cue from Nehru, who had repeatedly stated that a secular state did not mean that religion ceased to be an important

[21] Mehran Kamrava (ed.), *The New Voices of Islam: Reforming Politics and Modernity—A Reader* (London, 2006), p. 145; Tazeen M. Murshid, *The Sacred and the Secular: Bengal Muslim Discourses, 1871–1977* (Calcutta, 1995), p. 434.

[22] Alam Khundmiri, *Secularism, Islam and Modernity* (New Delhi, 2001).

[23] Hasan, *Legacy of a Divided Nation*, p. 250.

[24] Mushirul Haq, *Islam in Secular India* (Simla, 1972), pp. 4, 84.

[25] Ziya-ul-Hasan Faruqi, 'Indian Muslims and the Ideology of the Secular State in India', in D.E. Smith (ed.), *South Asian Politics and Religion* (Princeton, NJ, 1966), p. 149.

factor in the life of an individual. 'It means,' he stated in Parliament in 1950, 'that the state and religion are not tied up together. It simply means the repetition of the cardinal doctrine of modern democractic practice that is the separation of the state from religion and the full protection of every religion.[26]

For Syed Abul Ala Mawdudi (b. 1903), the establishment, realization, and pursuit of religion meant a superstructure of social conduct and political action raised on the base of the 'divine Khilafat', the 'divine sovereignty', entirely different from the secular state. After 1947, though, the Jamaat-e Islami in India reached the inescapable conclusion that democracy and secularism, which their mentor had so fiercely derided, protected them against majoritarianism.

'The idea of the monolithic Muslim vote is one myth they (politicians) ought to revisit. It's best to think of the Muslim citizen as just that, a citizen of a secular republic,' observed a recent newspaper editorial.[27] In the 1990s, admittedly, the demolition of the Babri Masjid and the alarming increase in the stridency of the Sangh Parivar had offended Muslim sensibilities, but they realized that they could not afford to lose faith in secularism. Even though 'secular' formations have taken the 'Muslim vote' for granted and have adamantly not heeded their demands, the Muslim electorates have added value to secularism, in marked contrast to those who reject secularism on the grounds that it does injustice to Hindu historical heritage and turns 'epistemic error into a political blunder'.[28] Despite their tales of betrayal, they have, historically, aligned themselves not with specifically Muslim parties (Kerala is an exception), but with secular parties. Alliances with progressive intent have been forged; such alliances cut across the religious divide.[29] The CPI (M)'s chief ally in Bengal has been the Muslims, who constitute 25 per cent of the population. This is regardless of the fact that the

[26] Uma Iyengar (ed.), *The Oxford India Nehru* (New Delhi, 2007), p. 361.

[27] *Times of India*, 12 September 2007, p. 20.

[28] Amartya Sen, 'Secularism and its Discontents', in Rajeev Bhargava (ed.), *Secularism and its Critics* (New Delhi, 1988); Javeed Alam, *Who wants Democracy?* (New Delhi, 2004).

[29] S.M.A.K. Fakhri, 'Tamil Muslims and the Self-Respect Movement', in Mushirul Hasan (ed.), *Living with Secularism: The Destiny of India's Muslims* (New Delhi, 2007), pp. 91–118. See also, Yoginder Sikand, *Muslims in India since 1947: Islamic Perspectives on Inter-faith Relations* (London, 2004); and *Muslims in India: Contemporary Social and Political Discourses* (Delhi, 2006).

religious-minded find the CPI (M) ideology antithetical to their faith. As in the six Muslim societies of Asia, so also in India, political trends are more likely to work in favour of forces and organizations that integrate Muslim values and moderate Islamic politics into broad-based platforms that go beyond exclusively religious concerns.[30]

It is not as if men of religion do not invoke moral and spiritual goals or that they are not wary of the more materialistic promises of secular nationalists. But even they, notwithstanding their reactionary role during the Shah Bano controversy in April 1985,[31] are convinced of the validity of secular nationalism. A consensus exists, regardless of the doctrinal differences between the Deobandis, the Barelwis, and the Ahl-e Hadith, on the Western versions of nationalism providing a vision of what they would like themselves and their country to become. In other words, contrary to Mark Juergensmeyer's assertion,[32] religious and secular leaders alike, look askance at the mixing of religion with politics. This attitude may not have produced any spectacular results, but it has certainly created spaces for a creative, though inconclusive, dialogue on reforms and innovation and on the direction of change and progress.[33]

The final point is this: today, the inheritors of what might be called the Azad-Ajmal-Ansari legacy have succeeded, on the one hand, in connecting Western education with modernization and, on the other, in building bridges with the non-Muslims. Even though their efforts have gone unnoticed, they work unobtrusively, within their own chosen domain, to break down the segments of the traditional order to create a common culture capable of integrating citizens.[34] This common culture,

---

[30] Zoya Hasan (ed.), *Democracy in Muslim Societies: The Asian Experience* (New Delhi, 2007), p. 40.

[31] The controversy was over the Supreme Court judgement on the right of Shah Bano, a divorcee, to seek and secure maintenance from her former husband. This claim was widely contested and the Rajiv Gandhi government had to introduce legislation in Parliament which reversed the Supreme Court verdict. See Zoya Hasan, 'Gender Politics, Legal Reform, and the Muslim Community in India', in Patricia Jeffery and Amrita Basu (eds), *Resisting the Sacred and the Secular: Women's Activism and Politicized Religion in South Asia* (New Delhi, 1999).

[32] Mark Juergensmeyer, *Religious Nationalism Confronts the Secular State* (California, 1993), pp. 23–4.

[33] Hasan, *Living with Secularism*; Mushirul Hasan (ed.), *Will Secular India Survive* (New Delhi, 2004).

[34] S.A. Akbarabadi, 'Islam and Other Religions', in *Islam* (Patiala, 1969), pp. 103–16.

in Lucknow, Bhopal, and Hyderabad, is no other than composite culture. Little is known of local committees, sabhas, and *biradaris* that serve, often informally, as platforms for promoting a common culture. Without using the vocabulary of social scientists, the 'children of Rifaa',[35] so to speak, believe in the coming together of different faiths and ideologies, plead for a spirit of compassion, fraternity, tolerance and reasonableness, and try to build a *Naya Shivala* (New Temple) to promote inter-faith dialogue.

Among the leading public intellectuals after Independence, Mujeeb affirmed that those believing in the one God and His guidance should think not in the light of Islamic theology and history only, but in the context of world history. They must know how the human conscience has operated among all the peoples of the world at all times, in the light of the status which the Quran assigns to man in creation, and the directives it has given: 'O believers, be you securers of justice, witnesses for God', and 'Let there be one nation of you, calling to good and bidding to honour and forbidding dishonour.' Mujeeb emphasized the need for studying religions, not to see how far they have deviated from but how close they are in essence to the fundamental human faith.[36]

Mujeeb and Abid Husain left it to others to build upon the foundations so carefully laid.[37] They include Imtiaz Ahmad, 'whose anthropology of Muslim India seems to have much in common with scholarship long associated with the Jamia Millia Islamia',[38] and K.G. Saiyidain (1907–91), who was firmly committed to the view that Indian culture is a composite to which many different religions and traditions have contributed. He stated that the Muslim contributions were 'so many and so varied and they are so securely woven into the total pattern of Indian

---

[35] See Guy Sorman, *The Children of Rifaa: In Search of Moderate Islam* (New Delhi, 2004).

[36] Mujeeb, *Islamic Influence on Indian Society*, p. 48.

[37] They are: A.A.A. Fyzee, K.G. Saiyidain, T. Lokhandwala, S. Maqbul Ahmad, Rafiq Zakaria (1920–2005), Khaliq Ahmad Nizami, S.A.I. Tirmizi, S. Vahiduddin, M.S. Agwani, Alam Khundmiri, Jamal Khwaja, Anwar Moazzam, Saeed Naqvi, Hasan Suroor, Rasheed Talib, and A.G. Noorani, who writes of the Muslims not letting 'mistaken notions of identity' hinder their participation in the struggle for a just society and the leaders of secular political parties assisting them in participation 'by responding to the genuine needs of Muslims, while enlisting them in the common struggle'. A.G. Noorani, 'Muslim Identity: Self Image and Political Aspirations', in Mushirul Hasan (ed.), *Islam, Communities and the Nation: Muslim Identities in South Asia and Beyond* (New Delhi, 1998), p. 138.

[38] Francis Robinson, *Islam and Muslim History in South Asia* (New Delhi, 2000).

culture that they cannot be disentangled and removed without weakening and impoverishing the whole pattern'.[39]

Some, if not all of them, struggle to knit together intellectual discourse, strategic activism, and holistic spirituality. Asghar Ali Engineer, a writer-activist, negotiates between his radicalism, now diluted in order to suit the exigencies of Bohra politics, and 'spiritual activism', that is 'to augment the abstract epistemology of reform discourse over revelation and human meaning towards acts of kindness and good, by joining them into a single process—change of heart, body and soul for participants hoping to create a meaningful alternative in governing Islamic affairs worldwide'.[40]

It is commonly agreed that the faithful cannot be denied the right to lead their lives in accordance with the Quran or to regard the Prophet, whose life has always been as crucial to the unfolding Islamic ideal as it is today, as the model of a Perfect Man.[41] At the same time they should not regard themselves as the sole possessors and upholders of true belief but acknowledge the right of non-Muslims to profess their own faiths. Through their writings, a number of public intellectuals have promoted, though not without stiff resistance, the idea of Unity of Existence (wahdatal-wujud) expounded by the great thinker Ibn Arabi (1165–1240). In so doing, they have drawn upon resources from Indian as well as the composite Sufi tradition.

The message is loud and clear. Instead of the imaginary civilizational clash between 'Islam' and 'the West',[42] the 'latitudinarian tendencies' should intermingle with the antinomian trends in Hinduism itself to reinforce the phenomenon of Hindu–Muslim rapprochement. An average

[39] Quoted in Imtiaz Ahmad, 'Basic Conflict of "We" and "They" between Religious Traditions, between Hindus, Muslims and Christians', in Imtiaz Ahmad, Partha S. Ghosh, Helmut Reifeld (eds), *Pluralism and Equality: Values in Indian Society and Politics* (New Delhi, 2000), pp. 156–79.

[40] Amina Wadud, *Inside the Gender Jihad* (Oxford, 2006).

[41] Karen Armstrong, *Muhammad: Prophet for Our Time* (London, 2006), p. 14.

[42] Martha Nussbaum talks of a clash within virtually all modern nations—between people who are prepared to live with others who are different on terms of equal respect, and those who seek the protection of homogeneity, achieved through the domination of a single religious and ethnic tradition. The real clash of civilizations, according to her, is not out there, between admirable Westerners and Muslim zealots, but 'within each person, as we oscillate uneasily between self-protective aggression and the ability to live in the world with others'. Martha Nussbaum, *The Clash Within: Democracy, Religious Violence and India's Future* (Cambridge, MA, 2007).

Muslim should maintain, rather than abrogate, his right to hold an independent opinion about right and wrong, good and evil, and, above all, act according to his conscience and remind himself that he must be 'securer of justice' not only for his brethren but the international community, of Muslims and non-Muslims, to which we belong. Iqbal had alluded to this in *Naya Shivala*. With its lyrical quality and tone of cheerfulness and hope, he had called upon the Hindus and Muslims to cultivate decent values which spring from a common tradition, to recognize each other as equals and treat the sister faiths with fundamental respect.[43]

Arguably, the Muslim communities are not answerable to anybody else; yet their well-wishers across the wide spectrum of informed opinion would not like them to be overwhelmed by the forces of reaction and bigotry within their own ranks. Local and regional leaders sound hollow and insincere because they merely repeat the slogans and the catchwords and ideals of progress. Moreover, they are disinterested in Muslim affairs and are content if someone deals with Muslim affairs for them. In a nutshell, they get excited about politics when their pockets are affected; they do not really believe in themselves or their civic responsibilities towards say reforming the charitable endowments (*auqaf*) and removing gender asymmetries in Islamic ritual practice. Still analysts expect an organized group, working largely within the parameters of some institution, to take the lead in disseminating ideas of progress, rationality, and enlightenment. While castigating the leadership chiefly on the

[43] I shall tell the truth, O Brahmin, but take it not as an offence:
    The idols in thy temple have decayed.
    Thou hast learnt from these images to bear ill-will to thine own people.
    And God has taught the [Muslim] preacher the ways of strife.
    My heart was sick: I turned away both from the temple and the Ka'abah,
    From the sermons of the preacher and from thy fairy tales, O Brahmin
    To thee images of stone embody the divine—
    For me, every particle of my country's dust is a deity.
    Come, let us remove all that causes estrangement
    Let us reconcile those that have turned away from each other, remove all
      signs of division.
    Desolation has reigned for long in the habitation of my heart—
    Come, let us build a new temple in our land.
    Let our holy places be higher than any on the earth,
    Let us raise its pinnacle till it touches the lapel of the sky;
    Let us awake every morning to sing the sweetest songs;
    And give all worshippers the wine of love to drink.
    There is power, there is peace in the songs of devotees—
    The salvation of all dwellers on the earth is love.

grounds that it has not done enough to prioritize education on its agenda and instead concentrates on preserving the Muslim personal law and the 'minority character' of the Aligarh Muslim University,[44] Asghar Ali Engineer sees a silver lining in an otherwise dismal picture:

The Muslims have to sink or swim in the Indian political ocean and from all available signs it appears Muslim masses have decided to swim even if the ocean is choppy. If right now the future of Muslims is not bright it is not dismal either. Given little more wisdom and pragmatic approach Muslims can succeed in shaping their future in democratic India even if secularism is undulating.[45]

In *Vettamangalam Elelphant*, Thoppil Mohamed Meeran (b. 1944), the great Malayalam writer, dwells on aspects of inter-community inter-mingling, the fusion of religio-cultural practices, their variety and richness. He describes popular singers, actors, and costumes: these develop into signs whose semiotic richness evokes the spontaneous and collective *jouissance* of Hindus and Muslims alike. Soon though this sharing of a unique and long-standing experience is ruptured. The elephant procession, once a joyous occasion for all, now fills Muslims with foreboding. Sad that his children were caught up in the communal cauldron, the Muslim narrator lamented that they would neither have access to a rich cultural tradition nor the opportunity to enjoy what he had so cherished all his life.

Why wasn't it easy any more to regard the Vettamangalam elephant as an animal, like any other, that was led along a public road belonging to one and all, to the sea that made no distinction between man and animal? Why couldn't the people accompanying the elephant be seen as no different from others? How did the two emerge as symbols meant to strike fear in the minds of a few, with an equally fearsome response? To whom belonged those secret hands that leavened human hearts with poison? Thoughts criss-crossed, in search of dim path-marks, converging presently on Naina's oft-repeated story of his betrayal by none other than his own man.[46]

India will remain quintessentially secular and pluralistic if no child is ever prevented from participating in the elephant procession. That is when one can share the poet's optimism:

[44] Rafiq Zakaria, *Indian Muslims: Where Have They Gone Wrong?* (Mumbai, 2005).
[45] A.A. Engineer, *Secular Perspective* (Mumbai), 16 March–15 April 2001.
[46] Mushirul Hasan and M. Asaduddin (eds), *Image and Representation: Stories of Muslim Lives in India* (New Delhi, 2000), p. 140.

Gul huii jaati hai afsurda sulagti huii shaam,
Dhul ke niklegi abhi chashma-e mehtaab se raat.

The fire of the sad smouldering evening is being extinguished,
In a moment the night will disappear washed by the stream of moonlight.

—Faiz

'The writing of history is a matter of conscience', wrote Leopold von Ranke (1795–1886) memorably. 'Remember your moral responsibility to our readers', admonished Gooch, the British historian. These are the practical issues which this book has endeavoured to address, and both are in a sense historical. I hope my approach and the purpose underpinning it will justify themselves in terms of the aim outlined at the very outset in the Introduction.

Glossary

Ahrar	'the free'; a political party founded in the Punjab in the 1930s.
ajlaf	literally, 'the low-born'.
akhlaq	morals, ethics.
alim	learned man, scholar in the Islamic religious sciences; pl. ulama.
Allah-o-Akbar	God is great.
anjuman	assembly, meeting; e.g., Anjuman-e Khuddam-i Kaaba
ashraf	'the high born', i.e. Syed and Sheikhzada.
auqaf	charitable endowments, a pious foundation, pl. of waqf.
Dar al-harb	literally, 'the abode of war'.
Dar al-Islam	literally, 'the abode of Islam'.
Dar al-ulum	literally, 'the abode of science', e.g., the Dar al-ulum at Deoband.
dargah	a Muslim shrine; seat of the head of an order or its branches.
divan	a collection of poetry; in Mughal times the name of the chief revenue official.

faqir	an ascetic, Hindu or Muslim beggar.
fatawa	plural of fatwa, a religious decree, or a legal counsel.
ghazal	celebrated poetic form in the Persian, Turkish, and Urdu traditions, usually a short love poem not longer than fourteen verses.
ghazi	a hero, a warrior, fighter for the true faith.
hadith	literally, 'a saying'; Prophetic traditions.
imam	prayer leader.
imambara	literally, 'the enclosure of the imams'; place for commemorating Muharram.
jamiyat	an association or conference, as the Jamiyat al-ulama.
jihad	'an effort, or striving', i.e., in the interest of the spread and defence of Islam.
Khalifa	a successor, viceregent, or deputy.
khanqah	a monastery of the Sufi or darwesh.
Khilafat	the office of the Khalifa.
madaris	plural of madarsa, a Muslim school.
majlis	mourning assembly, especially during Muharram.
maktab	A primary school commonly attached to a mosque.
marsiya	elegy.
mela	fair, exhibition.
millat	religious community.
miyan	in India a term of respect; 'master', 'good sir'.
mohalla	subdivision of a city; a ward or a quarter of a city; neighbourhood.
Muharram	the first month of the Muslim calendar observed to commemorate the martyrdom

	of Imam Husain, the grandson of the Prophet.
mulla, maulvi, or maulana	a Muslim doctor of law.
murid	literally, 'one who strives'; a disciple of a pir.
murshid	literally, 'one who guides aright'; spiritual guide.
mushaira	an assembly of poets.
Nadwat at-ulama	religious seminary founded by Maulana Shibli Numani at Lucknow in 1894.
Nawab	title given to dignitaries, especially regional rulers; also, an honorific plural of a Naib.
pir	a Sufi teacher or director.
qawwali	Muslim hymn or devotional songs sung in praise of the Prophet, his family, and the Sufi saints.
qazi	a judge.
salam	greetings.
sabha	association.
Syed	used to denote the descendants of the Prophet Mohammad.
Sheikh	a term used to denote a religious teacher; also one of the four caste divisions among, Indian Muslims. Originally, a designation of those Muslims who claimed to be descended from the first or second Khalifa or from the Prophet's uncle.
Sharif	the noble or high castes—Syed, Sheikh, Mughal, and Pathan.
Shia	'party', the party of Ali, son-in-law of the Prophet. The Shias claim that the first three Khalifas usurped his right to be the first Khalifa.

sharia	the path to be followed; the divine law based on the Quran.
silsilah	a chain, an order.
Sufi	a Muslim mystic, usually part of an established order (silsilah).
swaraj	rule over self; self-government.
taluqdar	recipients of proprietary rights, after 1858, from the British.
tazia	literally, 'a consolation'. Replicas of the tomb of Husain and his companions brought out during Muharram.
tazkira	biography; memoirs of eminent men of letters.
ulama	plural of alim: learned men, scholars in the Islamic religious sciences.
Urs	used as a term for the ceremonies observed at the anniversary of the death of a saint (pir or murshid).
zakat	alm-giving.
zamindar	a landholder.
zenana	women's part of a Muslim household.

Chronology

1878	Vernacular Press Act passed.
1882	Ripon repeals Vernacular Press Act.
1883	C.P. Ilbert's Criminal Procedure Amendment Bill introduced.
	First session of the National Conference held at Calcutta.
1884	Ilbert Bill amended and finally passed.
1885	Inauguration of Bombay Presidency Association.
	First Congress session held in Bombay.
1894	Elgin takes office as Governor-General.
1898	Death of Syed Ahmad Khan.
1899	Curzon takes over as Governor-General.
1905	Partition of Bengal leading to widespread public agitation in and outside the province.
1906	Minto receives Muslim deputation (1 October) led by the Aga Khan.
	The All-India Muslim League founded at Dacca.
1912	Delhi proclaimed a province.
	Abul Kalam Azad publishes *Al-Hilal*.
1913	Indian Criminal Law Amendment Act passed.

1914–18   First World War.

1915   Gandhi arrives in Bombay.
           Annie Besant announces the formation of her Home
           Rule League.

1917   Gandhi tried for his role in Champaran.
           Annie Besant interned by the Madras government.
           Rowlatt (Sedition) Committee appointed.

1918   Rowlatt (Sedition) Committee report submitted;
           Montagu-Chelmsford report on constitutional
           reform published.

1919   Gandhi takes over *Young India* and *Navajivan*;
           introduction of the Rowlatt Bills marked by an all-India hartal.
           General Dyer imposes curfew, followed by the
           Jallianwala Bagh massacre at Amritsar.
           The Hunter Committee of Inquiry into the Punjab
           massacres begins its work.
           Government of India Act, 1919
           (also Montagu-Chelmsford Reforms) becomes law.
           Treaty of Versailles; League of Nations formed;
           the Third (Communist) International is founded.

1921   Scheme of reforms under the Government of India Act,
           1919, put into operation.
           Moplah Rebellion in Malabar.

1922   The Chauri Chaura incident occurs, leading to Gandhi's
           suspension of the Non-Cooperation Movement.

1925   Death of C.R. Das.
           The All-India Congress Committee permits the Swaraj
           Party to work in the legislatures.

1928   Simon Commission reaches Bombay; marked by an
           all-India hartal.
           All-Parties Conference considers Nehru Report.

1929   All-Parties Conference adjourned sine die.
           Thirty-one members of the Communist Party arrested in
           connection with the Meerut conspiracy case.
           Under Jinnah's leadership, the All-Parties Muslim
           Conference formulates its 'fourteen points'.

Irwin announces Dominion Status as the political goal of British policy in India.

1930   The Congress adopts Civil Disobedience Resolution. Gandhi begins his Salt satyagraha with the Dandi March. Simon Commission report published. First Round Table Conference in London.

1931   Gandhi–Irwin Pact concluded (March); Gandhi sails for England (August) to attend the Second Round Table Conference (September–November); returns to Bombay (December).

1932   Whitehall announces Communal Award; Poona Pact regarding scheduled caste representation signed. Third Round Table Conference (November–December) held.

1933   White Paper on constitutional reforms published. Gandhi starts the weekly *Harijan*; is arrested and later (8 May) released. Civil disobedience temporarily suspended (May); is restarted (August); Gandhi arrested (1 August) and released (23 August).

1934   Congress policy on the Communal Award leads to the birth of the Nationalist Party. Jinnah returns from London to head the Muslim League.

1935   Rehmat Ali publishes a leaflet on the formation of Pakistan. The Government of India Bill, 1935, receives royal assent, becomes an act.

1936   The Congress, Muslim League, and other political parties campaigns for elections to the provincial legislatures and to the Central Legislative Assembly under the Act of 1935.

1937   The Congress permits its members to accept office under the Government of India Act of 1935. The All-India National Education Conference under Gandhi's leadership formulates a new education policy.

1939   The British induct India into the Second World War;
                Linlithgow declares Dominion Status for India as his
                government's ultimate goal. Congress ministries resign
                from office in the provinces; Jinnah declares 22
                December as a 'Day of Deliverance' for Muslims.

1939–45   Second World War.

1940   Lahore Session of Muslim League adopts the Pakistan
                Resolution.

                Linlithgow announces a new constitutional (August)
                offer which the Congress rejects but the Muslim League
                welcomes.

                The Congress starts (17 October) and later suspends
                (17 December) individual Civil Disobedience.

1941   Gandhi absolved of the responsibility of leading a
                satyagraha movement.
                Germany invades Russia; the proclamation of the
                Atlantic Charter (British Prime Minister Churchill
                affirms it does *not* apply to India); Japan attacks
                the USA.

1942   Cripps fails to break the political deadlock;
                the Congress and League reject his proposals.
                The Congress passes (9 August) the Quit India
                resolution; its leaders are arrested.

1943   The Karachi session of the Muslim League adopts
                the slogan 'Divide and Quit'.

1945   Landslide Labour Party victory in the British general
                elections (June).
                Wavell's Simla conference fails to break the political
                deadlock. Atom bombs dropped on Hiroshima and
                Nagasaki towards the end of the Second World War;
                Labour Government comes to power in Britain;
                United Nations Organisation (UNO) formed.

1946   British parliamentary delegation in India;
                Wavell announces Whitehall's intention of setting up a
                politically representative Executive Council at the centre.

Three-member British Cabinet Mission arrives (March)
and, after consultations, issues its proposals (May).
Elections to Constituent Assembly completed.
The Muslim League repudiates (29 July) the Cabinet
Mission Plan, and after Nehru is invited to form an
interim government (6 August) proclaims 'Direct
Action Day' (16 August). The 'Great Calcutta killing'
follows.
The Interim Government sworn in (2 September);
joined by the League (13 October).

Nehru, Baldev Singh, Jinnah, Liaquat Ali Khan, and
Wavell visit London (3–6 December) to break the
political impasse.
The Constituent Assembly convened (9 December).

1947   The Muslim League declares that the Cabinet Mission
Plan had failed and that the Constituent Assembly is illegal.
Attlee announces the end (June 1948) of British rule;
Mountbatten is sworn in (March) as the last Viceroy
and Governor-General; he presents (3 June) his plan for
partition and announces (9 June) the transfer of power
(14–15 August) to the separate Dominions of India and
Pakistan.
Indian Independence Bill introduced (4 July) in
Parliament; passed (15–16) July) and receives royal
assent (18 July).
Pakistan's Constituent Assembly meet (11 August) and
elect Jinnah as President who is sworn in as Governor-
General; Pakistan is born (14 August); India attains
Independence (15 August).

Bibliography

Aggarwal, Ravina. *Beyond Lines of Control: Performance and Politics on the Disputed Borders of Ladakh* (London, 2004).

Ahmad, Aziz. *Islamic Culture in the Indian Environment* (London, 1964).

———. 'Indian Muslims and the Ideology of the Secular State in India', in D.E. Smith (ed.), *South Asian Politics and Religion* (Princeton, NJ, 1966).

———. *Islamic Modernism in India and Pakistan, 1857–1964* (New Delhi, 1967).

———. *An Intellectual History of Islam in India* (Edinburgh, 1969).

———. 'India and Pakistan', in P.M. Holt, Ann K.S. Lambton, and Bernard Lewis (eds), *The Cambridge History of Islam*, vol. 2A (Cambridge, 1970).

Ahmad, Aziz and G.E. Von Gruenbaum (eds). *Muslim Self-statement in India and Pakistan 1857–1968* (Wiesbaden, 1970).

Ahmad, Imtiaz. 'For a Sociology of India', *Contributions to Indian Sociology*, vol. 6, 1972.

———. 'Basic Conflict of "We" and "They" between Religious Traditions, between Hindus, Muslims and Christians', in Imtiaz Ahmad, Partha S. Ghosh, Helmut Reifeld (eds), *Pluralism and Equality: Values in Indian Society and Politics* (New Delhi, 2000).

———. 'Muslim Educational Backwardness—An Inferential Analysis', *Economic and Political Weekly*, vol. 16, 1981.

Ahmad, Nazir. *The Bride's Mirror: Mirat ul-'Arus: A Tale of Life in New Delhi a Hundred Years Ago*. Translated from the Urdu by G.E. Ward, with an Afterword by Frances W. Pritchett (New Delhi, 2001).

———. *The Repentance of Nussooh* (*Taubat-Al-Nasuh*). Translated from the Urdu by M. Kempson, edited by C.M. Naim (New Delhi, 2004).

Ahmad, Qeyamuddin. *The Wahhabi Movement in India* (New Delhi, 1994; first edition, 1966).

Ahmad, Salim (ed.). *Lahore 1947* (New Delhi, 2001).

Ahmed, Akbar S. *Discovering Islam: Making Sense of Muslim History and Society* (London, 1988).

——. *Jinnah, Pakistan and Islamic Identity: The Search for Saladin* (Karachi, 1997).

Ahmed, Rafiuddin. *The Bengali Muslims 1871–1906: A Quest for Identity* (New Delhi, 1981).

——. 'Conflicts and Contradictions in Bengali Islam: Problems of Change and Adjustment', in Katherine P. Ewing (ed.) *Shariat and Ambiguity in South Asian Islam* (New Delhi, 1988).

Akbarabadi, S.A. 'Islam and Other Religions', in *Islam* (Patiala, 1969).

Akhtar, Javed. 'Progressive Writers' Movement in Urdu Literature', *Indian Literature*, vol. 142, 2007

Alam, Javeed. *Who wants Democracy?* (New Delhi, 2004).

Alam, Muzaffar, Francoise 'Nalini' Delvoye, and Marc Gaborieau (eds), *The Making of Indo-Persian Culture: Indian and French Studies* (New Delhi, 2000).

Alavi, Hamza. 'The State in Postcolonial Societies: Pakistan and Bangladesh', in Kathleen Gough and Hari P. Sharma (eds), *Imperialism and Revolution in South Asia* (New York, 1973).

Ali, Ahmed. *Twilight in Delhi* (London, 1940).

Ali, Meer Hasan. *Observations on the Mussulmans of India*, in 2 vols. (London, 1832).

Ali, Mohamed. *My Life A Fragment: An Autobiographical Sketch of Maulana Mohamed Ali*, edited by Mushirul Hasan (New Delhi, 1999).

Allen, Charles (ed.). *Plain Tales from the Raj* (London, 1975).

All Parties Conference 1928. *Report of the Committee Appointed by the Conference to determine the principles of the Constitution for India* (Allahabad, 1928).

Amin, Shahid. 'On Retelling the Muslim Conquest of North India', in Partha Chatterjee and Anjan Ghose (eds), *History and the Present* (New Delhi, 2002).

——. 'Representing the Musalman: Then and Now, Now and Then', in Shail Mayaram, M.S.S. Pandian, and Ajay Skaria (eds), *Muslims, Dalits, and the Fabrications of History: Subaltern Studies XII* (New Delhi, 2005).

Andrews, C.F. *Zakaullah of Delhi*. With an Introduction by Mushirul Hasan and Margrit Pernau (New Delhi, 2003).

Ansari, Iqbal A. 'Course of the Law on Riots and Terror', *Economic and Political Weekly*, 1 September 2007.

Ansari, Sarah F.D. *Sufi Saints and State Power: The Pirs of Sind, 1843–1947* (Cambridge, 1992).

——. *Life after Partition: Migration, Community and Strife in Sind 1947–1962* (Karachi, 2002).

Armstrong, Karen. *Muhammad: Prophet for Our Time* (London, 2006).

Ashraf, Mujeeb. *Muslim Attitudes towards British Rule and Western Culture in India* (New Delhi, 1982).

Assayag, Jackie. *At the Confluence of Two Rivers: Muslims and Hindus in South India* (New Delhi, 2004).

Azad, Abul Kalam. *Basic Concepts of the Quran.* Prepared by Syed Abdul Latif (Hyderabad, 1958).

——. *India Wins Freedom: An Autobiographical Narrative* (Bombay, 1959).

Baljon, J.M.S. *Modern Muslim Interpretations, 1880–1960* (Brill, 1968)

Basu, Sajal. *Communalism, Ethnicity and State Politics* (Jaipur, 2000).

Bayly, C.A. *The Local Roots of Indian Politics—Allahabad 1880–1920* (Oxford, 1975).

——. *Indian Society and the Making of the British Empire* (New Delhi, 1987).

——. *Rulers, Townsmen and Bazaars: North Indian Society in the Age of British Expansion 1770–1870* (New Delhi, 2002 edition).

Bayly, Susan. *Saints, Goddesses and Kings: Muslims and Christians in South Indian Society 1700–1900* (Cambridge, 1990).

Benegal, Shyam. 'Secularism and Popular Indian Cinema', in A.D. Needham and Rajeshwari Sunder Rajan (eds), *The Crisis of Secularism in India* (New Delhi, 2007).

Bhalla, Alok (ed.). *Stories about the Partition of India*, 3 vols (New Delhi, 1994).

Bhargava, Rajeev. 'India's Secular Constitution', in Zoya Hasan, E. Sridharan, and R. Sudarshan (eds), *India's Living Constitution: Ideas, Practices, Controversies* (New Delhi, 2002).

Bhattacharya, Sabyasachi (ed.). *Rethinking 1857* (New Delhi, 2007).

Blake, Stephen P. *Shahjahanabad: The Sovereign City in Mughal India 1639–1739* (New Delhi, 1993).

Blunt, W.S. *India under Ripon: A Private Diary* (London, 1909).

Bonnett, Alastair. *The Idea of the West: Culture, Politics and History* (New York, 2004).

Bose, Sugata and Ayesha Jalal. *Nationalism, Democracy and Development* (New Delhi, 1997).

Brass, Paul R. *Religion, Language and Politics in Northern India* (Cambridge, 1974).

——. *Theft of an Idol: Text and Context in the Representation of Collective Violence* (Princeton, NJ, 1997).

Brittlebank, Kate. *Tipu Sultan's Search for Legitimacy* (New Delhi, 1997).

Broomfield, J.H. *Elite Conflict in a Plural Society: Twentieth-century Bengal* (Bombay, 1968).

Brosius, Christiane. *Empowering Visions: The Politics of Representation of Hindu Nationalism* (London, 2005).

Buehler, Arthur. *Sufi Heirs of the Prophet: The Indian Naqshbandiyya and the Rise of the Mediating Sufi Shaykh* (Columbia, 1998).

Butterfield, Herbert. *The Whig Interpretation of History* (London, 1921; 1973).

Cell, John W. *Hailey: A Study in British Imperialism, 1872–1969* (Cambridge, 1992).

Chakrabarty, Bidyut. *The Partition of Bengal and Assam 1932–1947* (New Delhi, 2004).

Chakrabarty, Basudeb. *India Partition Fiction in English and in English Translation: A Text on Hindu–Muslim Relations* (Calcutta, 2007).

Chakravarty, Paula and Srinivas Lankala. 'Media, Terror and Islam: The Shifting Landscape and Culture Talk in India', in Amrita Basu and Sripu Roy (eds), *Violence and Democracy in India* (Calcutta, 2007).

Chakravarty, Uma. et al., 'Khurja Riots 1900: Understanding the Conjuncture', *Economic and Political Weekly*, 2 May 1992.

Chandra, Bipan. *Communalism in Modern India* (New Delhi, 1984).

Chandra, Sudhir 'Communal Consciousness in Late 19th Century', in Mushirul Hasan (ed.), *Communal and Pan-Islamic Trends in Colonial India* (New Delhi, 1985 revised and enlarged edition).

———. *The Oppressive Present: Literature and Social Consciousness in Colonial India* (New Delhi, 1992).

Chatterjee, Kumkum. 'Discovering India: Travel, History and Identity in Late Nineteenth- and Early Twentieth-century India', in Daud Ali (ed.), *Invoking the Past: The Uses of History in South Asia* (New Delhi, 1999).

Chatterjee, Partha. 'Agrarian Relations and Communalism in Bengal, 1926–1935', in Ranajit Guha (ed.), *Subaltern Studies I: Writings on South Asian History and Society* (New Delhi, 1982).

———. *Nationalist Thought and the Colonial World: A Derivative Discourse* (New Delhi, 1987).

———. *The Nation and Its Fragments: Colonial and Postcolonial Histories* (New Delhi, 1994).

Chatterji, Joya. *Bengal Divided: Hindu Communalism and Partition, 1932–1947* (Cambridge, 1995).

———. 'The Making of a Borderline: The Radcliffe Award for Bengal', in Ian Talbot and Gurharpal Singh (eds), *Region and Partition: Bengal, Punjab and the Partition of the Subcontinent* (New Delhi, 1999).

———. 'Right or Charity? The Debate over Relief and Rehabilitation in West Bengal', in Suvir Kaul (ed.), *The Partition of Memory: The Afterlife of the Division of India* (New Delhi, 2001).

Chattopadhyaya, Kamaladevi, *Inner Recesses Outer Spaces: Memoirs* (New Delhi, 1986).

Chaudhuri, Nirad C. . *The Autobiography of an Unknown Indian* (New York, 1951).

———. *The Continent of Circe* (London, 1965).

———. *The Intellectual in India* (New Delhi, 1967).

———. *Culture in the Vanity Bag* (Bombay, 1976).

———. *Hinduism: A Religion to Live By* (New Delhi, 1979).

———. *Thy Hand Great Anarch! India, 1921–1952* (London, 1987).

Cobban, Alfred. *The Social Interpretation of the French Revolution* (Cambridge, 1964).

Cole, J.R.I. *Roots of North Indian Shi'sm in Iraq and Iran: Religion and State in Awadh 1772–1859* (Berkeley, 1968).

Copland, Ian. 'Islam and the Moral Economy', in Asim Roy (ed.), *Islam in History and Politics: Perspective from South Asia* (New Delhi, 2006).

Cragg, Kenneth. *The Pen and the Faith: Eight Modern Muslim Writers and the Quran* (Delhi, 1988 reprint).

Currie, P.M. *The Shrine and Cult of Muin-al-din Chishti of Ajmer* (New Delhi, 1989).

Currim, Mumtaz and George Michell. *Dargahs: Abodes of the Saints* (New Delhi, 2004).

Dale, S.F. *Islamic Society on the South Asian Frontier: The Mappilas of Malabar 1498–1922* (Oxford, 1980).

Dalmia, Vasudha. *The Nationalization of the Hindu Traditions: Bharatendu Harischandra and Nineteenth-century Banaras* (New Delhi, 1997).

Dalrymple, William. *City of Djinns: A Year in Delhi* (Delhi, 1993).

———. *The Last Mughal: The Fall of a Dynasty, 1857* (New Delhi, 2007).

Darling, Malcolm. *Apprentice to Power: India 1904–8* (London, 1936).

Das, Sisir Kumar (ed.). *The English Writings of Rabindranath Tagore, vol. 3: A Miscellany* (New Delhi, 1996).

Datta, Nonica. 'Transcending Religious Identities: Amrita Pritam and Partition', in Satish Saberwal and Mushirul Hasan (eds), *Assertive Religious Identities: India and Europe* (New Delhi, 2006).

Datta, Pradip Kumar. *Carving Blocs, Communal Ideology in Early Twentieth-century Bengal* (New Delhi, 1999).

———. 'Bangla Sahitya and the Vicissitudes of Bengali Identity in the Latter of the Nineteenth Century', in Sambudha Sen (ed.), *Mastering Western Texts: Essays on Literature and Society* (New Delhi, 2003).

Datta, V.N. *Maulana Azad* (Delhi, 1990).

———. *Islam and the Modern Age*, vol. 34, August-October 2003.

Demant, Peter R. *Islam vs. Islamism* (London, 2006),

Desai, Anita. *In Custody* (New Delhi, 1994).

Desai, Meghnad. 'Our Economic Growth: 1947–2007', *India Sixty, IIC Quarterly*, spring 2007.

De Tassy, Garcin. *Muslim Festivals in India and Other Essays*. Translated and edited by M. Waseem (New Delhi, 1997).

Douglas, I.H. *Abul Kalam Azad: An Intellectual and Religious Biography*. Edited by Gail Minault and Christian W. Troll (New Delhi, 1988).

Dudoignon, Stephane A., Komatsu Hisao, and Kosugi Yasushi (eds). *Intellectuals in the Modern Islamic World* (London, 2007).

Duetsch, Karl K. 'Communication Theory and Political Integration,' in P.E. Jacob and J.V. Toscano, *The Integration of Political Communities* (Philadelphia, 1964).

Duggal, K.S. *Abducted Not and Other Stories of Partition Holocaust* (New Delhi, 2007).

Dutta, Krishna and Andrew Robinson (eds). *Selected Letters of Rabindranath Tagore* (Cambridge, 1997).

Eaton, Richard (ed.). *The Rise of Islam and the Bengal Frontier, 1204–1760* (Delhi, 1997).

Eaton, Richard. *India's Islamic Traditions, 711–1750* (New Delhi, 2003).

Edib, Halide. *The Conflict of East and West in Turkey* (Delhi, 1935).

——. *Inside India*. With an Introduction and Notes by Mushirul Hasan (New Delhi, 2002).

Ehlers, Eckart and Krafft, Thomas (eds). *Shahjahanabad/Old Delhi: Tradition and Colonial Change* (New Delhi, 2003, 2nd edition).

Eikelman, Dale F. and James Piscatori. *Muslim Politics* (Delhi, 1997).

Engineer, Asghar Ali. *The Bohras* (New Delhi, 1980).

——. *Secular Perspective* (Bombay), 16 March–15 April 2001.

Esposito, John L. and John O. Voll (eds). *Makers of Contemporary Islam* (New York, 2001).

Ewing, Katherine P. (ed.). *Shari'at and Ambiguity in South Asian Islam* (New Delhi, 1988).

Faiz, Faiz Ahmed. *Poems by Faiz*. Translated with an Introduction and Notes by V.G. Kiernan (New Delhi, 1971).

Fakhri, S.M.A.K. 'Tamil Muslims and the Self-Respect Movement', in Mushirul Hasan (ed.), *Living with Secularism: The Destiny of India's Muslims* (New Delhi, 2007).

Farmer, Victoria L. 'Mass Media: Images, Mobilization, and Communalism', in David Ludden (ed.), *Contesting the Nation: Religion, Community, and the Politics of Democracy in India* (Philadelphia, 1999).

Faruqi, Ziya-ul-Hasan, 'Indian Muslims and the Ideology of the Secular State in India', in D.E. Smith (ed.), *South Asian Politics and Religion* (Princeton, NJ, 1966)

Fazalbhoy, Nasreen, 'Sociology of Muslims in India', *Economic and Political Weekly*, 28 June 1997.

Fisher, Michael H. *Conterflows to Colonialism: Indian Travellers and Settlers in Britain, 1600–1857* (New Delhi, 2006).

——. *Beyond the Three Seas: Travellers' Tales of Mughal India* (New Delhi, 2007).

Flemming, Leslie. *Another Lonely Voice: The Life and Works of Saadat Hasan Manto*. Translated by Tahira Naqvi (Lahore, 1985).

Francisco, Jason. 'In the Heat of Fratricide: The Literature of India's Partition Burning Freshly', reprinted in Mushirul Hasan (ed.), *Inventing Boundaries: Gender, Politics and the Partition of India* (New Delhi, 2002).

Fraser, Bashabi (ed.). *Bengal Partition Stories: An Unclosed Chapter* (London, 2006).

Friedmann, Yohanan. *Prophecy Continuous: Aspects of Religious Thought and Its Medieval Background* (London, 1989).

Frietag, Sandria B. *Collective Action and Community. Public Arenas and the Emergence of Communalism in North India* (Berkeley, 1989).

——. (ed.). *Culture and Power in Banaras: Community, Performance, and Environment, 1800–1980* (New Delhi, 1989).

Frykenberg, R. E. (ed.). *Delhi through the Ages: Essays in Urban History* (New Delhi, 1986).

Gaenzle, Martin and Jorg Gengnagel (eds). *Visualizing Space in Benares: Images, Maps and the Praxis of Representation* (Wiesbaden, 2006).

Gandhi, M.K. *Hind Swaraj and Other Writings*. Edited by Anthony J. Parel (New Delhi, 2004 reprint).

Geyl, Peter. *Debates with Historians* (The Hague, 1955).

——. *Encounters in History* (London, 1962).

Ghosh, Papiya. *Partition and the South Asian Diaspora Extending the Subcontinent* (New Delhi, 2007).

Ghose, Sagarika. 'Minority Report', *Indian Express*, 13 July 2003.

Gibb, H.A.R. *Modern Trends in Islam* (Illinois, 1945).

Gilmartin, David. 'Customary Law and Shari'at in Punjab', in Katherine P. Ewing (ed.), *Shari'at and Ambiguity in South Asian Islam* (New Delhi, 1988).

——. 'A Networked Civilization', in Miriam Cooke and Bruce B. Lawrence (eds), *Muslim Networks: From Medieval Scholars to Modern Feminist* (New Delhi, 2005).

Gopal, S. (ed.). *Selected Works of Jawaharlal Nehru*, second series, vol. 15, part 1.

Gottschalk, Peter. *Beyond Hindu and Muslim: Multiple Identity in Narratives from Village India* (New Delhi, 2000)

Graff, Violette (ed.). *Lucknow: Memories of a City* (New Delhi, 1997).

Graham, G.F.I. *The Life and Work of Syed Ahmed Khan* (London, 1885).

Green, Nile. *Indian Sufism since the Seventeenth Century: Saints, Books, and Empires in the Muslim Deccan* (London, 2006).

Greenfeld, Liah. Nationalism: Five Roads to Modernity (London, 1992).

——. 'Transcending the Nation's Worth', *Daedalus*, Summer 1993.

Gruenbaum, G.E. *Islam* (London, 1955).

Guha, Ramachandra. *India after Gandhi: The History of the World's Largest Democracy* (New Delhi, 2007).

Guha, Ranajit (ed.). *Subaltern Studies I: Writings on South Asian History and Society* (New Delhi, 1982).

——. (ed.). *Subaltern Studies II: Writings on South Asian History and Society* (New Delhi, 1983).

——. (ed.). *Subaltern Studies VI: Writings on South Asian History and Society* (New Delhi, 1989).

Gupta, Dipankar. *The Context of Ethnicity: Sikh Identity in a Comparative Perspective* (New Delhi, 1996).

Gupta, Jyotirindra Das. *Language Conflict and National Development: Group Politics and National Language Policy in India* (Berkeley, 1970).

Gupta, Narayani. *Delhi between Two Empires, 1803–1931: Society, Government and Urban Growth* (New Delhi, 1981).

Gupta, Suman. *V.S. Naipaul* (Plymouth, 1999).

Hall, Stuart. 'Introduction', in Stuart Hall and Paul Du Gay (eds), *Questions of Cultural Identity* (London, 1997).

Hansen, Kathryn and David Lelyveld (eds). *A Wilderness of Possibilities: Urdu Studies in Transnational Perspectives* (New Delhi, 2005).

Haq, Mushirul. *Islam in Secular India* (Simla, 1972).

Hardy, Peter. *The Muslims of British India* (Cambridge, 1972).

Hasan, Mohibbul. *The History of Tipu Sultan* (Calcutta, 1971).

——. *Kashmir under the Sultans* (New Delhi, 2006 reprint).

Hasan, Mushirul. *Nationalism and Communal Politics in India, 1916–1928* (New Delhi, 1979).

——. (ed.). *Communal and Pan-Islamic Trends in Colonial India* (revised edition) (New Delhi, 1985).

——. *A Nationalist Conscience: M.A. Ansari, the Congress and the Raj* (New Delhi, 1987).

——. 'The Myth of Unity: Colonial and National Narratives', in David Ludden (ed.), *Contesting the Nation: Religion, Community, and the Politics of Democracy in India* (Philadelphia, 1996).

——. (ed.). *Legacy of a Divided Nation: India's Muslims since Independence* (New Delhi, 1997).

——. 'Traditional Rites and Contested Meanings: Sectarian Strife in Colonial Lucknow', in Violette Graff (ed.), *Lucknow: Memories of a City* (New Delhi, 1997).

——. (ed.). *India Partitioned: The Other Face of Freedom* (New Delhi, 1997).

——. (ed.). *Islam, Communities and the Nation: Muslim Identities in South Asia and Beyond* (New Delhi, 1998).

——. (ed.). *Knowledge, Power and Politics: Educational Institutions in India* (New Delhi, 1998).

——. (ed.). *Inventing Boundaries: Gender, Politics and the Partition of India* (New Delhi, 2000).

——. (ed.) *Islam and Indian Nationalism: Reflections on Maulana Abul Kalam Azad* (New Delhi, 2001 reprint).

——. (ed.). *Will Secular India Survive* (New Delhi, 2004).

——. *From Pluralism to Separatism: Qasbas in Colonial Awadh* (New Delhi, 2004).

——. *A Moral Reckoning: Muslim Intellectuals in Nineteenth-century Delhi* (New Delhi, 2005).

——. *The Nehrus: Personal Histories* (New Delhi, 2006).

——. (ed.). *Living with Secularism: The Destiny of India's Muslims* (New Delhi, 2006).

——. (ed.). *Nehru's India: Select Speeches* (New Delhi, 2006).

——. *Wit and Humour in Colonial India* (New Delhi, 2007).

Hasan, Mushirul and Asim Roy (eds). *Living Together Separately: Cultural India in History and Politics* (New Delhi, 2005).

Hasan, Mushirul and Margrit Pernau (eds). *Regionalizing Pan-Islamism: Documents on the Khilafat Movement* (New Delhi, 2005).

Hasan, Mushirul and M. Asaduddin (eds). *Image and Representation: Stories of Muslim Lives in India* (New Delhi, 2000).

Hasan, Mushirul and Narayani Gupta (eds). *India's Colonial Encounter: Essays in Memory of Eric Stokes* (New Delhi, 2004, second revised and enlarged edition).

Hasan, Mushirul and Rakhshanda Jalil. *Partners in Freedom: Jamia Millia Islamia* (New Delhi, 2007).

Hasan, Zoya. 'Gender Politics, Legal Reform, and the Muslim Community in India', in Patricia Jeffery and Amrita Basu (eds), *Resisting the Sacred and the Secular: Women's Activism and Politicized Religion in South Asia* (New Delhi, 1999).

——. (ed.). *Democracy in Muslim Societies: The Asian Experience* (New Delhi, 2007).

——. 'Bridging a Growing Divide? The Indian National Congress and Indian Democracy', *Contemporary South Asia*, vol. 15, no. 4, December 2006.

Hay, Stephen N. *Asian Ideas of East and West: Tagore and His Critics in Japan, China, and India* (Bombay, 1970).

Hollinger, David A. *Post Ethnic America: Beyond Multiculturalism* (New York, 1995).

Hobsbawm, E.J. *The Age of Revolution, 1789–1848* (Delhi, 1992).

Hodson, H.V. *The Great Divide: Britain–India–Pakistan* (Karachi, 1977 edn).

Hoodbhoy, Pervez. 'Jinnah and the Islamic State: Setting the Record Straight', *Economic and Political Weekly'*, 11 August 2007.

Hosain, Attia. *Sunlight on a Broken Column* (New Delhi, 1992).

Hourani, Albert. *Islam in European Thought* (Cambridge, 1991).

Howarth, Toby M. *The Twelver Shia as a Muslim Minority in India: Pulpit of Tears* (London, 2005).

Husain, S. Abid. *The National Culture of India* (revised edition, Bombay, 1961).

——. *Gandhi and Communal Unity* (Delhi, 1969).

Husain, Intizar. *The Seventh Door and Other Stories*. Edited and with an Introduction by Muhammad Umar Memon (London, 1998).

Imamuddin, Muhammad (ed.). *Mukammil Majmua Lectures wa Speeches, 1863 to 1898* (Lahore, 1900).

Inayatullah, Sohail and Gail Boxwell (eds). *Islam, Postmodernism and Other Futures* (London, 1985).

Iqbal, Mohammad. *The Reconstruction of Religious Thought in Islam* (Lahore, 1944).

Israel, Milton and N.K. Wagle (eds). *Islamic Society: Essays in Honour of Professor Aziz Ahmad* (New Delhi, 1983).

Irwin, H.C. *The Garden of India* (London, 1980).

Iyengar, Uma. (ed.). *The Oxford India Nehru* (New Delhi, 2007).

Jacob, P.E. and Toscano, J.V. *The Integration of Political Communities* (Philadelphia: Lippocott, 1964).

Jain, Girilal. *The Hindu Phenomenon* (Delhi, 1994).

Jalal, Ayesha. *The Sole Spokesman: Jinnah, the Muslim League and the Demand for Pakistan* (Cambridge, 1985).

——. *Democracy and Authoritarianism in South Asia: A Comparative and Historical Perspective* (Cambridge, 1995).

——. 'Ideology and the Struggle for Democratic Institutions', in Victoria Schofeld (ed.), *Old Roads New Highways* (Karachi, 1997).

Jalal, Ayesha. *Self and Sovereignty: Individual and Community in South Asian Islam since 1850* (New Delhi, 2001).

Jalil, Rakhshanda. *Invisible City: The Hidden Monuments of Delhi* (New Delhi, 2008).

Jameson, Fredrick. *Archaeologies of the Future: The Desire Called Utopia and Other Science Fictions* (London, 2007).

Jeffery, Patricia, Roger Jeffery, and Craig Jeffrey, 'The Mother's Lap and the Civilizing Mission: Madrasa Education and Rural Muslim Girls in Western Uttar Pradesh', in Zoya Hasan and Ritu Menon (eds), *In a Minority: Essays on Muslim Women in India* (New Delhi, 2005).

——. 'Investing in the Future: Education in the Social and Cultural Reproduction of Muslims in UP', in Mushirul Hasan (ed.), *Living with Secularism: The Destiny of India's Muslims* (New Delhi, 2007).

Juergensmeyer, Mark. *Religious Nationalism Confronts the Secular State* (California, 1993).

Kakar, Sudhir. *The Colour of Nothingness* (New Delhi, 1996).

Kalam, M.A. 'Conditioned Lives', *Economic and Political Weekly*, 10 March 2007

Kamrava, Mehran (ed.). *The New Voices of Islam: Reforming Politics and Modernity—A Reader* (London, 2006).

Kaul, Suvir (ed.). *The Partition of Memory: The Afterlife of the Division of India* (New Delhi, 2001).

Kaur, Ravinder. *Since 1947: Partition Narratives among Punjabi Migrants of Delhi* (New Delhi, 2007).

Kaviraj, Sudipta. *The Unhappy Consciousness: Bankimchandra Chattopadhyay and the Formation of Nationalist Discourse in India,* (New Delhi, 1998).

Kazmi, Fareed. 'Muslim Socials and the Female Protagonist; Seeing a Dominant Discourse at Work', in A.D. Needham and Rajeshwari Sunder Rajan (eds), *The Crisis of Secularism in India* (New Delhi, 2007).

Kesavan, Mukul. 'Urdu, Awadh and the Tawaif: The Islamicite Roots of Hindi Cinema', in Zoya Hasan (ed.), *Forging Identities: Gender, Communities and the State in India* (New Delhi, 1994).

Khalidi, Omar, *Muslims in Indian Economy* (New Delhi, 2006).

Khan, Dominique-Sila and Zawahir Moir, 'Co-existence and Communalism: The Shrine of Piranas in Gujarat', in Asim Roy (ed.), *Islam in History and Politics: Perspectives from South Asia* (New Delhi, 2006).

Khan, Gulfishan. *Indian Muslim Perceptions of the West during the Eighteenth Century* (Karachi, 1998).

Khan, M. Ishaq. *Kashmir's Transition to Islam: The Role of Muslim Rishis* (New Delhi, 1994).

Khan, Muin-ud-Din Ahmad. *History of the Faraidi Movement in Bengal, 1818–1906* (Karachi, 1965).

Khan, Yasmin. *The Great Partition: The Making of India and Pakistan* (New Delhi, 2007).

Khosla, Gopal Das. *Stern Reckoning: A Survey of Events Leading up to and Following the Partition of India* (New Delhi, 1989).

Khundmiri, Alam. *Secularism, Islam and Modernity* (New Delhi, 2001).

Kidwai, Sabina. 'Images and Representations of Muslim Women in the Media, 1990–2001', in Zoya Hasan and Ritu Menon (eds), *In a Minority: Essays on Muslim Women in India,* (New Delhi, 2005).

Kiernan, Victor (ed.). *Poems of Faiz* (London, 1971).

———. (ed.). *Poems from Iqbal* (Lahore, 1999 edition).

———. *Across Time and Continents: A Tribute.* Edited by Prakash Karat (New Delhi, 2003).

Kondo, Mitsuhiro, 'Hindu Nationalists and their Critique of Monotheism: The Relationship between Nation, Religion, and Violence', in Mushirul Hasan and Nariaki Nakazato (eds), *The Unfinished Agenda: Nation-Building in South Asia* (Delhi, 2001).

Kozlowski, Gregory C., 'Muslim Women and the Control of Property in North India', *The Indian Economic and Social History Review,* vol. 24, no. 2, 1987

Krishna, K.B. *The Problem of Minorities or Communal Representation in India* (London, 1939).

Kumar, Arun. *Cultural and Educational Rights of the Minorities under Indian Constitution* (New Delhi, 1985)

Kumar, Krishna. *Prejudice and Pride: School Histories of the Freedom Struggle in India and Pakistan* (New Delhi, 2004).

Kumar, Nita. 'Work and Leisure in the Formation of Identity: Muslim weavers in a Hindu City', in Sandria B. Frietag (ed.), *Culture and Power in Banaras. Community, Performance, and Environment, 1800–1980* (New Delhi, 1989).

———. *The Artisans of Banaras: Popular Culture and Identity, 1880–1986* (Delhi, 1995).

Kumar, Sukrita Paul. *Narrating Partition: Texts, Interpretations, Ideas* (Delhi, 2004).

Kumar, Sunil. *The Prsent in Delhi's Past* (New Delhi, 2002).

Lavan, Spencer. *The Ahmadiyah Movement: A History and Perspective* (New Delhi, 1974).

Lawrence, Walter Roper. *The India We Served* (London, 1928).

Lacy, Greighton. *India Insights* (Delhi, 1972).

Lehri, Chandralekha. *Socio-Demographic Profile of Muslims: Study of Bhopal City* (Jaipur, 1977).

Lelyveld, David. *Aligarh's First Generation: Muslim Solidarity in British India* (Princeton, NJ, 1978).

———. 'The Fate of Hindustani: Colonial Language and the Project of a National Language', in Carol A. Breckenridge and Peter van der Veer (eds), *Orientalism and the Postcolonial Predicament: Perspectives on South Asia* (Philadelphia, 1993).

Lewis, Bernard. *Islam and the West* (New York, 1993).

Lichtheim, George, *Europe in the Twentieth Century* (London, 1974).

Liebeskind, Claudia. *Piety on Its Knees, Three Sufi Traditions in South Asia in Modern Times* (New Delhi, 1998).

Llewellyn-Jones, Rosie. *A Fatal Friendship: The Nawabs, the Brtitish and the City of Lucknow* (New Delhi, 1985).

———. *Engaging Scoundrels: The Tales of Lucknow* (New Delhi, 2000).

Lokhandwala, S.T. (ed.). *India and Contemporary Islam* (Simla, 1971).

Ludden, David (ed.). *Contesting the Nation: Religion, Community, and the Politics of Democracy in India* (Philadelphia, 1996).

Lutfullah. *Seamless Boundaries: Lutfullah's Narrative beyond East and West.* Edited, annotated, and with an introduction by Mushirul Hasan (New Delhi, 2007).

Madan, T.N. *Modern Myths, Locked Minds: Secularism and Fundamentalism in India* (New Delhi, 1998).

———. (ed.). *Muslim Communities of South Asia: Culture, Society and Power* (Delhi, 2001, 3rd enlarged edition).

Madani, Maulana Hussain Ahmad. *Composite Nationalism and Islam.* Translated by Mohammad Anwer Hussain and Hasan Imam (Delhi, 2005).

Mahajan, Gurpreet. *Identities and Rights: Aspects of Liberal Democracy in India* (Delhi, 1988).

Mahajan, Sucheta. *Independence and Partition: The Erosion of Colonial Power in India* (New Delhi, 2000).

Mahmood Tahir (ed.). *Politics of Minority Educational Institutions* (New Delhi, 2007).

Majumdar, A.K. 'Writings on the Transfer of Power, 1945–47', in B.R. Nanda (ed.), *Essays in Modern Indian History* (New Delhi, 1980).

Makatib-i Shibli, vol. 1 (Azamgarh, 1924).

Malhotra, Inder. 'Nehru's Luminous Legacy', in Ira Pande (ed.), *India 60* (New Delhi, 2007).

Malik, Iftikhar H. 'Regionalism or Personality Cult? Allama and the Tehreek-e Khaksar in pre-1947 Punjab', in Ian Talbot and Gurharpal Singh (eds), *Region and Partition: Bengal, Punjab and the Partition of the Subcontinent* (New Delhi, 1999).

Malik, Jamal (ed.). *Perspectives of Mutual Encounters in South Asian History 1760–1860* (Brill, 2000).

Malik, Jamal and Helmut Reifeld (eds). *Religious Pluralism in South Asia and Europe* (New Delhi, 2005).

Mamdani, Mahmood. *Good Muslim, Bad Muslim: Islam, the USA, and the Global War against Terror* (Delhi, 2005).

Manchanda, Rita, 'Militarized Hindu Nationalism and the Mass Media: Shaping a Hindutva Public Discourse', in John McGuire and Ian Copland (eds), *Hindu Nationalism and Governance* (New Delhi, 2007).

Mani, Lata. *Contentious Traditions: The Debate on Sati in Colonial India* (New Delhi, 1998).

Mann, E.S. *Boundaries and Identities: Muslims, Work and Status in Aligarh* (Delhi, 1992).

Manto, Saadat Hasan. *Kingdom's End and Other Stories*. Translated from the Urdu by Khalid Hasan. (New Delhi, 1989).

Mason, Philip (ed.). *India and Ceylon: Unity and Diversity* (London, 1967).

Manzar, Hasan. *A Requiem for the Earth: Selected Stories* (Karachi, 1998).

Massignon, L. *La Passion d'al Hallaj* (Paris, 1922). Translated by Hervert Mason, *The Passion of al-Hallaj* (Princeton, NJ, 1982).

Mayaram, Shail. *Resisting Régimes: Myth, Memory and the Shaping of a Muslim Identity* (Delhi, 1997).

———. 'Living Together: Ajmer as a paradigm for the (South) Asian City', in Mushirul Hasan and Asim Roy (eds), *Living Together Separately: Cultural India in History and Politics* (2004).

McDonough, Sheila. 'The Spirit of Jamia Millia Islamia as Exemplified in the Writings of Syed Abid Husain', in Robert D. Baird (ed.), *Religion in Modern India* (New Delhi, 1981).

Mecklai, Noorel-nissa Sultanali, 'Abrogated Identity: Muslim Representation in Hindi Popular Cinema' (Unpublished Ph.D. thesis, Edith Cowan University, Western Australia, 2006).

Mehrunissa (Princess of Rampur). *An Extraordinary Life* (Delhi, 2000).

Mehta, Asoka and Achyut Patwardhan. *The Communal Triangle in India* (Allahabad, 1942).

Memon, Muhammad Umar (ed.). *An Epic Unwritten: The Penguin Book of Partition Stories in Urdu* (New Delhi, 1998).

Menon, Ritu (ed.). *No Woman's Land* (New Delhi, 2004), p. 44 Ritu Menon (ed.), *No Woman's Land* (New Delhi, 2004).

Metcalf, Barbara Daly. *Islamic Revival in British India: Deoband 1860–1900* (Princeton, NJ, 1982).

———. (ed.). *Moral Conduct and Authority: The Place of Adab in South Asian Islam* (London, 1984).

———. *Perfecting Women: Maulana Ashraf Ali Thanawi's Bihishti Zewar* (Berkeley, 1990).

———. Presidential Address: 'Too Little Too Much. Reflection on Muslims in the History of India', *Journal of Asian Studies*, vol. 54, 1995.

———. *Islamic Contestations: Essays on Muslims in India and Pakistan* (New Delhi, 2004).

———. 'Observant Muslims, Secular Indians: The Political Vision of Maulana Husain Ahmad Madani, 1938–57', Dipesh Chakrabarty, Rochona Majumdar, and Sartori Andrew (eds), *From the Colonial to the Postcolonial* (New Delhi, 2007)

Miller, R.E. *Mapila Muslims of Kerala: A Study of Islamic Trends* (New Delhi, 1992, rev. edn.).

———. *The Khilafat Movement: Religious Symbolism and Mobilization in India* (New Delhi, 1982).

Milton-Edwards, Beverly. *Islam and Politics in the Contemporary World* (London, 2004).

Minault, Gail. *Secluded Scholars: Women's Education and Muslim Social Reform in Colonial India* (New Delhi, 1998).

Mir, Ali Husaini and Raza Mir. A Celebration of Progressive Urdu Poetry: Anthems of Resistance (New Delhi, 2006).

Moon, Penderel. Divide and Quit (New Delhi, 1988).

Moraes, Frank. Jawaharlal Nehru: A Biography (New York, 1956).

———. Witness to an Era (Delhi, 1973).

———. (ed.). Science, Philosophy and Culture: Essays Presented in Honour of Humayun Kabir's Sixty-Second Birthday (Bombay, 1965).

Mujeeb, Mohammad. Education and Traditional Values (Meerut, 1965).

———. The Indian Muslims (London, 1967).

———. Ghalib (Delhi, 1969).

———. Akbar (New Delhi, 1969).

———. 'The Partition of India in Retrospect', in C.H. Philips and D.A. Wainright (eds.), The Partition of India: Policies and Perspectives (London, 1970).

———. Dr. Zakir Husain, A Biography (New Delhi, 1972).

———. Islamic Influence on Indian Society (Meerut, 1972).

———. 'Guru Nanak through Muslim Eyes', Islam and the Modern Age (Delhi, August–October 2003).

———. 'The Discovery of India', Islam and the Modern Age (Delhi), August–October 2003.

———. 'Approach to the Study of Medieval Indian History', in Special Issue on Professor Mohammed Mujeeb, Islam and the Modern Age, vol. 34, Nos. 3–4, (Delhi, August–October 2003).

Murshid, Tazeen M. The Sacred and the Secular: Bengal Muslim Discourses, 1871–1977 (Calcutta, 1995).

Naipaul, V.S. Among the Believers: The Islamic Journey (New Delhi, 1981)

———. India: A Million Mutinies (New Delhi, 1990).

———. Beyond Belief: Islamic Excursions among the Converted People (1998).

Nanda, B.R. (ed.). Selected Works of Govind Ballabh Pant, vol. 11 (New Delhi, 1998)

Nandy, Ashis. The Illegitimacy of Nationalism (New Delhi, 1994).

Nandy, Ashis, Shikha Trivedy, Shail Mayaram, Achyut Yagnik, The Ramjanmabhumi Movement and Fear of the Self (New Delhi, 1995).

Naqvi, Tahira (ed.). My Friend, My Enemy: Essays, Reminiscences, Portraits (New Delhi, 2000).

Nasr, Vali. The Shia Revival: How Conflicts within Islam Will Shape the Future (New York, 2006).

Nathan, R. Progress of Education in India 1896–97 to 1901–2, vol. 1 (Calcutta, 1904).

Nayar, Pramod K. (ed.). The Trial of Bahadur Shah (New Delhi, 2007).

Nehru, Jawaharlal. An Autobiography (London, 1936).

———. Glimpses of World History (London, 1939).

———. The Discovery of India (Calcutta, 1946 reprint).

———. A Bunch of Old Letters (New Delhi, 1958).

Nixon, Rob. *London Calling: V.S. Naipaul, Postcolonial Mandarin* (Oxford, 1992).

Nizami, K.A. (ed.). *Collected Works of Professor Mohammad Habib*, vol. 2 (Delhi, 1981).

Noorani, A.G. *President Zakir Husain: A Quest for Excellence* (Bombay, 1967).

———. (ed.). *The Muslims of India: A Documentary Record* (New Delhi, 2003).

———. 'Muslim Identity: Self Image and Political Aspirations', in Mushirul Hasan (ed.), *Islam, Communities and the Nation: Muslim Identities in South Asia and Beyond* (New Delhi, 1998).

Nussbaum, Martha C. *The Clash within: Democracy, Religious Violence, and India's Future* (Cambridge: Massachusetts, 2007).

Oldenburg, Veena. *The Making of Colonial Lucknow, 1856–1877* (Princeton, NJ, 1984).

Oesterheld, Christina and Claus Peter (eds). *Of Clowns and Gods, Brahmans and Babus: Humour in South Asian Literatures* (New Delhi, 1999).

Pandey, Gyanendra, 'A Rural Base for Congress: The United Provinces, 1920–40', in D.A. Low (ed.), *Congress and the Raj: Facets of the Indian Struggle 1917–47* (London, 1977).

———. *The Ascendancy of the Congress in Uttar Pradesh 1926–34: A Study in Imperfect Mobilization* (New Delhi, 1978).

———. 'Encounters and Calamities': The History of a North Indian Qasba in the Nineteenth Century', in Ranajit Guha (ed.), *Subaltern Studies II: Writings on South Asian History and Society* (New Delhi, 1983), pp. 60–129.

———. 'The Colonial Construction of "Communalism": British Writings on Banaras in the Nineteenth Century', in Veena Das (ed.), *Mirrors of Violence: Communities, Riots and Survivors in South Asia* (New Delhi, 1990).

———. *The Construction of Communalism in Colonial North India* (New Delhi, 1990).

———. *Remembering Partition* (Cambridge, 2001).

———. *Routine Violence, Nations, Fragments, Histories* (New Delhi, 2006).

Panikkar, K.N., *Colonialism, Culture and Resistance* (New Delhi, 2007).

Pernau, Margrit. *The Passing of Patrimonialism: Politics and Political Culture in Hyderabad 1911–1948* (New Delhi, 2000).

———. 'Multiple Identities and Communities; Re-Contextualizing Religion', in Jamal Malik and Helmut Reifeld (eds), *Religious Pluralism in South Asia and Europe* (New Delhi, 2005).

———. (ed.). *The New Delhi College: Traditional Elites, the Colonial State, and Education before 1857* (New Delhi, 2007).

Philips, C.H. (ed.). *The Evolution of India and Pakistan, 1858 to 1947. Select Documents* (London, 1962).

Philips, C.H and D.A. Wainright (eds). 'The Partition of India in Retrospect'. *The Partition of India: Policies and Perspectives* (London, 1970).

Pirzada, Sharifuddin (ed.). *Foundations of Pakistan: All-India Muslim League Documents: 1906–1947* (Karachi, 1970).

Poole, Elizabeth. *Media Representation of British Muslims: Reporting Islam* (London, 2002).

Powell, Avril A. *Muslims and Missionaries in Pre-Mutiny India* (London, 1993).

Prasad, Leela. *Ethics in Everyday Hindu Life: Narration and Tradition in a South Indian Town* (New Delhi, 2007)

Prasad, Rajendra. *Autobiography* (Bombay, 1957).

Pritchet, Frances W. *Nets of Awareness: Urdu Poetry and its Critics* (Berkeley, 1994).

Pugh, Judith F. 'Divination and Ideology in the Banaras Hindu Community', in Katherine P. Ewing (ed.), *Shariat and Ambiguity in South Asian Islam* (New Delhi, 1988).

Pyarelal, *Mahatma Gandhi: The Last Phase*, vol. 1, Book One, (Ahmedabad, 1956).

Rahman, Fazlur. *Islam* (London, 1966).

Rahman, Tariq. *Denizens of Alien Worlds: A Study of Education, Inequality and Polarization in Pakistan* (Karachi, 2004).

Rai, Mridu. *Hindu Rulers, Muslim Subjects: Islam, Rights, and the History of Kashmir* (New Delhi, 2004).

Rai, Sudha. *V.S. Naipaul: A Study in Expatriate Sensibility* (New Delhi, 1982)

Ramadan, Tariq. *Western Muslims and the Future of Islam* (New York, 2004).

Rao, Anupama. 'Ambedkar and the Politics of Minority: A Reading', in Dipesh Chakrabarty, Rochona Majumdar, and Andrew Sartori (eds), *From the Colonial to the Postcolonial* (New Delhi, 2007).

Raychaudhuri, Tapan. *Europe Reconsidered: Perception of the West in Nineteenth Century Bengal* (New Delhi, 1988).

Ray, Rajat Kanta. 'Revolutionaries, Pan-Islamists and Bolsheviks: Maulana Abul Kalam Azad and the Political Underworld in Calcutta, 1905–1925', in Mushirul Hasan (ed.). *Communal and Pan-Islamic Trends in Colonial India* (New Delhi, 1987).

———. (ed.). *Mind, Body, and Society: Life and Mentality in Colonial Bengal* (Calcutta, 1995).

Ray, Sibnarayan (ed.). *Selected Works of M.N. Roy*, vol. 4 (New Delhi, 1997).

Reetz, Dietrich. *Islam in the Public Sphere: Religious Groups in India, 1900–1947* (New Delhi, 2006).

Reeves, P.D. (ed.). *Sleeman in Oudh: An Abridgement of W.H. Sleeman's Journey through the Kingdom of Oude in 1949–50* (Cambridge, 1971).

Reid, H.S. *Report on Indigeneous Education and Vernacular Schools* (Agra, 1852)

Reuben, Bunny. *Dilip Kumar: Star Legend of Indian Cinema* (New Delhi, 2005 Impression), p. 459.

Rizvi, S.A.A. 'The Breakdown of Traditional Society', in *The Cambridge History of Islam* (Cambridge, 1972), vol. 2.

Robb, Peter. *Liberalism, Modernity, and the Nation* (New Delhi, 2007).

Robinson, Francis. *Separatism among Indian Muslims: The Politics of the United Provinces' Muslims, 1860–1923* (Cambridge, 1974).

Robinson, Francis. 'Nation Formation: The Brass Thesis and Muslim Seprartism', and Reply by Paul Brass, *Journal of Commonwealth and Comparative Politics*, vol. 15, no. 13, November 1977.

———. 'The Ulama of Farangi Mahall and their *Adab*', in Barbara Daly Metcalf (ed.), *Moral Conduct and Authority: The Place of Adab in South Asian Islam* (London, 1984).

———. 'Islam and Muslim Separatism', in Mushirul Hasan (ed.), *Communal and Pan-Islamic Trends in Colonial India* (New Delhi, 1987).

———. 'Technology and Religious Change: Islam and the Impact of Print', *Modern Asian Studies*, vol. 27, no. 1, February 1993.

———. *Islam and Muslim History in South Asia* (New Delhi, 2000).

———. *The Ulama of Farangi Mahall and Islamic Culture in South Asia* (New Delhi, 2001).

———. *Islam, South Asia and the West* (New Delhi, 2007).

Robinson, Rowena. *Tremors of Violence: Muslim Survivors of Ethnic Strife in Western India* (New Delhi, 2005).

Roy, Asim. *The Islamic Syncretistic Tradition in Bengal* (Princeton, NJ, 1983).

———. *Islam in History and Politics: Perspectives from South Asia* (New Delhi, 2006).

Roy, M.N. *The Historical Role of Islam* (New Delhi, 1981 reprint).

Roy, Olivier, *Globalised Islam: The Search for a New Ummah* (London, 2004).

Reuben, Bunny. *Dilip Kumar: Star Legend of Indian Cinema* (New Delhi, 2005 Impression).

Russell, Ralph. 'Aziz Ahmad, South Asia, Islam and Urdu', in Milton Israel and N.K. Wagle (eds), *Islamic Society: Essays in Honour of Professor Aziz Ahmad* (New Delhi, 1983).

———. *The Pursuit of Urdu Literature: A Select History* (London, 1992).

Saberwal, Satish and Mushirul Hasan (eds). *Assertive Religious Identities: India and Europe* (New Delhi, 2006).

Sadiq, Muhammad. *A History of Urdu Literature* (New Delhi, 1995, 2nd edition).

Said, Edward W. *Representations of the Intellectual* (New York, 1996).

———. *Covering Islam, How the Media and the Experts Determine How We See the Rest of the World* (New York, 1981).

Saiyidain, K.G. *Islam and the Modern Age*, vol. 36, August-November 2005.

Salim, Ahmad (ed.). *Lahore 1947* (New Delhi, 2001).

Samad, Yunus. *A Nation in Turmoil: Nationalism and Ethnicity in Pakistan, 1937–1958* (New Delhi, 1995).

Sanyal, U. *Devotional Islam & Politics in British India: On Ahmad Riza Khan Barelwi and his Movement, 1870–1920* (New Delhi, 1996).

Sarkar, Sumit. *The Swadeshi Movement in Bengal, 1903–1908* (New Delhi, 1973).

———. 'Popular Movements and National Leadership 1945–47', *Economic and Political Weekly*, Annual Number, 1982.

Sarkar, Sumit. *Popular Movements and 'Middle Class' Leadership in Late Colonial India: Perspectives and Problems of a 'History from Below'* (Calcutta, 1983).

Sarkar, Susobhan. *Bengal Renaissance and Other Essays* (New Delhi, 1970).

Sarkar, Tanika. 'Imagining Hindurashtra: The Hindu and the Muslim in Bankim Chandra's Writings', in David Ludden (ed.), *Contesting the Nation: Religion, Community, and the Politics of Democracy in India* (Philadelphia, 1996).

Saxena, N.C. 'Public Employment and Educational Backwardness among Muslims in India', *Political Science Review*, vol. 22, no. 2, pp. 119–61.

Sayeed, Khalid Bin. *Western Dominance and Political Islam: Challenges and Response* (Karachi, 1995).

Schimmel, Annemarie. *Gabriel's Wing: A Study into the Religious Ideas of Sir Muhammad Iqbal* (Leiden, 1963).

——. *Islam in the Indian Subcontinent* (Leiden, 1980).

——. *As through a Veil: Mystical Poetry in Islam* (New York, 1982).

Schubel, Vernon James. *Religious Performance in Contemporary Islam: Shia Devotional Rituals in South Asia* (South Carolina, 1993).

——. 'Karbala as Sacred Space among North American Shia', Barbara Daly Metcalf (ed.), *Making Muslim Space in North America and Europe* (Berkeley and Los Angeles, 1996).

Seal, Anil. *The Emergence of Indian Nationalism: Competition and Collaboration in the Later Nineteenth Century* (Cambridge, 1971).

——. 'Imperialism and Nationalism in India', *Modern Asian Studies*, vol. 3, 1973.

Sedgwick, Mark. *Islam and Muslims: A Guide to Diverse Experiences in the Modern World* (Boston, MA, 2006).

Sehgal, Squadron Leader Anil (ed.). *Ali Sardar Jafri: The Youth Boatman of Joy* (New Delhi, 2001).

Sen, Amartya. 'Secularism and its Discontents', in Rajeev Bhargava (ed.), *Secularism and its Critics* (New Delhi, 1988).

Sen, Amiya P. *Hindu Revivalism in Bengal 1872: Some Essays in Interpretation* (New Delhi, 1993).

Sen, Simonti. *Travels to Europe: Self and Other in Bengali Travel Narratives 1870–1910* (New Delhi, 2005).

Shackle, Christopher (ed.). *Urdu and Muslim South Asia: Studies in Honour of Ralph Russell* (New Delhi, 1991).

Shackle, Christopher and Javed Majeed (trans). *Hali's Musaddas: The Flow and Ebb of Islam* (New Delhi, 1997).

Shariff, Abusaleh. 'Socio-Economic and Demographic Differentials between Hindus and Muslims in India', *Economic and Political Weekly*, 18 November 1995, pp. 2947–53

Shaikh, Farzana. *Community and Consensus in Islam: Muslim Representation in Colonial India 1860–1947* (Cambridge, 1989).

Shani, Ornit. *Communalism, Caste and Hindu Nationalism: The Violence in Gujarat* (Cambridge, 2007).

Sharar, Abdul Halim. *Lucknow: The Last Phase of an Oriental Culture*. Translated and edited by E.S. Harcourt and Fakhir Hussain (London, 1975).

Sharma, Hari Dev (ed.). *Selected Works of Acharya Narendra Deva* (New Delhi, 1998), vol. 2.

Shaw, Bernard. *Prefaces by Bernard Shaw* (London, 1934).

Shourie, Arun. *A Secular Agenda* (New Delhi, 1993).

——. *Indian Controversies: Essays on Religion in Politics* (New Delhi, 1993).

——. *Worshipping False Gods: Ambedkar, and the Facts Which Have Been Erased* (New Delhi, 1997).

Shureef, Jaffur. *Qanoon-e-Islam*. Translated by G.A. Herklots (Madras, 1863).

Sikand, Yoginder. *Reflections of the Believers: Madrasas and Islamic Education in India* (New Delhi, 2001).

——. *The Origins and Development of the Tablighi Jamaat, 1920s-1990: A Cross-Country Comparative Study* (New Delhi, 2002).

——. *Muslims in India since 1947: Islamic Perspectives on Inter-faith Relations* (London, 2004).

——. *Muslims in India: Contemporary Social and Political Discourses* (Delhi, 2006).

——. 'The Reformist Sufism of the Tablighi Jamaat: The Case of the Meos of Mewat', in Mushirul Hasan (ed.), *Living with Secularism: The Destiny of India's Muslims* (New Delhi, 2007).

Singh, Khushwant. *Train to Pakistan* (New Delhi, 2007 reprint),

Singh, K.S. *People of India; Introduction* (Oxford, 2002, revised edition).

Singh, Patwant. *The Second Partition: Fault-Lines in India's Democracy* (New Delhi, 2007).

Skuy, David. 'Macaulay and the India Penal Code of 1862: The Myth of the Inherent Superiority and Modernity of the English Legal System in the Nineteenth Century', *Modern Asian Studies*, vol. 32, no. 3, 1998

Smith, Anthony D. 'State-making and Nation-building', in John A. Hall (ed.), *States in History* (Oxford, 1986).

Smith, D. E. *India as a Secular State*, (Princeton, NJ, 1963).

Smith, W.C. *Modern Islam in India* (Lahore, 1946).

——. *Islam in Modern History* (Princeton, NJ, 1957).

Sorman, Guy. *The Children of Rifaa: In Search of Moderate Islam* (New Delhi, 2004).

Spear, Percival. 'The Position of the Muslims before and after Partition', in Philip Mason (ed.), *India and Ceylon: Unity and Diversity* (London, 1967).

Subramanian, Lakshmi. 'Tagore and the Problem of Self-esteem', in Rajat Kanta Ray (ed.), *Mind Body and Society: Life and Mentality in Colonial Bengal* (Calcutta, 1995).

Suroor, Hasan. 'Debate or Denial: The Muslim Dilemma', *Hindu*, 17 July 2007.

Suvorova, Anna. *Muslim Saints of South Asia: The Eleventh to the Fifteenth Centuries* (London, 2006).

Talbot, Ian. *Punjab and the Raj 1849–1947* (Delhi, 1988).

——. *Freedom's Cry: The Popular Dimension in the Pakistan Movement and Partition Experiences in North-West India* (Karachi, 1996).

Talbot, Ian and Gurharpal Singh (eds). *Region and Partition: Bengal, Punjab and the Partition of the Subcontinent* (New Delhi, 1999).

Taleb, Mirza Abu. *Westward Bound: Travels of Mirza Abu Taleb.* Edited with an Introduction, by Mushirul Hasan (New Delhi, 2005)

Tan, Tai Young and Gyanesh Kudaisya. *The Aftermath of Partition in South Asia* (London, 2000).

Tandon, Prakash. *Punjabi Saga 1857–2000: The Monumental Story of Five Generations of a Remarkable Punjabi Family* (New Delhi, 2003, paperback edition).

Tanwar, Raghuvendra. *Reporting the Partition of Punjab 1947: Press, Public and Other Opinions* (New Delhi, 1996).

The Partition Omnibus. Introduction by Mushirul Hasan (New Delhi, 2002).

Thompson, Edward. *Rabindranath Tagore: Poet and Dramatist* (Oxford, 1926).

Tibi, Bassam. *Islam between Culture and Politics* (Harvard, 2001).

Toynbee, Arnold J. *Acquaintances* (London, 1967).

Troll, Christian W. (eds). *Muslim Shrines in India* (New Delhi, 1992).

Tully, Mark. *India's Unending Journey: Finding Balance in a Time of Change* (London, 2007),

Tyabji, Badrudding. *Memoirs of an Egoist*, vol. 1 (Delhi, n.d).

van der Veer, Peter. 'God Must be Liberated! A Hindu Liberation Movement in Ayodhya', *Modern Asian Studies*, vol. 21, no. 2, 1987.

——. 'The Concept of the Ideal Brahman as an Ideological Construct', in Gunter D. Southeimer and Herman Kulke (eds), *Hinduism Reconsidered* (Delhi, 1989).

——. *Religious Nationalism: Hindus and Muslims in India* (California, 1994).

Vitthal, B.P.R. 'Muslims of Hyderabad', *Economic and Political Weekly*, 13 July 2002

von, Tunzelmann, Alex. *Indian Summer: The Secret History of the End of an Empire* (London, 2007).

Waardenburg, Jacques. (ed.). *Muslim Perceptions of Other Religions: A Historical Survey* (New York, 1999).

——. (ed.). *Islam: Historical, Social and Political Perspectives* (Berlin, 2002)

Wadud, Amira. *Inside the Gender Jihad* (Oxford, 2006).

Waseem, M. (trans. and ed.). *On Becoming an Indian Muslim: French Essays on Aspects of Syncretism* (New Delhi, 2003).

Waseem, Mohammad. 'Functioning of Democracy in Pakistan', in Zoya Hasan (ed.), *Democracy in Muslim Societies: The Asian Experience* (New Delhi, 2007).

Weinberg, Leonard and Ami Pedahazur (eds). *Religious Fundamentalism and Political Extremism* (London, 2004).

Wilkinson, Steven I. *Votes and Violence: Electoral Competition and Communal Riots in India* (Cambridge, 2004).

Wolpert, Stanley. *Jinnah of Pakistan* (New York, 1984).

Zakaria, Rafiq. *Indian Muslims: Where Have They Gone Wrong?* (Bombay, 2005).

Zubrzycki, John. *The Last Nizam* (London, 2006).

Zutshi, Chitralekha. *Languages of Belonging: Islam, Regional Identity and the Making of Kashmir* (New Delhi, 2003).

Zutshi, Somnath. 'Women, Nation and the Outsider in Hindi Cinema', in Alok Bhalla and Sudhir Chandra (eds), *Indian Responses to Colonialism in the 19th Century* (New Delhi, 1993).

Index